THE EXILES OF FLORIDA

Death of Waxe-hadjo.

THE EXILES OF FLORIDA:

or
The crimes committed by our government against the maroons, who fled from South Carolina and other slave states, seeking protection under Spanish laws.

By Joshua R. Giddings

Black Classic Press
Baltimore
1997

THE EXILES OF FLORIDA

First Published 1858
Published by Black Classic Press 1997
All Rights Reserved.

Library of Congress Card Catalog Number 93–74117
ISBN 0–933121–47–4

Cover art by Carles Juzang

*Printed by BCP Digital Printing,
a division of Black Classic Press*

Founded in 1978, Black Classic Press specializes in bringing to light obscure and significant works by and about people of African descent. If our books are not in available in your area, ask your local bookseller to order them. Our current list of titles can be obtained by writing:

**Black Classic Press
c/o List
P.O. Box 13414
Baltimore, MD 21203**

Visit our website at www.blackclassic.com

A Young Press With Some Very Old Ideas

TO

MY CONSTITUENTS,

THE PEOPLE WHO HAVE SO LONG HONORED ME

WITH THEIR CONFIDENCE,

THIS WORK IS RESPECTFULLY DEDICATED.

J. R. GIDDINGS.

INTRODUCTION.

DISCARDING that code of morals which teaches the suppression of truth, for the purpose of upholding the honor, either of the Government, or of the individuals who wield its administration, the Author of the following work has endeavored to give a faithful record of those interesting events which appear directly connected with the Exiles of Florida.

Torn from their native land, their friends and homes, they were sold in the markets of Carolina and Georgia. Feeling the hand of oppression bearing heavily upon them, they fled to Florida, and, under Spanish laws, became free. Holding lands of the Spanish Crown, they became citizens of that Territory, entitled to protection. To regain possession of their truant bondmen, Georgia made war upon Florida, but failed to obtain her object.

At a time of profound peace, our army, acting under the direction of the Executive, invaded Florida, murdered many of these free men, and brought others to the United States and consigned them to slavery. An expensive and bloody war followed; but failing to capture more of the Exiles, our army was withdrawn.

This war was followed by diplomatic efforts. Florida was purchased; treaties with the Florida Indians were made and violated; gross frauds were perpetrated; dishonorable expedients were resorted to, and another war provoked. During its protracted continuance of seven years, bribery and treachery were practiced towards the Exiles and their allies, the Seminole Indians; flags of truce were violated; the pledged faith of the nation was disregarded. By these means the removal of the Exiles from Florida was effected. After they had settled in the Western Country, most of these iniquities were repeated, until they were driven from our nation and compelled to seek an asylum in Mexico.

Men who wielded the influence of Government for the consummation of these crimes, assiduously labored to suppress all knowledge of their guilt; to keep facts from the popular mind; to falsify the history of current events, and prevent an exposure of our national turpitude.

The object of this work is to meet that state of circumstances; to expose fraud, falsehood, treachery, and other crimes of public men, who have prostituted the powers of Government to the perpetration of murders, at the contemplation of which our humanity revolts.

The Author has designed to place before the public a faithful record of events appropriately falling within the purview of the proposed history; he has endeavored, as far as possible, to do justice to all concerned. Where the action of individuals is concerned, he has endeavored to make them speak for themselves, through official reports, orders, letters, or written evidences from their own hands; and he flatters himself that he has done no injustice to any person.

CONTENTS.

THE

EXILES OF FLORIDA.

CHAPTER I.

CIRCUMSTANCES ATTENDING THE EARLY HISTORY OF SLAVERY IN THE COLONIES.

Settlement of Florida — Boundaries of Carolina — Enslaving Indians — They flee from their Masters — Africans follow the example — Spanish policy in regard to Fugitive Slaves — Carolina demands the surrender of Exiles — Florida refuses — Colony of Georgia establish- ed — Its object — Exiles called Seminoles — Slavery introduced into Georgia — Seminole Indians separate from Creeks — Slaves escape from Georgia — Report of Committee of Safety — Report of General Lee — Treaty of Augusta — Treaty of Galphinton — Singular conduct of Georgia — War between Creeks and Georgia — Resolution of Congress — Treaty of Shoulderbone — Hostilities continue — Georgia calls on United States for assistance — Commissioners sent to negotiate Treaty — Failure — Col. Willett's mission — Chiefs, head men and Warriors repair to New York — Treaty formed — Secret article — Extraordinary covenants.

FLORIDA was originally settled by Spaniards, in 1558. They were the first people to engage in the African Slave trade, and sought to supply other nations with servants from the coast of Guinea. The Colonists held many slaves, expecting to accumulate wealth by the unrequited toil of their fellow-man.

1630.] Carolina by her first and second charters claimed a vast extent of country, embracing St. Augustine and most of Florida. This conflict of jurisdiction soon involved the Colonists in hostilities. The Carolinians also held many slaves. Profiting

1700.] by the labor of her servants, the people sought to increase their wealth by enslaving the Indians who resided in their vicinity. Hence in the early slave codes of that colony we find reference to " negro and *other* slaves."

When the boundaries of Florida and South Carolina became established, the Colonists found themselves separated by the territory now constituting the State of Georgia, at that time mostly occupied by the Creek Indians.

The efforts of the Carolinians to enslave the Indians, brought with them the natural and appropriate penalties. The Indians soon began to make their escape from service to the Indian country. This example was soon followed by the African slaves, who also fled to the Indian country, and, in order to secure themselves from pursuit, continued their journey into Florida.

We are unable to fix the precise time when the persons thus exiled constituted a separate community. Their numbers had become so great in 1736, that they were formed into companies, and relied on by the Floridians as allies to aid in the defense of that territory. They were also permitted to occupy lands upon the same terms that were granted to the citizens of Spain; indeed, they in all respects became free subjects of the Spanish crown. Probably to this early and steady policy of the Spanish Government, we may attribute the establishment and continuance of this community of Exiles in that territory.[1]

1738.] A messenger was sent by the Colonial Government of South Carolina to demand the return of those fugitive slaves who had found an asylum in Florida. The demand was made upon the Governor of St. Augustine, but was promptly rejected. This was the commencement of a controversy which has continued for more than a century, involving our nation in a vast expenditure of blood and treasure, and it yet remains undetermined.

The constant escape of slaves, and the difficulties resulting therefrom, constituted the principal object for establishing a free colony between South Carolina and Florida, which was called Georgia [2]

(1) Vide Bancroft's and Hildreth's Histories of the United States.
(2) Vide both Histories above cited.

It was thought that this colony, being free, would afford the planters of Carolina protection against the further escape of their slaves from service.

These Exiles were by the Creek Indians called "Seminoles," which in their dialect signifies "runaways," and the term being frequently used while conversing with the Indians, came into almost constant practice among the whites; and although it has now come to be applied to a certain tribe of Indians, yet it was originally used in reference to these Exiles long before the Seminole Indians had separated from the Creeks.

Some eight years after the Colony of Georgia was first established, efforts were made to introduce Slavery among its people. The ordinary argument, that it would extend the Christian religion, was brought to bear upon Whitfield and Habersham, and the Saltzbergers and Moravians, until they consented to try the experiment, and Georgia became thenceforth a Slaveholding Colony, whose frontier bordered directly upon Florida; bringing the slaves of her planters into the very neighborhood of those Exiles who had long been free under Spanish laws.

1750.] A difficulty arose among the Creek Indians, which eventually becoming irreconcilable, a chief named Seacoffee, with a large number of followers, left that tribe—at that time residing within the present limits of Georgia and Alabama—and continuing their journey south entered the Territory of Florida, and, under the Spanish colonial policy, were incorporated with the Spanish population, entitled to lands wherever they could find them unoccupied, and to the protection of Spanish laws.[1]

From the year 1750, Seacoffee and his followers rejected all Creek authority, refused to be represented in Creek councils, held themselves independent of Creek laws, elected their own chiefs, and in all respects became a separate Tribe, embracing the Mickasukies, with whom they united. They settled in the vicinity of the Exiles, associated with them, and a mutual sympathy and respect existing,

(1) Vide Schoolcraft's History of Indian Tribes.

some of their people intermarried, thereby strengthening the ties of friendship, and the Indians having fled from oppression and taken refuge under Spanish laws, were also called Seminoles, or "runaways."

After Georgia became a Slaveholding Colony, we are led to believe the practice of slaves leaving their masters, which existed in South Carolina, became frequent in Georgia. But we have no definite information on this subject until about the commencement of the Revolutionary War (1775), when the Council of Safety for that colony sent to Congress a communication setting forth, that a large force of Continental troops was necessary to *prevent their slaves from deserting their masters.*[1] It was about the first communication sent to Congress after it met, in 1776, and shows that her people then sought to make the nation bear the burthens of their slavery, by furnishing a military force sufficient to hold her bondmen in fear ; and if she adheres to that policy now, it merely illustrates the consistency of her people in relying upon the freemen of the North to uphold her system of oppression.

1776.] General Lee, commanding the military forces in that colony, called the particular attention of Congress to the fact, that slaves belonging to the planters, fled from servitude and sought freedom among the "*Exiles of Florida.*"

There also yet remained in Georgia many descendants of those who, at the establishment of that colony and since that time, had opposed the institution of Slavery. These people desired to testify their abhorrence of human servitude. They assembled in large numbers, in the district of Darien, and publicly resolved as follows : " To show the world that we are not influenced by any contracted " or interested motives, but by a general philanthropy for all man- " kind, of whatever climate, language or *complexion*, we hereby " declare our disapprobation and abhorrence of slavery in America." The public avowal of these doctrines, naturally encouraged slaves to seek their freedom by such means as they possessed. One day's

(1) Vide American Archives, Vol. I. Fifth Series : 1852.

travel would place some of them among friends, and in the enjoyment of liberty; and they were sure to be kindly received and respectfully treated, soon as they could reach their brethren in Florida. Of course many availed themselves of this opportunity to escape from service.

The Exiles remained in the undisturbed enjoyment of liberty during the war of the Revolution. The Creeks were a powerful and warlike people, whose friendship was courted during the sanguinary struggle that secured our National Independence. During those turbulent times it would not have been prudent for a master to pursue his slave through the Creek country, or to have brought him back to Georgia if once arrested.

The Exiles being thus free from annoyance, cultivated the friendship of their savage neighbors; rendered themselves useful to the Indians, both as laborers and in council. They also manifested much judgment in the selection of their lands for cultivation—locating their principal settlements on the rich bottoms lying along the Appalachicola and the Suwanee Rivers. Here they opened plantations, and many of them became wealthy in flocks and herds.

1783.] Immediately after the close of the war, the authorities of Georgia are said to have entered into a treaty with the Creek Indians, at Augusta, in which it is alleged that the Creeks agreed to grant to that State a large tract of land, and to restore such slaves as were then resident among the Creeks. But we find no copy of this treaty in print, or in manuscript. As early as 1789, only six years after it was said to have been negotiated, Hugh Knox, Secretary of War, in a communication to Congress, declared that no copy of this treaty was then in the possession of Congress; and it has not been since reprinted. Indeed, it is believed never to have been printed.

1785.] The difficulty between Georgia and the Creeks becoming more serious, the aid of the Continental Congress was invoked, for the purpose of securing that State in the enjoyment of what her people declared to be their rights. Congress appointed three commissioners to examine the existing causes of difficulty, and if possible to negotiate a treaty with the Creeks that should secure justice to all the people of the United States.

Communities, like individuals, often exhibit in early life those characteristics which distinguish their mature age, and become ruling passions when senility marks the downhill of life. Thus Georgia, in her very infancy, exhibited that desire for controlling our National Government which subsequently marked her manhood. Possessing no power under the Constitution to enter into any treaty except by consent of Congress, her Executive appointed three Commissioners to attend and supervise the action of those appointed by the Federal Legislature. The time and place for holding the treaty had been arranged with the Indians by the Governor of Georgia. At Galphinton,[1] the place appointed, the Commissioners of the United States met those of Georgia, who presented them with the form of a treaty fully drawn out and ready for signatures, and demanded of the Commissioners of the United States its adoption. This extraordinary proceeding was treated by the Federal Commissioners in a dignified and appropriate manner, in their report to Congress. One important provision of this inchoate treaty stipulated for the return to the people of Georgia of such fugitive negroes as were then in the Indian country, and of such as might thereafter flee from bondage.

The Commissioners appointed by Congress waited at Galphinton

---

(1) This was the residence of George Galphin, an Indian trader, who, in 1773, aided in obtaining a treaty by which the Creek Indians ceded a large tract of land to the British Government. Georgia succeeded the British Government in its title to these lands, by the treaty of peace in 1783. Some fifty years afterwards, the descendants of Galphin petitioned the State of Georgia for compensation, on account of the services rendered by Galphin in obtaining the treaty of 1773. But the Legislature repudiated the claim. The heirs, or rather descendants of Galphin, then applied to Congress, who never had either legal or beneficial interest in the lands obtained by the treaty. The Representatives from Georgia and from the South generally supported the claim. Northern men yielded their objections to this absurd demand, and in 1848 a bill passed both Houses of Congress by which the descendants of Galphin, and their attorneys and agents, obtained from our National Treasury $243,871 86. and the term " Galphin " has since become synonymous with " peculation " upon the public Treasury.

several days, and finding only *two* of the one hundred towns composing the Creek tribe represented in the council about to be held, they refused to regard them as authorized to act for the Creek nation, and would not consent to enter upon any negotiation with them as representatives of that tribe. This course was not in accordance with the ideas of the Commissioners appointed by Georgia. After those of the United States had left, they proceeded to enter into a treaty with the representatives from the two towns, who professed to act for the whole Creek nation.

This pretended treaty gave the State of Georgia a large territory; and the eighth article provided, that " the Indians shall restore all " the negroes, horses and other property, that are or may hereafter " be among them, belonging to the citizens of this State, or to any " other person whatever, to such person as the governor shall " appoint." [1]

This attempt to make a treaty by the State of Georgia, in direct violation of the articles of Confederation, and to bind the Creek nation by an act of the representatives of only two of their towns, constitutes the first official transaction of which we have documentary evidence, in that long train of events which has for seventy years involved our nation in difficulty, and the Exiles of Florida in persecutions and cruelties unequaled under Republican governments.

The Commissioners of the United States made report of their proceedings to Congress; and those of Georgia reported to the governor of that State.[2] Their report was transmitted to the Legislature, and that body, with an arrogance that commands our admiration, passed strong resolutions denouncing the action of the Federal Commissioners, commending the action of those of Georgia, and asserting her State sovereignty in language somewhat bombastic.

(1) Vide Report of Hugh Knox, Secretary of War, to the President, dated July 6, 1789. American State Papers. Vol. V. page 15, where the Treaty is recited in full.

(2) Vide papers accompanying the Report of the Secretary of War, above referred to, marked A, and numbered 1, 2 and 3.

1786.] Soon after the making of this pretended treaty, the Creeks commenced hostilities, murdering the people on the frontiers of Georgia, and burning their dwellings. The Spanish authorities of Florida were charged with fomenting these difficulties, and the Congress of the United States felt constrained to interfere.[1] The Commissioners previously appointed to form a treaty with the Creeks, were, by a resolution of the Continental Congress, adopted Oct. 26, instructed to obtain a treaty 1787.] with the Indians which would secure a return of all prisoners, of whatever age, sex or complexion, and to *restore all fugitive slaves belonging to citizens of the United States.*[2]

This resolution was the first act on the part of the Continental Congress in favor of restoring fugitive slaves. It was adopted under the articles of Confederation, before the adoption of our present constitution, and of course constitutes no precedent under our present government; yet it introduced a practice that has long agitated the nation, and may yet lead to important and even sanguinary results.

1788.] Without awaiting the action of Congress, the authorities of Georgia, by her agents, entered into another treaty, at a place called " Shoulderbone," by which the Creeks appear to have acknowledged the violation of the Treaty of Galphinton, and again stipulated to observe its covenants.[3]

We have no reliable information as to the number of the Creek towns represented at the making of this third treaty by Georgia. The whole transaction was by the State, in her own name, by her own authority, without consent of Congress, and all papers relating to it, if any exist, would of course be among the manuscript files of that State. It is believed that Georgia never printed any of these treaties; and we can only state their contents from recitals

---

(1) Vide letter of James White to Major General Knox, of the 24th May, 1787. American State Papers, Vol. II, Indian Affairs.

(2) American State Papers, Vol. V, page 25.

(3) Vide Documents accompanying the Treaty of New York; Am. State Papers, Vol. I, Indian Affairs.

which we find among the State papers of the Federal Government. It is however certain, that the Creeks denied that any such treaty had been entered into; and they continued hostilities, as though no such treaty had been thought of by them. This pretended Treaty of Shoulderbone exerted no more moral influence among the Creeks than did that of Galphinton. The war continued between the people of Georgia and the Creeks. The savages appeared to be aroused to indignation by what they regarded as palpable frauds. Excited at such efforts to impose upon them stipulations degrading to their character, they prosecuted the war with increased bitterness.

The natural results of such turpitude, induced Georgia to be one of the first in the sisterhood of States to adopt the Federal Constitution (Aug. 28). Her statesmen expected it to relieve their State from the burthens of the war which then devastated her border.

1788.]

Soon as the Federal Government was organized under the constitution, the authorities of Georgia invoked its aid, to protect her people from the indignation of the Creek Indians.

1789.]

General Washington, President of the United States, at once appointed Commissioners to repair to the Indian country, ascertain the real difficulty, and if able, they were directed to negotiate a suitable treaty, in the name of the United States. The State of Georgia claimed title to the territory ceded by the treaties of Galphinton and Shoulderbone; while the Creeks entirely repudiated them, declaring them fraudulent, denying their validity, and refusing to abide by their stipulations. The governor of Georgia placed in the hands of the Commissioners of the United States, a list of property which had been lost since the close of the Revolution by the people of Georgia, for which they demanded indemnity of the Creeks. This list contained the names of one hundred and ten negroes, who were said to have left their masters *during the Revolution*, and found an asylum among the Creeks. The Treaty of Galphinton contained a stipulation on the part of the Creeks, to return all prisoners, of whatever age, sex or color, and all negroes belonging to the citizens of Georgia, "*then residing with the Creeks.*"

Arrangements had already been made with the chiefs, warriors and principal men of the Creek nation, to meet the Commissioners of the United States at Rock Landing, on the Oconee River. The Commissioners were received by the Indians with great respect and formality; but soon as they learned that the Commissioners were not authorized to restore their lands, they broke off all negotiation, promising to remain in peace, however, until an opportunity should be presented for further negotiations.

The failure of this mission was followed by the appointment of Col. Willett, an intrepid officer of the Revolution, who was authorized to proceed to the Creek nation, and, if possible, to induce its chiefs and headmen to repair to New York, where they could negotiate a new treaty, without the interference of the authorities or people of Georgia.

Col. Willett was successful. He induced the principal chief, McGillivray, the son of a distinguished Indian trader, together with twenty-eight other chiefs and warriors, to come on to New York, for the purpose of forming a treaty with the United States, and settling all difficulties previously existing between Georgia and their nation. On their way to New York, they were received at Philadelphia, by the authorities of that city, with great ceremony and respect. Their vanity was flattered, and every effort made to induce them to believe peace with the United States would be important to both parties.

At New York they found Congress in session. Here they mingled with the great men of our nation. The "Columbian Order," or "Tammany Society," was active in its attentions. They escorted the delegation to the city, and entertained them with a public dinner; and made McGillivray, the principal chief, a member of their society. In this way, the minds of the Indians were prepared for entering into the treaty which followed.

1790.] There was, among the people of the entire nation, an intense anxiety to render every part of the Union satisfied and pleased with the Federal Government, then just formed, as they felt that their only hope of prosperity depended upon a continuance of the federal union. There was also a general sympathy throughout the nation with the slaveholders of the South, who were supposed to have suffered much, by the loss of their servants, during the war of the Revolution; few people at that time realizing the moral guilt of holding their fellow-men in bondage.

While the revolutionary contest was going on, many slaves in the Southern States escaped from the service of their masters, and, under the proclamations of various British commanders, enlisted into the service of his Britannic Majesty; and having taken the oath of allegiance to the crown of England, were regarded as British subjects. Others escaped with their families, and getting on board British vessels, sailed to the West Indies, where they settled as "*free persons.*" Thus, while one class of masters had sustained great losses by the enlistment of their slaves, another class had suffered by the escape of their bondmen, through the aid of British vessels; while a third sustained an equal loss by the escape of their servants to the Seminoles in Florida. These three different interests united in claiming the aid of government to regain possession of their slaves, or to obtain indemnity for their loss.

The timely arrival of Mr. Pinckney, secured the insertion of a clause in the Treaty of Paris, providing that his Britannic Majesty should withdraw his troops from all American forts, arsenals, shipyards, etc., without destroying ordnance or military stores, or "carrying away any negroes or other property of the inhabitants." This provision was regarded by the slaveholders of the South as securing a compensation to all those whose slaves had enlisted in the British army, as well as to those whose slaves had escaped to the British West India Islands by aid of English vessels; while those whose servants were quietly living with the Seminoles, had not been provided for by the treaty of peace.[1] These circumstances rendered the owners of the Exiles more clamorous for the interposition of the State Government, inasmuch as the federal authority had entirely omitted to notice their interests, while it was supposed to have secured a compensation to the other two classes of claimants.

It was under these circumstances, that General Washington proceeded to the negotiation of the first treaty, entered into under our present form of government. The chiefs, headmen and warriors of the Creek nation were present at New York : Georgia was also there by her senators and representatives, who carefully watched over her interests; and General Knox, the Secretary of War, was appointed commissioner to negotiate a treaty, thus to be formed, under the personal supervision of the President.

The object of the President was effected, a treaty was formed, and bears date August 1, 1790. It constitutes the title-page of our diplomatic history. This first exercise of our treaty-making power under the constitution, was put forth for the benefit of the Slave interests of Georgia. It surrendered up to the Creeks certain lands, which the authorities of Georgia claimed to hold under the treaty of Galphinton, but retained substantially the stipulation for the surrender of negroes, which had been inserted in that extraordinary compact.

By the third article of this new treaty, it was stipulated as follows :

"The Creek nation shall deliver, as soon as practicable, to the
"commanding officer of the troops of the United States stationed
"at Rock Landing, on the Oconee River, all citizens of the United
"States, white inhabitants or negroes, who are now prisoners in
"any part of the said nation. And if any such prisoners or
"negroes should not be so delivered, on or before the first day of

(1) The reader need not be informed, that these demands of indemnity for slaves were promptly rejected by the English government ; and Jay's Treaty of 1794, surrendered them forever.

" June ensuing, the governor of Georgia may empower three
" persons to repair to the said nation, in order to claim and receive
" such prisoners and negroes."

Historians have referred to this clause as containing merely a
stipulation for the surrender of *prisoners ;* [1] but the manner in
which the term "*negroes*" stands connected in the disjunctive form
with that of "prisoners," would appear to justify, at least to some
extent, the subsequent construction put upon it, so far as regarded
negroes then resident with the Creeks ; but it certainly makes no
allusion to those who were residing with the Seminoles in Florida.

It is a remarkable feature of this treaty, that the Creek
chiefs, principal men and warriors should, in its first article,
profess to act, not only for the Upper and Lower Creek Towns, but
for the Seminoles who were in Florida, protected by Spanish laws.
They had not been invited to attend the negotiation, had sent no
delegate, were wholly unrepresented in the Council; indeed, so far
as we are informed, were wholly ignorant of the objects which had
called such a council, and of the fact even that a council was held,
or a treaty negotiated.

Our fathers had just passed through seven years of war and
bloodshed, rather than submit to "*taxation without representation ;*" but this attempt to bind the Seminole Indians to surrender
up the Exiles, who were their friends and neighbors, and who now
stood connected with them by marriage, and in all the relations of
domestic life, without their consent or knowledge, constitutes an
inconsistency which can only be accounted for by the desire then
prevalent, to gratify and please those who wielded the slaveholding
influence of our nation.

Another extraordinary feature of this treaty may be found in the
secret article, by which the United States stipulated to pay the
Creeks fifteen hundred dollars annually, in all coming time. The
reason for making this stipulation secret is not to be learned from
any documentary authority before the public, and cannot now be

(1) Hildreth, in his History of the United States, speaks of in that light.

accounted for, except from the delicacy which the authorities of our nation then felt in taxing the people of the free States, to pay southern Indians for the return of those Exiles. And it is interesting at this day to look back and reflect, that for nearly seventy years the people of the nation have contributed their funds to sustain the authority of those slaveholders of Georgia over their bondmen, while Northern statesmen have constantly assured their constituents, they have nothing to do with that institution.

It would be uncharitable to believe, that General Washington was at that time conscious that he was thus precipitating our nation upon a policy destined to involve its government in difficulties, whose termination would be uncertain.

After the treaty had been agreed to by the parties making it, General Washington met the chiefs, headmen and warriors, assembled in the Hall of Representatives, in the presence of members of Congress and a large concourse of spectators. The treaty was publicly read, and to each article the Indians expressed their assent, and signed it in the presence of the people, each receiving from the President a string of wampum. The President then shook hands with each, which concluded the ceremonies of the day.

The treaty was transmitted on the following day to the Senate, accompanied by a Message from the President, saying : "I flatter "myself that this treaty will be productive of present peace and "prosperity to our Southern frontier. It is to be expected, also, that "it will be the means of firmly attaching the Creeks and neighboring "tribes to the interests of the United States." The President also alluded in his message to the treaty of Galphinton, as containing a stipulation to cede to Georgia certain other lands, which it was believed would be detrimental to the interests of the Indians, and, therefore, that covenant had been disregarded in the "treaty of New York." In another Message to the Senate, on the eleventh of August, the President says : "This treaty may be regarded as "the main foundation of the future peace and prosperity of the "Southwestern frontier of the United States."

On the ninth of August, a motion was made in the Senate to refer the treaty to a select committee, which was rejected by a vote of ten nays to eight yeas; and on the twelfth, it was approved by a vote of fifteen yeas to four nays; but we have no report of any discussion upon the subject, nor do we know at this day the objections which dictated the votes given against its ratification.[1]

(1) Vide Annals of Congress, Vol. I, pages 1068-70-74.

CHAPTER II.

FURTHER EFFORTS TO RESTORE EXILES.

Seminoles repudiate Treaty of New York — Attempts to induce Spanish authorities to deliver up the Exiles — Their refusal —Lower Creeks hostile to Treaty — McGillivray — His parentage and character — Georgia hostile to Treaty — Makes war upon Creeks — General Washington announces failure to maintain Peace — General Knox's recommendation — Decision of United States Court — Exertions — Combination of various classes of Claimants — Washington finds his influence powerless — Appoints Judge Jay — Failure of claims on England — Condition and habits of Exiles — Effect on Slaves of Georgia — Treaty of Colerain — Commissioners of Georgia leave Council in disgust — Election of the elder Adams — His Administration — Election of Jefferson — His Administration.

THE long pending difficulties between Georgia and the neighboring tribes of Indians were now (1791) believed to be permanently settled, and it was thought the new government would proceed in the discharge of its duties without further perplexity. But it was soon found impossible for the Creeks to comply with their stipulations. The Seminoles refused to recognize the treaty, insisting that they were not bound by any compact, arrangement or agreement, made by the United States and the Creeks, to which they were not a party, and of which they had no notice ; that they were a separate, independent tribe ; that this fact was well known to both Creeks and the United States ; and that the attempt of those parties to declare what the Seminoles should do, or should not do, was insulting to their dignity, to their self-respect, and only worthy of their contempt. They therefore wholly discarded the treaty, and repudiated all its provisions. They resided in Florida, under the jurisdiction of Spanish laws, subject only to the crown of Spain.

There they enjoyed that liberty so congenial to savages, as well as civilized men. The Creeks dared not attempt to bring back the Exiles by force, and the Government of the United States was unwilling to invade a Spanish colony for the purpose of recapturing those who had escaped from the bonds of oppression, and had become legally *free.*

1792.] In this state of affairs, an agent by the name of Seagrove was sent to Florida for the purpose of negotiating with the Spanish authorities for the return of the Exiles. He had been agent to the Creek Indians, and well understood their views in regard to the treaty. When he reached Florida, he found the authorities of that Province entirely opposed to the surrender of any subjects of the Spanish crown to slavery. The Exiles were regarded as holding the same rights which the white citizens held; and it was evident, that the representatives of the King of Spain encouraged both the Seminole Indians and Exiles, to refuse compliance with the treaty of New York.[1]

Nor was the Creek nation united upon this subject. The "lower Creeks," or those who resided on the southern frontier of Georgia, were not zealous in their support of the treaty; and it was said that McGillivray, the principal chief of the Creeks, was himself becoming unfriendly to the United States, and rather disposed to unite with the Spanish authorities. This man exerted great influence with the Indians. He was the son of an Indian trader, a Scotchman, by a Creek woman, the daughter of a distinguished chief. He had received a good English education; but his father had joined the English during the Revolution, and he, having been offended by some leading men of Georgia, had taken up his residence with the Indians and become their principal chief, in whom they reposed implicit confidence.

Amid these difficulties, the people of Georgia manifested an equal hostility to the treaty, inasmuch as it surrendered a large ter-

(1) Vide Correspondence on this subject between Seagrove and the War Department. American State Papers, Vol. V, pages 304-5, 320, 336, 387, and 392.

2

ritory to that State, which the authorities of Georgia pretended to have obtained by the treaty of Galphinton. The general feeling in that State was far from being satisfied with the action of the Federal Government. Seagrove, writing to the Secretary of War on this subject, declared, that "to such lengths have matters gone, "that they (the Georgians) now consider the troops and servants "of the United States who are placed among them, nearly as great "enemies as they do the Indians." [1]

Under these circumstances, the Governor of Georgia was addressed, by order of the President; but he evidently participated in the popular feeling of his State. While the Spanish authorities and Seminoles, both Indians and Exiles, repudiated the treaty of New York, Governor Tellfair, of Georgia, declared that the people of his State "*would recognize no treaty in which her commissioners were not consulted.*" Instead of observing its stipulations of peace, he proceeded to raise an army; invaded the Creek country, attacked one of their towns said to be friendly to Georgia, killed some of their people, took others prisoners, burned their dwellings, and destroyed their crops.

1794.] The Creeks declared their inability to return the Exiles, [2] and, on the thirtieth of January, General Washington, in a Special Message to Congress, announced the failure of all efforts to maintain tranquillity between the people of Georgia and the Creek Indians. Such were the difficulties surrounding the subject of regaining the Exiles, that General Knox, Secretary of War, in a written communication addressed to the President, recommended that Congress should make an appropriation to their owners, from the public treasury, as the only practicable manner in which that matter could be settled. [3] This communication was transmitted to Congress by the President, accompanied by a special message, recommending it to the consideration of that body; but the mem-

---

(1) American State Papers, "Indian Affairs." Vol. II, p. 305.
(2) Vide talk of principal Chief at Treaty of Colerain.
(3) Vide Annals of Congress of that date.

bers appeared unwilling to adopt the policy thus suggested. They seem to have entertained doubts as to the propriety of appropriating the money of the people to pay for fugitive slaves. They respectfully laid the Message, and the recommendation of the Secretary of War, upon the table, and ordered them to be printed.[1]

The claimants of the Exiles were again encouraged and strengthened in their expectations by the excitement prevailing in the southern portion of the Union, arising from a decision of the Circuit Court of the United States, held at Richmond, Virginia. At the commencement of the war, the States prohibited the collection of debts due British subjects from citizens of the Colonies. These debts had remained unpaid for some sixteen years; and although the debtors entertained an expectation of paying them at some future period, many intended meeting those demands by the funds which they supposed would be awarded them as indemnity for slaves carried away in British vessels during the Revolution, and for those enlisted into the British army.

These laws, enacted at the commencement of the Revolution, were declared by the Court to have been superseded by the treaty of peace, in 1783; and the debtors in the several States thus became liable to the payment of those debts, while their demands of indemnity for slaves were pending, and the British Government had thus far refused to acknowledge their validity. These claimants became impatient of delay, and demanded that another treaty be formed with England, by which they could obtain indemnity for the loss of their slaves. These uniting with those who claimed a return of the Exiles in Florida, constituted an influential portion of the people of the Southern States, whose joint influence was exerted to involve the Government in the support of slavery.

Notwithstanding these clamors, the Government was powerless as to obtaining relief for either class. The British Ministry

(1) Vide papers accompanying the Treaty of Colerain. American State Papers, Vol. I, "Indian Affairs."

refused indemnity, and the Seminoles, supported and encouraged by the Spanish authorities, were inexorable in their refusal to surrender the Exiles.

At that early period of our history, the subject of slavery greatly perplexed the Federal Administration; nor was the genius, or the influence of Washington, sufficiently powerful to silence the malcontents. He was fortunate in selecting Judge Jay, of New York, as a Minister Plenipotentiary, for negotiating a treaty with Great Britain. This illustrious patriot possessed great purity of character; had long been distinguished for his devotion to the welfare of the nation; and, although a Northern man, Southern slave claimants could raise no objection to him.

But every step towards the adjustment of the claims arising for slaves carried away by the English ships, or enlisted into the British army, had the effect to render the owners of Exiles more importunate. There was only one recourse, however, left for the Administration; they could do no more than to call on the Creeks for a new treaty, in order to adjust these claims.

1795.] As the President was about to take measures for obtaining another treaty with the Creeks, news arrived from England that Judge Jay, in forming a new treaty with the British Crown, had been constrained to surrender all claims of our citizens for slaves carried from the United States in British vessels during the war, or for those who had enlisted into the British service. This news created much excitement among the slaveholders of the Southern States. The treaty was denounced by the public Press, and a strong effort was made to defeat its approval by the Senate But failing in that, the slave power was rallied in opposition to making any appropriation, by the House of Representatives, for carrying the treaty into effect, and perhaps at no time since the Union was formed, has it been in greater danger of disruption; but the friends of the treaty prevailed in both Houses of Congress, and it became a paramount law of the nation.

While these incidents were transpiring, the Exiles were engaged in cultivating their lands, extending their plantations and increasing their flocks and herds, and consolidating their friendships with the Indians around them. Of all these facts the bondmen of Georgia had full knowledge. It were impossible for them to contemplate their friends, in the enjoyment of these rights and privileges, without a strong desire to share in those blessings of freedom. The example of the Exiles was thus constantly exerting an influence upon those who remained in bondage. Many of them sought opportunities to flee into Florida, where they, in like manner, became free subjects of Spain.

This condition of things induced General Washington to make another effort to remedy existing evils, and prevent their recurrence in future. He took measures to obtain the attendance of the Chiefs, head men and warriors of the Creek nation, at a place called Colerain, for the purpose of forming another treaty. He again appointed Benjamin Hawkins, George Clymer and Andrew Pickens, Commissioners, to meet the Indians in Council, and agree upon the proper adjustment of pending difficulties. These men were interested in the institution of Slavery, and were supposed to be perfectly acceptable to the claimants, as well as to the authorities of Georgia.

1796.]

The parties met at the place appointed, and proceeded to the consideration of the proposed treaty. The Creeks were not disposed to make further grants of territory ; nor were they able to give any better assurance for the return of the Exiles than had been given at New York. They insisted that, by the treaty of New York, they were only bound to return those negroes who had been captured *since* the treaty of peace between the United States and Great Britain ; these they had delivered up, so far as they were able to surrender them. They admitted there were more negroes among them, whom they might probably obtain at some future day, and expressed a willingness to do so. It is however evident, from the talk of the various Chiefs, that they had no idea of returning those Exiles who were residing in Florida—no allusion being made to them by either of the Commissioners, on the part of the United States, nor by the Indians. The Council was also attended by Commissioners on the part of Georgia, who attempted to dictate the manner of transacting the business, and, even in offensive language, charged the Commissioners of the United States with improper conduct; but in no instance did they name the Seminoles, nor allude to any obligation, on the part of the Creeks, to return the Exiles resident among the Seminoles. It should however be borne in mind, that these Commissioners on behalf of Georgia left the council in disgust, before the close of the negotiation. In the treaty itself, however, there is a stipulation that the treaty of New York shall remain in force, except such parts as were expressly changed by that entered into at Colerain; and that portion of the treaty of New York by which the Creeks assumed to bind the Seminoles, was not changed.[1]

The seventh article of the Treaty of Colerain reads as follows:—
" The Creek nation shall deliver, as soon as practicable, to the
" Superintendent of Indian Affairs, at such place as he may direct,
" all the citizens of the United States, white inhabitants and negroes,
" who are now prisoners in any part of the said nation, agreeably to
" the treaty at New York; and also all citizens, white inhabitants,
" negroes and property, taken since the signing of that treaty. And
" if any such prisoners, negroes, or property, should not be delivered
" on or before the first day of January next, the Governor of Georgia
" may empower three persons to repair to the said nation, in order to
" claim and receive such prisoners, negroes and property, under the
" direction of the President of the United States." This stipulation
was understood by the Creeks, and they were willing to perform it;
but it is very obvious, from all the circumstances, that they had no
idea of binding the Seminoles to return the Exiles resident in
Florida.

(1) Vide the papers accompanying this Treaty when submitted to the Senate. They are collected in the second volume of American State Papers, entitled " Indian Affairs." They will afford much interesting matter as to the doctrines of " State Rights " and Nullification, which it is unnecessary to embrace in this work.

The State of Georgia obtained very little territory by this treaty, and no further indemnity for the loss of their fugitive bondmen. The people of that State, therefore, were greatly dissatisfied with it. But the extraordinary feature of this treaty, consists in the subsequent construction placed upon it by the authorities of Georgia, who, twenty-five years subsequently, insisted that the Seminoles were in fact a part of the Creek tribe, bound by the Creek treaties, and that the Creek nation were under obligation to compel the Seminoles to observe treaties made by the Creeks.

In each of the treaties made between the State of Georgia and the Creeks, as well as in that made at New York, between the United States and the Creek nation, attempts had been made to bind the Seminoles, although that tribe had steadily and uniformly denied the authority of the Creeks to bind them; and being sustained by the Spanish authorities, it became evident that all further efforts to induce them to submit to the government of the Creeks would be useless. This independence they had maintained for nearly half a century. They had in no instance acknowledged the authority of the Creeks since they left Georgia, in 1750; nor is it reasonable to suppose the authorities of that State, or those of the United States, were ignorant of that important circumstance.

The flagrant injustice of holding the Creeks responsible for fugitive slaves resident in Florida, and under protection of the Spanish crown, must be obvious to every reader; and the inquiry will at once arise, Why did the Creek chiefs at New York consent to such a stipulation? The answer *perhaps* mays be found in the secret article of that treaty, giving to the Creeks fifteen hundred dollars annually, *forever*, and to McGillivray *twelve hundred dollars during life*, and to six other chiefs *one hundred dollars annually*. These direct and positive bribes could not fail to have effect. The necessity for keeping this article secret from the Indians generally, and from the people of the United States, is very apparent; as the propriety of thus taking money, drawn from the free States to bribe Indian chiefs to obligate their nation to seize and return fugitive slaves, would have been doubted by savages as well as civilized men. But the duty of the Creeks to seize and return the Exiles was legally recognized by the treaty of Colerain, which admitted the treaty of New York to be in force. This was regarded as a continuance of the claims of Georgia, although the Creeks appear to have had no idea of entering into such stipulations.

1797.]   Many circumstances now combined to quiet the apprehensions of the fugitive bondmen in Florida. The elder Adams had been elected President in the autumn of 1796, and assumed the duties of his office on the fourth of March following. A descendant of the Pilgrims, he had been reared and educated among the lovers of liberty; he had long served in Congress; he had reported upon the rights of the people of the Colonies in 1774, and was chairman of the committee who reported the Declaration of Independence, in 1776, and to its doctrines he had ever exhibited an unfaltering devotion. From such an Administration the claimants in Georgia could expect but little aid.

Another consideration, cheering to the friends of Freedom, was the total failure of the claims on Great Britain, for slaves lost during the War of the Revolution. The influence of those claimants was no longer felt in the Government. The public indignation was also somewhat excited against the institution of Slavery by incidents of a barbarous character, which had then recently transpired in North Carolina. After the promulgation of the Declaration of Independence, the Quakers of that State, conscious of its momentous truths, proceeded in good faith to emancipate their slaves; believing that the only mode in which they could evince their adherence to its doctrines.

The advocates of oppression were offended at this practical recognition of the "equal right of all men to liberty," and, to manifest their abhorrence of such doctrines, arrested the slaves so emancipated as *fugitives from labor*. The Quakers, ever true to their convictions of justice, lent their influence, and contributed their funds, to test the legal rights of the persons thus set at liberty, before the proper tribunals of the State ; and the question was carried to the Court of Appeals, where a final judgment was rendered in favor of their freedom. This decision appears to have disappointed general expectation among the advocates of slavery, and created much excitement throughout the State.

At the next session of the Legislature, an act was passed authorizing persons possessing landed property to seize and reënslave the people thus emancipated. But the planters of that State were usually possessed of wealth and intelligence, and, holding principles of honor, they refused to perform so degrading a service ; and the liberated negroes continued to enjoy their freedom.

But the opponents of liberty became so clamorous against the example thus set in favor of freedom, that the Legislature passed an amendatory act, authorizing *any person* to seize, imprison and sell, as slaves, any negro who had been emancipated in said State, *except those who had served in the army of the United States during the war of the Revolution.*

Persons of desperate character, gamblers, slave-dealers and horse thieves, were now authorized to gratify their cupidity, by seizing and selling persons who had for years enjoyed their liberty ; and the scenes which followed, were in no respect creditable to the State, to the civilization or Christianity of the age. Emancipated families were broken up and separated for ever. In some instances the wife escaped, while the husband was captured. Parents were seized, and their children escaped. Bloodhounds were employed to chase down those who fled to the forests and swamps, in order to avoid men more cruel than bloodhounds.

The Quakers, so far as able, assisted these persecuted people to escape to other States. Some left North Carolina on board ships ; others fled north by land ; and many reached the free States, where their descendants yet live. But even our free States did not afford a safe retreat from the cruelty of inexorable slave-catchers. Those free persons were seized in Philadelphia, and, under the fugitive slave law of 1793, were imprisoned in that city ; and, what excites still greater wonder, were delivered up and carried back to bondage.[1]

Some of these people, while in Pennsylvania, sent petitions to Congress, praying protection against such barbarity; and great excitement was aroused among Southern members by the presentation of such petitions. The Quakers of that State, and of New Jersey, also sent petitions to Congress, praying that these people may be protected against such piratical persecution. The popular feeling of the nation was shocked at these things, and great indignation against the institution, generally, was aroused.

We have no record of further attempts on the part of the claimants to obtain a return of the Exiles, after the Treaty of Colerain, until the close of Mr. Adams's administration. During that period, the fugitives remained quietly in their homes, undisturbed by their former masters. Their numbers were often increased by new arrivals, as well as by the natural laws of population, and they began to assume the appearance of an established community.

In 1801, Mr. Jefferson entered upon the duties of President. He had himself penned the Declaration of Independence, and manifested a deep devotion to its doctrines. Nor do we find that any attempt was made by him for the return of the Exiles; nor were there any measures adopted to obtain indemnity for the loss of the claimants during the eight years of his Administration.

In 1802, a new law regulating intercourse with the Indian tribes was enacted, by which the holders of slaves were secured for the price or value of any bondmen who should leave his master and take up his residence with any Indian tribe resident in the United States, or Territories thereof — at least such was the construction given to this statute.

The Creeks, Cherokees, and other Southern tribes, had gradually adopted the institution of Slavery, so long practiced by their

---

(1) Vide Annals of IVth Congress, 2d Session.

more civilized neighbors, and thus became interested in every effort to extinguish the hope cherished among their own bondmen, of regaining freedom by fleeing from their masters. And many circumstances now appeared to favor the idea, that no more attempts would be made to compel a return of the Exiles to bondage.

CHAPTER III.

HOSTILIITES MAINTAINED BY GEORGIA.

Mr. Madison's election — His character — Desire of people of Georgia to enslave Exiles — They demand annexation of Florida — Congress passes a law for taking possession of that Territory — General Mathews appointed Commissioner — Declares insurrection — Takes possession of Amelia Island — Spanish Government demands explanation — The President disavows acts of Mathews — Governor Mitchell succeeds Mathews — Georgia raises an Army — Florida invaded — Troops surrounded by savage foes — Their danger — Their retreat — Stealing Slaves — Lower Creeks join Seminoles — Georgia demands their surrender — Chiefs refuse — Georgia complains — President refuses to interfere — Another invasion of Florida — Towns burned; Cattle stolen — Troops withdrawn from Amelia Island — Public attention directed toward our Northern frontier — Lord Cockrane enters Chesapeake Bay — Issues Proclamation to Slaves — Dismay of Slaveholders — Slaves go on board British ships — Several vessels enter Appalachicola Bay — Col. Nichols lands there with Troops — Gathers around him Exiles and Indians — Builds a Fort, arms it, and places Military Stores in its Magazines — Treaty of Peace with England — Provision in regard to Slaves taken away during War — Claimants of the Exiles encouraged — Col. Nichols delivers Fort to the Exiles — Their plantations, wealth, and social condition — Our Army — General Gaines represents Fort as in possession of Outlaws — Plans for its destruction — Correspondence — General Jackson's order — Col. Clinch's Expedition — Met by Sailing-Master Loomis and two gun-boats — Fort blown up — Destruction of human life — Negroes captured and enslaved — Property taken — Claimed by Governor of Florida — First Seminole War commenced.

WHEN Mr. Madison assumed the duties of President (March 4, 1809), the Exiles were quietly enjoying their freedom; each sitting under his own vine and fig-tree, without molestation or fear. Many had been born in the Seminole country, and now saw around them children and grand-children, in the enjoyment of all the necessaries of life. Many, even of those who fled from Georgia after the formation of that colony, had departed to their final rest; but their children and friends had been comparatively free from persecutions since the Treaty of Colerain, in 1796. Discarding all connection with the Creeks, and living under protection of Spain, and feeling their right to liberty was "self-evident," they believed the United States to have tacitly admitted their claims to freedom. With these impressions, they dwelt in conscious security, believing no further attempts would be made to reënslave them. Mr. Madison had penned the memorable Address of Congress to the people of the United States, published near the close of the old Confederation, in which was reiterated, in glowing language, the doctrines of the Declaration of Independence; and in the Convention that framed the Constitution, he had declared "it would be wrong to admit, in that instrument, that *man can hold property in man.*"

1810.] The people of Georgia were not satisfied with the existing state of things. They were greatly excited at seeing those who had once been slaves, in South Carolina and in Georgia, now live quietly and happily in the enjoyment of liberty, with their flocks and their herds, their wives and their little ones, around them; but they were on Spanish soil, protected by Spanish laws. The only mode of enslaving them was, firstly, to obtain jurisdiction of the Territory; and the annexation of Florida to the United States was, accordingly, urged upon the Federal Government.

Spain had acquired her American territories by conquest, and was too proud to part with them. An excitement, however, was raised in favor of its annexation; and this anxiety to secure the slave interests of the South, soon extended to Congress, 1811.] and infused itself into the Executive policy of the nation. A law was passed by the two Houses, in secret session, and approved by the President, for taking possession of Florida. Gen. Mathews, a slaveholder of Georgia, was appointed Commissioner for that purpose. A few malcontents were found in the northeastern part of the Territory; their numbers were increased by men of desperate fortunes from Georgia; and an insurrection was proclaimed by the Acting General. Mathews, commanding the insurgents, took possession of Amelia Island, and of the country opposite to it on the main land. The Spanish Government, on learning the outrage, remonstrated with our Executive, who disavowed the acts of Mathews, whom he recalled; and proceeded to appoint General Mitchell, the Governor of Georgia, to act as Commissioner, in place of Mathews.

Mitchell, however, continued to hold military possession of the island and part of the main land, and, in fact, continued to carry forward the policy which Mathews had inaugurated. These things occurred while our nation was professedly at peace with Spain, and constituted a most flagrant violation of our national faith.

1812.]   The Executive of Georgia, apparently entertaining the idea that his State was competent to declare war and make peace, raised an army, which, under the command of the Adjutant General, entered Florida with the avowed intention of exterminating the Seminoles, who had so long refused to surrender the Exiles; while the real object was the recapture and reënslavement of the refugees. The Creeks of the Lower Towns, however, took sides with the Seminoles, in opposing this piratical foray of slave-catchers. The army having penetrated a hundred miles or more into Florida, found itself surrounded with hostile savages. Their supplies were cut off; the men, reduced almost to a state of starvation, were compelled to retrace their steps; and with great loss the survivors reached Georgia. But they robbed those Spanish inhabitants who fell in their way of all their provisions, and left them to suffer for the want of food. Nor were the Georgians satisfied with taking such provisions as were necessary to support life; they also took with them a large number of slaves, owned by Spanish masters, with whom they resided.[1]

(1) The claims of these ancient Spanish inhabitants for indemnity against those robberies, have been pressed upon the consideration of Congress for the last twenty-five years, and were recently pending before the Court of Claims. When the bill for their relief was under discussion before the House of Representatives, in 1843, Hon. John Quincy Adams presented a list of some ninety slaves, for the loss of whom the owners claimed compensation from the United States. But the discussions which arose on private bills were not at that time reported; and neither this exhibit, nor the speech of Mr. Adams, are to be found in the Congressional Debates of that day.

The people, and the authorities of Georgia, were greatly incensed at the Creek Indians, who had assisted the Seminoles in defending themselves; and the Governor of that State demanded of the chiefs a surrender of those individuals who had thus offended against the sovereignty of that commonwealth. The chiefs refused to deliver up their brethren, and the Governor complained to the President of this disregard of slaveholding comity by the Creeks.

The Federal authorities appear to have felt very little interest in the matter, and Georgia determined to redress her own grievances. The Legislature of that State, deeming their interests neglected by the Federal Government, passed resolutions declaring the occupation of Florida essential to the safety and welfare of their people, whether Congress authorized it or not; and they passed an act for raising a force " *to reduce St. Augustine and punish the Indians.*"

Under this declaration of war by the sovereign power of Georgia, another army was raised. Hunters, trappers, vagabonds, and men of desperate fortunes, were collected from that State, from East Tennessee, and from other Southern States, to the number of five hundred; and Florida was again invaded. This expedition was more successful, in some respects, than the first. They burned two or three of the smaller Seminole towns, destroyed several cornfields that had been planted by the Exiles, and drove back to Georgia large herds of cattle, which they had stolen from the negroes; yet the principal object of the Expedition failed : They were unable to capture an individual, or family, of the Exiles. There were no Spanish inhabitants in that part of Florida from whom they could capture slaves, and they were compelled to return without human victims, but with the loss of several individuals of their own party. Thus, after a struggle of more than two years (ending May, 1813), the State of Georgia found itself unable to conquer Florida or the Seminoles, or to capture the Exiles. Further prosecution of the war was given up, the troops were withdrawn from Amelia Island, and peace was restored.

This extraordinary proceeding, on the part of Georgia, appears to have excited very little attention at the time; probably in consequence of the more important operations that were then being carried forward, upon our Northern and Northwestern frontiers. Harrison at Tippecanoe, and at Maumee; and Scott and Van Rensselaer at Queenston, and along the Niagara frontier, were gallantly confronting the British army, aided by powerful allies from the various neighboring tribes of savages; and so greatly was the attention of the people of the Northern States absorbed in these operations, that they were scarcely conscious of the slave-catching forays carried on by the State of Georgia. Indeed, during these operations, the public men of that State were among the most vehement advocates for a strict construction of the Federal Constitution, and for maintaining the American Union.

1814.] These transactions upon our Southern frontier, called attention of British Ministers to the Seminoles and the Exiles. A hostile fleet entered Chesapeake Bay, under Lord Cochrane, who issued a proclamation inviting all persons (meaning slaves), who desired to emigrate from the United States, to come with their families on board his Britannic Majesty's ships of war; assuring them of the privilege of entering his Majesty's naval service, or of settling with their families, as *free* persons, in either of the British West India Islands. This proclamation was widely circulated, and spread very general consternation along our Southern seaboard: it gave the slaveholders of Georgia occasion to look to their own protection, and to secure the fidelity of those bondmen who yet remained in the service of their masters.[1]

Two British sloops of war and some smaller vessels suddenly appeared in Appalachicola Bay, where they landed a body of troops,

---

(1) Many slaves actually fled from their masters and found an asylum on board British vessels. Some sixty, belonging to a planter named Forbes, who resided in Georgia, left his plantation and took shelter on board the ship commanded by Lord Cochrane. They were transported to Jamaica, where they settled and lived as other free people. After the restoration of peace, Forbes sued his Lordship, before the British courts, for damages sustained by the loss of these slaves. The case elicited much learning in regard to the law of Slavery, and, next to that of Sommerset, may be regarded as the most important on that subject ever litigated before an English court.

Negro Abraham.

under Lieut. Colonel Nichols, of the British Army, for the purpose of lending support and protection to the Exiles and their Indian allies. He opened communications with them, furnished them with arms and ammunition, and soon drew around him a considerable force of Indians as well as negroes. His encampment was on the east side of the Appalachicola River, some thirty miles above its mouth. In November, he completed a strong fort on the bank of that stream. Some eight pieces of heavy ordnance were mounted upon its walls, and its magazine was well stored with the material of war.[1] It was evidently intended as a defense against the forays of slave-catchers, who were not expected to bring with them heavy artillery. The plan was well conceived. Even the plundering expeditions authorized by the State of Georgia, would have been unable to make any impression on this fortification. But neither Nichols, nor the Exiles, appear to have anticipated the employment of the United States navy in a piratical work, discarded by most Christian nations and people, and allowed to be carried on only upon the African coast.

The British fleet withdrew from the coast of Georgia, and the slaveholders of that State were relieved, for a time, from those apprehensions of slave insurrection which had been excited by the proclamation of Lord Cochrane.

In the meantime the Treaty of Ghent was ratified, and peace restored to the country. In that treaty the interests of Slavery

(1) "Monette," in his "History of the Valley of the Mississippi," says Woodbine erected this fort in the summer of 1816; and such were the representations made before the Committee appointed in 1819, to investigate the conduct of General Jackson, in taking possession of Florida. But the reader will notice the Letter of General Gaines, hereafter quoted, which bears date on the 14th May, 1815, and *officially* informed the Secretary of War that "*negroes and outlaws have taken possession of* a FORT ON THE APPALACHICOLA RIVER." This was more than a year before the time of erecting the fort, according to "Monette."

The parapet of the fort was said to be fifteen feet high and eighteen thick, situated upon a gentle cliff, with a fine stream emptying into the river near its base, and a swamp in the rear, which protected it from the approach of artillery by land. On its walls were mounted one thirty-two pounder, three twenty-four pounders, two nine pounders, two six pounders, and one brass five and a half-inch howitzer. Vide Official Report of Sailing-Master Loomis.

3

had not been forgotten; and the same stipulations were inserted, in regard to the withdrawal of his Majesty's troops and navy, "without taking or carrying away any negroes or other property "of the citizens," which characterized the treaty of 1782. The owners of slaves who had fled from service under the proclamation of Lord Cochrane, now determined to obtain compensation for their loss. This general feeling again aroused the cupidity of those whose fathers had once claimed to own those Exiles, who fled from Georgia some thirty or forty years previously.

In the spring of 1815, Colonel Nichols and his troops withdrew from Florida, leaving the fort, with its entire armament and magazine of military stores, in the possession of the Exiles, who resided in the vicinity. Their plantations extended along the river several miles, above and below the fort.[1] Many of them possessed large herds of cattle and horses, which roamed in the forests, gathering their food, both in summer and winter, without expense or trouble to their owners.

The Pioneer Exiles from South Carolina had settled here long before the Colony of Georgia existed. Several generations had lived to manhood and died in those forest-homes. To their descendants it had become consecrated by "many an oft told tale" of early adventure, of hardship and suffering; the recollection of which had been retained in tradition, told in story, and sung in their rude lays. Here were the graves of their ancestors, around whose memories were clustered the fondest recollections of the human mind. The climate was genial. They were surrounded by extensive forests, and far removed from the habitations of those enemies of freedom who sought to enslave them; and they regarded themselves as secure in the enjoyment of liberty. Shut out from the cares and strifes of more civilized men, they were happy in their own social solitude. So far from seeking to injure the people of

---

(1) This is the official account of Sailing-Master Loomis, who commanded the naval expedition subsequently sent to reduce this fortress.

"Monette," in his History of the Valley of the Mississippi, says, " *Near the Fort the fields were fine*, and extended along the river nearly *fifty miles.*"

the United States, they were only anxious to be exempt, and entirely free from all contact with our population or Government; while they faithfully maintained their allegiance to the Spanish crown.

1815.] Peace with Great Britain, however, had left our army without active employment. A portion of it was stationed along our Southern frontier of Georgia, to maintain peace with the Indians. The authorities and people of Georgia maintained social and friendly relations with the officers and men of the army. By means of Indian spies, the real condition of the Exiles was also ascertained and well understood. What means were used to excite the feelings or prejudices of the military officers against these unoffending Exiles, is not known at this day. Most of the officers commanding in the South were, however, slaveholders, and probably felt a strong sympathy with the people of Georgia in their indignation against them, for obtaining and enjoying liberty without permission of their masters.

General Gaines, commanding on the Southern frontier of Georgia, making Fort Scott his head-quarters, wrote the Secretary of War (May 14), saying, " certain negroes and outlaws have taken " possession of a fort on the Appalachicola River, in the Territory " of Florida." He assured the Secretary, that he should keep watch of them. He charged them with no crime, imputed to them no hostile acts. He was conscious that they had taken possession of the fort solely for their own protection; but he styled them *negroes*, which, in the language of that day among slaveholders, was regarded as an imputation of guilt; and *outlaw* was supposed to be a proper term with which to characterize those who had fled from bondage and sworn allegiance to another government.[1]

(1) The reader will at once see, that these people were as much under the protection of Spain, as the fugitive slaves now in Canada are under the protection of British laws. They were as clearly Spanish subjects as the latter are British subjects. By the law of nations, Spain had the same right to permit her black subjects to occupy " Blount's Fort," that the Queen of England has to permit Fort Malden to be occupied by her black subjects. The only distinction between the two cases is, Spain was weak and unable to maintain her national honor, and national rights; while England has the power to do both.

For more than a year subsequently to the date of this letter, General Gaines made the Exiles a subject of frequent communication to the War Department. In this official correspondence, he at all times spoke of them as "runaways," "outlaws," "pirates," "murderers," etc.; but in no instance did he charge them with any act hostile to the United States, or to any other people or government.

Of these communications the Exiles were ignorant. They continued in peaceful retirement, cultivating the earth, and gaining a support for themselves and families. In the autumn of 1815, they gathered their crops, provided for the support of the aged and infirm, as well as for their children. They carefully nursed the sick; they buried their dead; they lived in peace, and enjoyed the fruits of their labor. The following spring and summer found them in this enviable condition.

1816.]   While the Exiles living on the Appalachicola were thus pursuing the even tenor of their ways, plans were ripening among the slaveholders and military officers of our army for their destruction. A correspondence was opened by the Secretary of War with General Jackson, who commanded the Southwestern Military District of the United States, holding his head-quarters at Nashville, Tennessee. Various letters and communications passed between those officers in regard to this "Negro Fort," as they called it.

Power is never more dangerous than when wielded by military men. They usually feel ambitious to display their own prowess, and that of the troops under their command; and no person can read the communications of General Gaines, in regard to the Exiles who had gathered in and around this fort, without feeling conscious that he greatly desired to give to the people of the United States an example of the science and power by which they could destroy human life.[1]

(1) Vide the voluminous Correspondence on this subject contained in Ex. Doc. 119, 2d Session, XVth Congress.

At length, on the sixteenth of May, General Jackson wrote General Gaines, saying, "I have little doubt of the fact, that this "fort has been established by some villains for the purpose of "rapine and plunder, and that it ought to be blown up, regardless "of the ground on which it stands; and if your mind shall have "formed the same conclusion, destroy it and return the *stolen* "*negroes* and property to their rightful owners." [1]

Without attempting to criticise this order of General Jackson, we must regard a fort thus situated, at least sixty miles from the border of the United States, as a most singular instrument for the purpose of "rapine," or plundering our citizens. Nor could General Jackson have entertained any apprehensions from those who occupied the fort. The entire correspondence showed them to be *refugees*, seeking only to avoid our people; indeed, his very order shows this, for he directs General Gaines to return the "*stolen negroes* to their rightful owners." The use of opprobrious epithets is not often resorted to by men in high official stations: yet it is difficult to believe, that General Jackson supposed these negroes to have been stolen; for, neither in the official correspondence on this subject, nor in the papers accompanying it, embracing more than a hundred documentary pages, is there a hint that these negroes were "*stolen*," or that they had committed violence upon any person, or upon the property of any person whatever. They had sought their own liberty, and the charge of stealing themselves, was used like the other epithets of "outlaws," "pirates" and "murderers," to cast opprobrium upon the character of men who, if judged by their

(1) Perhaps no portion of our national history exhibits such disregard of international law, as this unprovoked invasion of Florida. For thirty years, the slaves of our Southern States have been in the habit of fleeing to the British Provinces. Here they are admitted to all the rights of citizenship, in the same manner as they were in Florida. They vote and hold office under British laws; and when our Government demanded that the English Ministry should disregard the rights of these people and return them to slavery, the British Minister contemptuously refused even to hold correspondence with our Secretary of State on a subject so abhorrent to every principle of national law and self-respect. Our Government coolly submitted to the scornful arrogance of England; but did not hesitate to invade Florida with an armed force, and to seize the faithful subjects of Spain, and enslave them-

love of liberty or their patriotism, would now occupy a position not less honorable in the history of our country than is assigned to the patriots of 1776.

Nor is it easy to discover the rule of international law, which authorized the Executive of the United States, or the officers of our army, to dictate to the crown of Spain in what part of his territory he should, or should not, erect fortresses; or the constitutional power which they held for invading the territory of a nation at peace with the United States, destroy a fort, and consign its occupants to slavery. But those were days of official arrogance on the one hand, and popular submission on the other. The Exiles, or their ancestors, had once been slaves. They now were cultivating the richest lands in Florida, and possessed wealth; they were occupying a strong fortress. Many slaves during the recent war had escaped from their masters, in Georgia, and some were supposed to be free subjects of Spain, living in Florida; and if the Exiles were permitted to enjoy their plantations and property in peace, it was evident that the institution in adjoining States would be in danger of a total overthrow. These facts were apparent to General Jackson, as well as to General Gaines and the slaveholders of Georgia.

General Gaines only awaited permission from his superior to carry out the designs of the slaveholders, who had become alarmed at the dangers to which their "peculiar institution" was subjected. Upon the receipt of the order above quoted, he detailed Lieut. Col. Clinch,[1] of the regular troops, with his regiment and five hundred friendly Creek Indians, under McIntosh, their principal chief, to carry out the directions of General Jackson. Colonel Clinch was directed to take with him two pieces of artillery, for the purpose of cannonading the fort if necessary.[2]

This commencement of the first Seminole war was, at the time,

(1) Hon. Duncan L. Clinch. He left the service in 1841, and was subsequently a Member of Congress for several years, and died in 1852.

(2) War was thus waged against Spain, by Executive authority, without consulting Congress; and no member of that body uttered a protest, or denunciation of the act.

unknown to the people of the United States. It was undertaken for the purposes stated in General Jackson's order, to "blow up the fort, and *return the negroes to their rightful owners.*" Historians have failed to expose the cause of hostilities, or the barbarous foray which plunged the nation into that bloody contest which cost the people millions of treasure and the sacrifice of hundreds of human lives.

It was July before the arrangements were fully made by Colonel Clinch and his savage allies for descending the river, with suitable artillery and supplies, to accomplish the object of their mission.[1] The Creeks, having entered into the treaties of New York and Colerain, by which they bound themselves, twenty years previously, to return those Exiles who fled from Georgia, and having failed to perform those stipulations, now cheerfully united with the American army in this first slave-catching expedition undertaken by the Federal Government.

Of these movements the Exiles had been informed by their neighbors, the friendly Creeks; for, among the Lower Creeks, were individuals who at all times sympathized with them, and kept them informed of the measures adopted for their destruction. All the families living on the river and in the vicinity of the fort, fled to it for protection. They had no idea of the advantages arising from scientific warfare; they believed their fortification impregnable. Colonel Nichols had erected it for the purpose of affording them protection, and they had no doubt of its efficiency for that purpose.

Such were the delays attending the journey, in consequence of difficulties in transporting heavy guns and provisions, that the

(1) In Ex. Doc. No. 119, 2d Session. XVth Congress, may be found the official correspondence between the War Department and General Jackson; also that between General Jackson and General Gaines, together with the orders of each, as well as the correspondence between the Secretary of the Navy and Commodore Patterson; and the order of the latter officer to Sailing-Master Loomis; and the final report of Sailing-Master Loomis and General Clinch. In none of these papers is there any act of hostility mentioned or referred to as having been committed by the Exiles, or the Seminole Indians, prior to their reaching the vicinity of the Fort.

troops did not reach the vicinity of the fort until the twenty-fourth of July. In the meantime, Commodore Patterson, in pursuance of orders from the naval department, had detailed Sailing-Master Loomis, with two gun-boats, to assist in carrying out the order of General Jackson.[1]

On the twenty-fourth of July, Colonel Clinch commenced a reconnoisance of the fort. On the twenty-fifth, he cleared away the brush and erected a battery, and placed upon it two long eighteen-pounders, and commenced a cannonade of the fortress. At the time of this investment, there were about three hundred Exiles in the fort, including women and children, besides thirty-four Seminole Indians:[2] yet in the official report of Colonel Clinch, he makes no mention of his fire being returned; nor does he say that any of his men were killed or wounded by the occupants of the fort.

On the twenty-sixth of July, Sailing-Master Loomis, with his command, reached a point on the river some two miles below the fort. Colonel Clinch met him at that place, for consultation, and informed him that his fire had thus far proved ineffectual, and that a nearer approach of artillery by land would be difficult.[3]

Judging from the language used in his official dispatch, Sailing-Master Loomis must have entertained some feelings of distrust towards Colonel Clinch, as they evidently separated in bad temper: yet no officer in the service of the United States ever exhibited greater prudence in his preparations, or more firmness in battle, than Colonel Clinch. He was, however, a man of kind and humane feelings, and high notions of honor. It has been supposed by many of his friends, that he shrank from the perpetration of the outrage which he had been detailed to commit.[4]

---

(1) Hildreth states that *three* gun-boats were detailed on that occasion; but the report of Sailing-Master Loomis speaks only of *two*.

(2) Hildreth states the number to have been about three hundred, partly Indians and partly negroes.

(3) Monette says this expedition was undertaken by Col. Clinch upon his own responsibility, to enable some boats laden with provisions to pass up the river. A strange misapprehension of facts, as shown by official documents.

(4) At this conference, Sailing-Master Loomis informed Colonel Clinch that, on the day

On the morning of the twenty-seventh, Loomis, with his boats, ascended the river and cast anchor opposite the fort, while Colonel Clinch and the Creek Indians took positions so as to cut off retreat by land. The cannonade was resumed, and the land and naval forces of the United States were engaged in throwing shot and shells for the purpose of murdering those friendless Exiles, those women and children, who had committed no other offense than that of having been born of parents who, a century previously, had been held in bondage. Mothers and children now shrieked with terror as the roar of cannon, the whistling of balls, the explosion of shells, the war-whoops of the savages, the groans of the wounded and dying, foretold the sad fate which awaited them. The stout-hearted old men cheered and encouraged their friends, declaring that death was to be preferred to slavery.

The struggle, however, was not protracted. The cannon balls not taking effect upon the embankments of earth, they prepared their furnaces and commenced the fire of hot shot, directed at the principal magazine. This mode proved more successful. A ball, fully heated, reached the powder in the magazine. The small size of the fort, and the great number of people in it, rendered the explosion unusually fatal. Many were entirely buried in the ruins, others were killed by falling timbers, while many bodies were torn in pieces. Limbs were separated from bodies to which they had been attached, and death, in all its horrid forms, was visible within that doomed fortress.[1]

Of three hundred and thirty-four souls within the fort, two hun-

previous, while a party of his men were on shore, they were fired on by Indians and one man killed. This was the first and only act of hostility against our troops. It was committed by *Indians*, not by *Exiles*; but it was subsequently seized upon and published as a justification for carrying out General Jackson's order, bearing date more than two months prior to the occurrence, directing General Gaines to destroy the fort and return the negroes to slavery.

(1) Monette says, "The scene in the fort was horrible beyond description. *Nearly the whole of the inmates were involved in indiscriminate destruction; not one-sixth of the whole escaped. The cries of the wounded, the groans of the dying, with the shouts and yells of the Indians, rendered the scene horrible beyond description.*"

dred and seventy were *instantly killed;* while of the sixty who remained, only *three* escaped without injury.[1] Two of the survivors—one negro and one Indian—were selected as supposed chiefs of the allied forces within the fort. They were delivered over to the Indians who accompanied Colonel Clinch, and were massacred within the fort, in the presence of our troops;[2] but no report on record shows the extent of torture to which they were subjected.

We have no reliable information as to the number who died of their wounds. They were placed on board the gun-boats, and their wounds were dressed by the surgeons; and those who recovered were afterwards delivered over to claimants in Georgia. Those who were slightly wounded, but able to travel, were taken back with Colonel Clinch to Georgia and delivered over to men who claimed to have descended from planters who, some three or four generations previously, owned the ancestors of the prisoners. There could be no proof of identity, nor was there any court authorized to take testimony, or enter decree in such case; but they were delivered over upon *claim,* taken to the interior, and sold to different planters. There they mingled with that mass of chattelized humanity which characterizes our Southern States, and were swallowed up in that tide of oppression which is now bearing three millions of human beings to untimely graves.

Sailing-Master Loomis informed the Naval Department, through Commodore Patterson, that the value of the property captured in the fort was "not less than two hundred thousand dollars." He also stated that a portion of this property was "delivered over by "Colonel Clinch to the Indians who had accompanied him, on the "*express agreement that they should share in the plunder.*" Another portion of property was held by Colonel Clinch, as necessary for the use of the troops. A list of the articles thus taken is

---

(1) Vide Official Report of Sailing-Master Loomis, Ex. Doc. 119: 2d Sess. XVth Cong.

(2) Some years since, the author wrote a short sketch of the general Massacre, but omitted this point as too revolting to the feelings of humanity, and too disgraceful to the American arms, to be laid before the popular mind in such an article; and he would most gladly have omitted it in this work, could he have done so consistently with his duty to the public.

given in the report : it embraces spades, shovels, pickaxes, swords, sword-belts, pistols and muskets. The remainder of the property was taken on board the gun-boats, and held subject to the order of the Secretary of the Navy.[1]

The Governor of Florida demanded, in the name of "his Most Christian Majesty the king of Spain," possession of the property thus captured in the fort ; denying the right of either our army or navy to invade the territory of Spain, and take and carry away property from its fortifications.

To this claim Sailing-Master Loomis replied, that the property did not belong to the Spanish crown, but to the Exiles, who were in possession of it, from whom it was taken by *conquest*. This correspondence between his Excellency the Governor of Florida and the Commander of the two gun-boats, was duly transmitted to our Government at Washington, and may now be found in our National Archives.[2]

Some twenty-two years subsequent to the capture of this property, and the massacre of those who were in possession of it, a bill was reported in the House of Representatives,[3] granting five thousand dollars to the officers, marines and sailors who constituted the crews of those gun-boats, as compensation for their *gallant* services. Whether the honorable Chairman of the Naval Committee who reported the bill, or any member of the House who voted for it, was aware of the true character of the services rendered, is a matter of doubt ; but the bill passed without opposition, became a law, and the people of the United States paid that bonus for the perpetration

(1) Monette says that three thousand stands of arms and six hundred barrels of powder were destroyed by the explosion. This is probably somewhat of an exaggeration. We have no fact to warrant the assertion, that there was any addition made to the stores left by Col. Nichols, when he delivered the fort to the Exiles. The same author states, that one magazine, containing one hundred and sixty barrels of powder, was left unharmed by the explosion ; but no mention of such fact is found in the Official Report, by Sailing-Master Loomis.

(2) Vide Documents before the Committee of Congress appointed to investigate the cause of General Jackson's invasion of Florida : XVth Congress, 2d Session.

(3) This bill was reported by Mr. Ingham of Connecticut, Chairman of the Committee on Naval Affairs.

of one of the darkest crimes which stains the history of any civilized nation.[1]

The official correspondence connected with this massacre was called for by resolution, adopted in the House of Representatives, and was communicated to that body at the second session of the fifteenth Congress. But no action appears to have been proposed in regard to it; nor does it appear that public attention was at that time particularly called to this most wanton sacrifice of human life.

In this massacre, nearly every Exile resident upon the Appalachicola River, including women and children, perished or was reënslaved. Their homes were left desolate; their plantations, and their herds of cattle and horses, became the property of those who first obtained possession of them. Probably one-third of all the Exiles at that time resident in Florida, perished in this massacre, or were reënslaved by Colonel Clinch; yet the atrocious character of the transaction appears to have attracted very little attention at the time. General Jackson was popular as a military officer, and the Administration of Mr. Madison was regarded with general favor. No member of Congress protested against the transaction, or made known its barbarity to the people; while the ablest members taxed their ingenuity, and brought all their rhetoric to bear, in vindication of those concerned in the outrage.[2]

While Mr. Clay and others severely condemned the technical invasion of Florida, as an act of hostility toward the King of Spain, they omitted all reference to this wanton massacre of the Exiles: nor have we been able to learn that any member even intimated that the bloody Seminole war of 1816–17 and 18, arose from efforts of our Government to sustain the interests of Slavery; or that our troops were employed to murder women and children because their ancestors had once been held in bondage, and to seize and

(1) Vide Statutes enacted at 2d Session, XXVIth Congress. The author was then a member of the House of Representatives, but had not learned to watch the movements of slaveholders and "their allies," so closely as subsequent experience taught him would be useful.

(2) Vide Speeches of Hon. George Poindexter and others on the Seminole War, in 1819.

carry back to toil and suffering those who escaped death in that barbarous massacre. The officers of Government, and historians of that day, appear to have avoided all reference to the fact, that the people thus murdered had been far longer in the wilderness than were the children of Israel; that they were contending for that Liberty which is the rightful inheritance of every human being. Indeed, more than twenty years elapsed after this massacre, before a distinguished Philanthropist gave to the public the first intimation that such a people as the Exiles had existed.[1]

(1) Hon. William Jay, of New York, published his Views of the action of the Federal Government in 1837.

CHAPTER IV

GENERAL HOSTILITIES.

The Troops along the Florida frontier become active — The Exiles on Suwanee and Withlacoochee prepare for War — General Gaines's representation of their numbers — Depredations committed during the Spring and Summer of 1817 — Massacre of Lieutenant Scott and his party — Its Effect upon the Country — Congress not consulted as to this War — General Gaines authorized to invade Florida — General Jackson ordered to the Field — Mr. Monroe assumes the Duties of President — His Cabinet — Character of Congress — Public Sentiment in regard to discussion of Subjects connected with Slavery — General Jackson concentrates his Army at Fort Scott — Proceeds to Mickasukie — Battle — Destruction of the Town — Marches to St. Marks — Indian Chiefs decoyed on board a Vessel — Hanged by order of General Jackson — The Army moves upon Suwanee — Its Situation — Exiles prepare for a decisive Battle — Severe Conflict — General Jackson takes the Town — Captures Indian Women and Children — Burns the Villages of that region – Returns to Pensacola — Capture and Trial of Arbuthnot and Ambrister — Their Execution — Invasion of Florida condemned by some of our Statesmen, and vindicated by others.

THE nation having been precipitated into war (1816), the Officers of Government, and the army, at once became active in carrying it on. Orders were sent to General Gaines, exhorting him to vigilance, caution and promptitude. He was on the southern frontier of Georgia, where it was naturally supposed the first blow, in retaliation for the massacre of Blount's Fort, would fall. His scouts were constantly on the alert, his outposts strengthened, and his troops kept in readiness for action.

The Seminole Indians had lost some thirty men, who had intermarried with the Exiles, and were in the fort at the time of the massacre. They entertain the opinion that the souls of their murdered friends are never at rest while their blood remains unavenged;

(46)

nor could it be supposed that the Exiles would feel no desire to visit retributive justice upon the murderers of their friends. Long did this desire continue, in the minds of the surviving Exiles, until, many years subsequently, their vengeance was satiated, their hands were stained, and their garments saturated, in the blood of our troops.

The surviving Exiles had their principal remaining settlements upon the Suwanee and Withlacoochee rivers, and in the Mickasukie towns. These settlements were on fertile lands, and were now relied upon to furnish provisions for their support during hostilities. Savages are usually impetuous; but the Exiles were more deliberate. Colonel Clinch had returned to Georgia; Sailing-Master Loomis was at Mobile Bay, and no circumstances demanded immediate action. They gathered their crops, obtained arms and ammunition from British and Spanish merchants, and made every preparation for hostilities. During the summer and autumn of 1816, General Gaines reported slight depredations on the frontiers of Georgia, but in February, 1817, he reported that larger bodies of Indians were collecting in some of their villages; and in one of his letters he stated that *seven hundred negroes* were collected at Suwanee, and were being daily drilled to the use of arms. This number of fighting men would indicate a larger population of Exiles than is warranted by subsequent information.

1817.] During the Spring and Summer, both parties were in a state of preparation — of constant readiness for war. A few predatory excursions to the frontier settlements, marked the action of the Indians and Exiles, while the army, under General Gaines, often sent parties into the Indian country, without any important incident or effect. The first effective blow was struck in November. A boat was ascending the Appalachicola river, with supplies for Fort Scott, under the escort of a Lieutenant and forty men, in company with a number of women and children. Information of this fact was communicated to the Exiles and Indians resident at Mickasukie, and a band of warriors at once hastened to

intercept them. They succeeded in drawing them into ambush, a
few miles below the mouth of Flint River, and the Lieutenant, and
all his men but six, and all the children, and all the women but
one, were massacred on the spot. Six soldiers escaped, and one
woman was spared and taken to Suwanee as a prisoner. Here she
was kept by the Exiles through the winter, and treated with great
kindness, residing in their families and sharing their hospitality.
She had thus an opportunity of learning their condition, and the
state of civilization to which they had attained, as well as their
desire to be at peace with mankind, in order to enjoy their own
rights and liberties.

This massacre was regarded by the country as a most barbarous
and wanton sacrifice of human life. The newspapers blazoned it
forth as an exhibition of savage barbarity. The deep indignation
of the people was invoked against the Seminoles, who were represented as alone responsible for the murder of Lieutenant Scott,
and his men. Probably nine-tenths of the Editors, thus assailing
the Seminoles, were not aware of the atrocious sacrifice of human
life at "Blount's Fort," in July of the previous year. Even the
1818.] President of the United States, in his Message (March
25), relating to these hostile movements of the Seminoles,
during the previous year, declared "*The hostilities of this Tribe
were unprovoked*," as though the record of the massacre at
"Blount's Fort" had been erased from the records of the moral
Universe. Notwithstanding our army had, in a time of profound
peace, invaded the Spanish Territory, marched sixty miles into its
interior, opened a cannonade upon "Blount's Fort," blown it up,
with an unprecedented massacre, in which both Seminole Indians
and negroes were slain, and two of their principal men given over
to barbarous torture ; yet, the President, in his Message, as if to
falsify the history of current events, declared that "as almost the
"whole of this Tribe inhabit the country within the limits of
"Florida, Spain was bound, by the Treaty of 1795, to restrain
"them from committing depredations against the United States."

Such were the efforts made to misrepresent facts, in relation to the first Seminole War. With its commencement, the people had nothing to do; they were not consulted, nor were their Representatives in Congress permitted to exercise any influence over the subject. The correspondence between General Gaines and the Secretary of War, in regard to the occupation of the fort by the Exiles, had commenced on the fourteenth of May, 1815. It was continued while Congress was in session, in 1815 and 1816, but no facts in regard to the plan of destroying it, and entering upon a war, for the purpose of murdering or enslaving the Exiles, had been communicated to Congress or the public.

Orders were now issued to General Gaines, authorizing him to carry the war into Florida, for the purpose of punishing the Seminoles. General Jackson was ordered to take the field, in person, with power to call on the States of Tennessee and Georgia for such militia as he might deem necessary, for the due prosecution of the war; and the most formidable arrangements were made for carrying on hostilities upon a large scale.

Mr. Monroe had assumed the duties of President in March, 1817. He had appointed Hon. John Quincy Adams Secretary of State, at the commencement of his administration; but the office of Secretary of War was not filled by a permanent appointment, for some months, in consequence of Governor Shelby's refusal to accept it, on account of his advanced age. It was finally conferred on Hon. John C. Calhoun, who, through his entire official life, was distinguished for his devotion to the institution of Slavery; and this war having been entered upon for the support of that institution, it may well be supposed that he exerted his utmost energies for its vigorous prosecution.

The fifteenth Congress assembled in December, 1817. Most of the members from the free States had not enjoyed the advantages of having served long in that body. They afterwards showed themselves able men; but the business of legislation requires experience, industry, and a perfect knowledge of the past

4

action of government. This cannot be obtained in one session, nor in one Congress; it can only be gathered by the labors of an active life. It is, therefore, not surprising that Congress granted to the War Department whatever funds the President required to carry on the war.

It is not our province to applaud, or condemn, public men; but history represents no member of the fifteenth Congress as having proclaimed the cause of this war, or the atrocious massacre which characterized its commencement. On the contrary, those who spoke on the subject, represented it as entirely owing to the Indian murders on the frontiers of Georgia, and to the massacre of Lieutenant Scott and his men. There was great delicacy exhibited, and had been for many years previously, in regard to the agitation of any question touching the institution of Slavery; and the people of the free and slave States appeared to feel that silence on that subject was obligatory upon every citizen who desired a continuance of the Union. These circumstances rendered it easy for the Administration to prosecute the war, with whatever force they deemed necessary for the speedy subjection of Indians and Exiles.

On entering the field of active service, General Jackson called on the State of Tennessee for two thousand troops. He repaired to Harford, on the Ockmulgee, where a body of volunteers, from Georgia, had already assembled, and organizing them, he requested the aid of the Creek Indians also. They readily volunteered, under the command of their chief, McIntosh, ready to share in the honors and dangers of the approaching campaign. With the Georgia volunteers and Creek Indians, General Jackson marched to Fort Scott, where he was joined by about one thousand regular troops.

With this force, he moved upon the Mickasukie towns, situated near the Lake of that name, some thirty miles south of the line of Georgia. It was the nearest place at which the Exiles had settled in considerable numbers. There were several small villages in the vicinity of this Lake, inhabited almost entirely by blacks.

A large quantity of provisions had been stored there. There were also several Seminole towns between Mickasukie Lake and Talla-hasse, on the west.

The Exiles appear to have viewed the approach of General Jackson with coolness and firmness. They had evidently calculated the result with perfect accuracy. Their women and children were removed to places of safety, and their herds of cattle were driven beyond the reach of the invading army; and some of their Indian allies followed the example thus set them by the Exiles; yet others were not equally careful in calculating future events.

Neither Indians nor negroes had made these towns their general rendezvous; nor did they expect a decisive battle to occur at that point; yet they prepared to meet General Jackson, and his army, in a becoming manner. Most of their forces were collected prior to the arrival of our troops. In making the requisite dispositions for battle, the Indians were formed in one body, and the negroes in another — each being under their respective chiefs.

General Jackson encountered the allied forces at some little distance from the Mickasukie towns, April first. The battle was of short duration. The Indians soon fled. The Exiles fought with greater obstinacy. Their fire was so fatal that a reinforcement was ordered to that part of the field, and the Exiles were driven from their position, leaving twelve of their number dead upon the field.

In his official report of this battle, General Jackson insisted that British officers had drilled the negroes, and British traders had furnished them ammunition. He also reported that he burned more than three hundred dwellings, and obtained a supply of provisions and cattle for his army.

The Exiles, generally, retreated to Suwance, and the Indians continued to hang around the American army, watching its move-ments. General Jackson, however, directed his course towards St. Marks, a Spanish fort, situated on the river of that name, some fifty miles southwest of Mickasukie Lake.

The American army reached St. Marks on the seventh of April, and remained there several days. One of the American vessels lying in Appalachicola Bay, hoisted British colors, in order to decoy some Indians who were looking at them from the shore. Two of the "Red Stick" band ventured on board; they were said to be chiefs, and in alliance with the Seminoles. General Jackson ordered them to be hanged, without trial or ceremony, justifying the act by charging them with having participated in the massacre of Lieutenant Scott and his party, during the previous autumn, apparently unconscious that, by his own orders, two hundred and seventy people, including innocent children and women, had been most wantonly and barbarously murdered at the fort on Appalachicola, and that Lieutenant Scott and *thirty* men were murdered in retaliation for that act, according to savage warfare. He appears to have felt it due to offended justice, that these men should die for being suspected of participating in that act of retaliation. In all these cases, the most assiduous efforts were exerted to misrepresent the real state of facts.

The time occupied in the approach and capture of Fort St. Marks, gave to the Exiles and Indians full opportunity to concentrate their forces at Suwanee. It constituted the most populous settlement of the Exiles, after the destruction of that upon the Appalachicola. It was regarded as their stronghold. Surrounded by swamps, it was approached only through narrow defiles, which rendered it difficult for an army to reach it. Here many of the Exiles had been born and reared to manhood. Here were their homes, their firesides. Here their chief, Nero, resided; and here they concentrated their whole force. They had removed their women and children, their provisions and cattle, to places of safety, and coolly awaited the approach of General Jackson's army.[1]

Scouting parties were, however, sent out to harrass his advance guard, and delay his approach, and render it more difficult; but,

(1) Monette says Arbuthnot sent word to the Negroes and Indians, notifying them of the approach of General Jackson; but the official report of that Officer shows that his advance guard was daily engaged in skirmishing with the Indians.

notwithstanding these obstacles, the army steadily advanced, and on the nineteenth of April reached the "Old Town" of "Suwanee," and found the allied forces in order of battle, prepared to contest the field. The Indians were again formed on the right, and the Exiles constituted the left wing, bringing them in conflict with the right wing of General Jackson's forces.

With the Exiles, there was no alternative other than war or slavery; and they greatly preferred death upon the battle field, to chains and the scourge. We may well suppose they would fight with some degree of desperation, under such circumstances; and the battle of Suwanee gave evidence of their devotion to freedom. They met the disciplined troops, who constituted General Jackson's army, with firmness and gallantry.[1] At the commencement, their fire was so fatal that the right wing of the American army faltered, and ceasing to advance, gave signs of falling back. But the left wing, opposed to the Indians, made a successful charge; the Indians gave way, and the reserve was suddenly brought into action to sustain the right wing, when a general charge was ordered, and the Exiles were compelled to fall back.[2]

General Jackson, in his official report of this battle, refers to the desperation with which the negroes fought, and says they left many dead upon the field, but does not mention their number. He entered the town and set fire to the buildings, and burned all the villages in the vicinity. He also captured some three hundred Indian women and children, while those belonging to the Exiles

(1) Vide General Jackson's Official Report of this battle, Ex. Doc. 175, 2d Session XVth Congress.

(2) Williams, in his History of Florida, states that three hundred and forty Negroes again rallied after the first retreat, and fought their pursuers, until *eighty* of their number, were killed on the field. "Monette" also states the same fact; but General Jackson, in all his Reports, evidently avoided, as far as possible, any notice of the Exiles, as a people. Indeed such was the policy of the Administration, and of its officers, and of all slaveholders. They then supposed, as they now do, that slavery must depend upon the supposed ignorance and stupidity of the colored people; and scarcely an instance can be found, where a slaveholder admits the slave to possess human intelligence or human feeling; indeed, to teach a slave to read the Scriptures, is regarded as an offense, in nearly every slave State, and punishable by fine and imprisonment.

had been carefully removed beyond the reach of the American army. This superior caution and provident care appears to mark the character of the Exiles in all their conduct; while the Indians appear to have practised none of these precautions.

But the allied forces, defeated, and their warriors scattered in various directions, were pursued by McIntosh and his Creek warriors, who had accompanied General Jackson, until fearing the Seminoles might rally in force against them, they returned and again united with the American army.

This battle substantially closed the war of 1818. It had been commenced for the destruction of the Exiles; they had shared in its dangers, and by their energy and boldness, had given intensity to its conflicts. From the time they united in the expedition for the destruction of Lieutenant Scott and his party, in November, 1817, until the close of the battle of Suwanee, they had been active participants in every skirmish, and had uniformly displayed great firmness; bearing testimony to the truth of those historians who have awarded to the African race the merit of great physical courage.

General Jackson appears to have spoken as little of the Exiles as duty would permit, when communicating with the Secretary of War; yet he was more free to complain of them in his correspondence with the Governor of Pensacola. In a letter to that officer, dated a few days after the battle of Suwanee, he says: "*Negroes* "*who have fled from their masters, citizens of the United States,* "*have raised the tomahawk, and, in the character of savage war-* "*fare, have spared neither age nor sex. Helpless women have* "*been massacred, and the cradle crimsoned with blood.*"

We can, at this day, scarcely believe that this eloquent description of savage barbarity was from the pen of a man whose order for the massacre of defenseless women and children, at the Fort on Appalachicola, bore date less than two years before writing this letter; nor can we readily comprehend the effrontery of him who thus attempted to justify the invasion of Florida, by reference to acts done by the Exiles long after the army under his command had entered that territory, and committed the most atrocious outrages ever perpetrated by civilized men upon an unoffending people.

After the battle of Suwanee, General Jackson returned to St. Marks, being unable to follow the Indians and Exiles into the more southern portions of Florida. While at St. Marks, he ordered a court-martial, constituting General Gaines president, in order to try Arbuthnot and Ambrister. The history of their trial and execution is familiar to the reader. The first and principal charge against Ambrister was, that he excited the *negroes* and Indians to commit murder upon the people of the United States; the second charge was for supplying them with arms. On these charges he was convicted and executed. It was also alleged, that he was present at the battle of Suwanee; and some writers say he commanded the Exiles on that occasion, and had previously taught them military discipline.

In May, General Jackson issued an Address to his troops, declaring the war at an end; and wrote the Executive, asking permission to retire to his home in Nashville, there being no further use for his services in the field.

The Exiles now returned to their homes. They had full leisure to contemplate their situation. Many of their best men had fallen. Nearly the entire population residing upon the Appalachicola River had been massacred. Their villages at Mickasukie and Suwanee had been burned; and it is probable that nearly one half of their entire population had been sacrificed, in this first war waged by the United States for the murder and recapture of fugitive slaves.

The invasion of Florida by General Jackson was condemned by many public men, and was approved by others with equal ability. Even the then Secretary of State, John Quincy Adams, in his correspondence with Don Onis, the Spanish Minister, defended the invasion with great ability. But in the discussions of this subject, we find no allusion to the massacre at "Blount's Fort;"[1] that

(1) Various names have been given this Fort. The author, having heretofore adopted

appears to have been regarded as a subject of too delicate a nature for public scrutiny. In the alcoves of our National Library, we find many volumes of documents touching this war, embracing some thousands of pages, in which there is the strongest censure expressed against the Seminoles for provoking the war, and condemnation for the barbarous manner in which they conducted it; but we search them in vain to find any condemnation, by American statesmen, of the object for which the war was commenced, or the unprovoked and worse than savage massacre which marked its beginning.

that of "Blount's Fort," prefers to continue that name. It was equally known, however, as the "Negro Fort," and as "Fort Nichols."

CHAPTER V.

THE first Seminole war, like most other wars, was attended with
great sacrifice of blood and treasure. It had corrupted the morals
of the nation ; but the Administration had entirely failed to attain
the objects for which it had been commenced. Not ten slaves had
been captured, if we except those who were wounded and taken
prisoners at "Blount's Fort," one half of whom had died of their
wounds. Under such circumstances, the Government could not,
with propriety, condescend to make a treaty with a community of
black men, whose ancestors had fled from slavery. Such act would,
in the opinion of slaveholders, have compromised the dignity of the
Slaveholding States; nor could they treat with the Seminole Indians
as a separate tribe, for the Administration was endeavoring to hold
the Creeks responsible for the acts of the Seminoles, who, the slaveholders insisted, were a part of the Creek tribe. The army was
therefore withdrawn from Florida, without any treaty whatever.
But the act of withdrawing the army and permitting the Exiles to

remain in a state of freedom and independence, constituted an acknowledgment of the inability of our Government to reënslave them, although it was constantly asserted that they were a degraded race, incapable of supporting themselves if set at liberty.

In looking over the official reports of our officers, the action of Congress, and the tone of the public press, we are forcibly impressed with the constant and unceasing efforts to hide from the popular mind of the nation the real questions involved in this war. Nor can we account for it upon any other hypothesis, than the popularity of President Monroe's Administration. The old Federal party had ceased to exist. They had been the only party opposed to Mr. Monroe; and no member of Congress appears to have possessed the requisite independence, information and ability, to take a position distinctly against his policy.

Soon as our army was withdrawn from Florida, peace was of course restored, and things remained as they were prior to the invasion under Colonel Clinch, in 1816. The Exiles were again left in peace, as they had been prior to the commencement of the war. Nothing had been gained to the United States by the vast expenditure of blood and treasure which attended the prosecution of hostilities. The Exiles had maintained their liberty for at least a century, and now they had set the American Government at defiance. These considerations operated upon the minds of the slave population of Georgia and Alabama, who now became more anxious to join them; and their numbers were thus increased almost daily by slaves from those States.

From 1790, our Government had endeavored to reënslave these people. No Northern statesmen objected to the policy; while those of the South had come to believe that, although the Union may not have been formed solely for the purpose of capturing slaves, yet that duty was regarded by them as *one* of its most important objects. It had now become evident that no military force could pursue them into their retired fastnesses, or seek them out when scattered among the hommocks, the swamps and everglades of that singular country.

Southern statesmen now turned their attention to the purchase of Florida. That would deprive the Indians and Exiles of the nominal protection of Spanish laws, and would bring them under the jurisdiction of the United States; they therefore addressed themselves to that policy with renewed assiduity. Recent events had convinced the authorities of Spain that it was impossible for them to maintain the dignity of the Spanish crown, or the sanctity of her soil from invasion against an American army, when in pursuit of fugitive slaves. She had seen her territory invaded; her forts at Pensacola and at St. Marks captured, and that upon the Appalachicola destroyed; her subjects massacred; her authority despised, and her rights as a nation treated with indignity by our army. There was, indeed, no other way for her but to accede to the proposition of the United States.

1819.] A treaty was negotiated (February 22), and in consideration of five millions of dollars, Florida was transferred to the United States, and the Seminoles were brought within the jurisdiction which they most dreaded.

The slaveholders of Georgia, who had so long pressed their claims for fugitive slaves, now became more clamorous. They saw, with intense interest, the pertinacity with which the Executive had pressed the claims of those who lost slaves, in the then recent war with England. Under the Treaty of Ghent, the President insisted upon full indemnity to those whose slaves had left the country, under British aid; and when the English ministry refused, and insisted upon the same construction as that placed upon the treaty of 1783, which contained the same words, the American Executive refused, and the question was referred to the umpirage of the Autocrat of Russia, who held an entire nation in slavery, and could not be expected to decide in any other manner, than that most favorable to the institution.[1]

(1) The people of the free States should understand, that almost every question touching slavery which has arisen between our Government and that of England, the latter has yielded, since the formation of Jay's Treaty in 1795.

The payment for slaves who were shipwrecked on board the Comet, the Encomium, and

1820.]   The influence of the slave power having increased so greatly since 1796, as to induce the British Government to change its policy, adopted at the framing of Jay's Treaty, was now believed competent to compel the Creek Indians to comply with the treaties of New York and Colerain. A quarter of a century had passed, since the signing of the last of these treaties, and they had been forgotten by many ; but the people of the free States, and their Representatives and Senators in Congress, had quietly submitted to this prostitution of our national character and influence, and none appeared to doubt the propriety of continuing these efforts.

1821.]   Georgia now demanded of the Federal Government a new treaty with the Creek Indians,[1] in order to obtain from them indemnity for the slaves she had lost, subsequent to the close of the Revolution, and prior to the act of 1802. To this demand the Federal Executive assented. The Secretary of War, Mr. Calhoun, with his attachment to the institution, could do no less than to exert what influence he was able to wield, in assisting Georgia to obtain a compensation for the loss of her slaves. On him devolved the burthen of selecting commissioners to negotiate the contemplated treaty. Careful to place the subject in the hands of men who would be likely to wield their power for the benefit of the " peculiar institution," he appointed General Andrew Pickens

---

the Enterprise, and found freedom by being landed on British soil, constitute rare instances in which slaveholding arrogance has proved successful in the arts of diplomacy. The case of the Creole constitutes another admirable illustration of successful effrontery. In this case, the slaves took possession of the ship, guided it to Nassau, a British Island, went on shore and became free. The officers of the slave ship demanded that the British authorities should seize the negroes, and return them to the ship. They refused. Daniel Webster, Secretary of State, became the voluntary Agent, Attorney and Solicitor, for the slave dealers, who should have been hanged, instead of receiving the encouragement of our Government. But the subject was submitted to the umpirage of a man, said to have once lived in Boston, who, principally upon the authority of Mr. Webster, decided that the people of the British government should pay the slave dealers for these parents and children ; and after fifteen years of continued effort, the money was obtained.

(1) Vide Letter from the Secretary of War to Messrs. Pickens and Flournoy, August 8, 1820. Am. State Papers, Vol. VI, p. 249.

of his own State, and General Thomas Flournoy of Georgia, to conduct the negotiation.

In his letters of instruction to those gentlemen, he was careful to inform them that the treaty was to be negotiated *for the benefit of Georgia;*[1] that she would also appoint commissioners to attend the negotiation, and watch over the interests of her people. The commissioners proceeded to make arrangements for the treaty. They appointed the time and place for holding it; employed an agent to furnish the requisite supplies, and made arrangements for the necessary payments. At this point a correspondence arose between them and the commissioners of Georgia, who assumed to dictate the terms on which the treaty was to be founded. The commissioners of the United States, finding those of Georgia inclined to dictate the course of action which they were to pursue, were unwilling to submit to such dictation, and reported the difficulty to the Secretary of War; while the commissioners on the part of Georgia, feeling perfect confidence in the devotion of that officer to the interests of slavery, made their report of the matter to him also.[2]

The Secretary returned an answer, reproving the commissioners whom he had himself appointed, so severely for their refusal to obey the dictation of those appointed by Georgia, that they both immediately resigned their offices, appearing to feel that their own self-respect must be compromised by acting under the instruction of the State Commissioners.[3]

Apparently determined to appoint no man who should again prove refractory, the Executive — probably at the instance of the Secretary of War — next selected as commissioner, in the place of Mr. Flournoy, David Meriwether, who had, up to the time of receiving the appointment, acted as commissioner on the part of

---

(1) Vide Letter of the Secretary of War to Gen. Flournoy, of the 19th of October, 1820. Ibid, 250.

(2) Vide Papers transmitted to Congress, in connection with the Treaty of "Indian Spring." Am. State Papers, "Indian Affairs," Vol. I, No. 174.

(3) Ibid.

Georgia. At the request of the Secretary of War, he resigned his office of commissioner on behalf of the State, and accepted the appointment from the Federal Government. Hon. D. M. Forney, of North Carolina, was selected as the other commissioner, in place of Mr. Pickens. These commissioners were expressly instructed to assist the State of Georgia in obtaining the objects for which she was striving.[1]

These preliminary arrangements could not fail to foreshadow the character of the treaty negotiated under such auspices. Anticipating no other motive for the treaty than the settlement of the boundary between the State of Georgia and the Creeks, the chiefs, head-men and principal warriors of the tribe assembled at the time and place appointed. After the ordinary formalities on such occasions, the commissioners on the part of the United States opened the business by simply stating, that the people of Georgia complained to the President that the Creeks had not returned the property (negroes, cattle and horses), which they were under obligations to return to their owners in Georgia, by the treaties of New York and Colerain.

The commissioners on the part of Georgia now delivered their talk, saying, that by the treaty of Augusta (1783), of Galphinton (1785), and of Shoulderbone (1786), the Creeks had agreed to return to their owners, negroes who had left their masters, and other property; that these treaties were all made before the formation of the government of the United States under their present Constitution; but they were ratified by the treaty of New York (1790), and of Colerain (1796), made with the United States, and Georgia now demanded compensation for the loss of her negroes and other property.

On the following day, General McIntosh, principal chief of the Creeks, replied, that he came to meet the commissioners of the United States, and had no expectation of meeting those of Georgia; nor had he or his friends any idea that such claims were to be pre-

(1) Ibid. Letter of Instructions contained in the papers referred to on preceding page.

sented. That the chief, McGillivray, when he returned, after the treaty of New York, informed them that they were to deliver up such negroes as were *then in the nation;* that they were to pay for none who had removed or died; that they all so understood that treaty, and that nothing was then said about any other claims than for *negroes;* that the *prisoners,* both black and white, were delivered up under the treaty of New York; that the claims now presented were also presented at the treaty of Colerain, in 1796, but the Creeks then absolutely refused to acknowledge any further obligation than that contained in the treaty of New York, and by that they were under obligation to surrender no property except persons held as prisoners, and negroes then in the nation. That many of these negroes were carried away by the British, during the war of 1812; that others were in the fort at Appalachicola, when he and his warriors went with Colonel Clinch and blew it up, and killed nearly all who were in it; and the others were with the *Seminoles,* and not with the Creeks.

To this answer the commissioners of Georgia replied, that by the treaties of Augusta, and Galphinton, and Shoulderbone, the Creeks were bound to deliver all negroes who had left their masters in Georgia; that, if they had done so, the British would not have carried them off, nor would they have been killed in the fort; that the *Seminoles were a part of the Creek nation,* who were responsible, not only for the slaves and their increase, but also for the loss of the labor which they would have performed had they remained in bondage.

Of the means used to obtain the treaty, we have no other information than appears of record. Those acquainted with the usual modes of negotiating Indian treaties, by the use of intoxicating liquors, by bribery, and those appliances generally used on such occasions, will not wonder at the stipulations contained in the Treaty of "Indian Spring."

By the first article, the Creeks ceded to the United States, for the benefit of Georgia, about five million acres of their most valuable territory. The second article provided for the reservation of certain lands, to be retained by those who were then living upon them. The third reserved certain lands for the use of the United States agency; and the fourth is in the following words:

"It is hereby stipulated and agreed, on the part of the United "States, as a consideration for the land ceded by the Creek nation, "by the first article, that there shall be paid to the Creek nation, "by the United States, ten thousand dollars in hand, the receipt "whereof is hereby acknowledged, forty thousand dollars as soon "as practicable after the ratification of this convention, five thou- "sand dollars annually for two years thereafter, sixteen thousand "dollars annually for five years thereafter, and ten thousand dollars "annually for six years thereafter; making in the whole fourteen "payments, in fourteen successive years, without interest, in money "or goods, and implements of husbandry, at the option of the "Creek Nation, seasonably signified, from time to time, through "the agent of the United States residing with said nation, to "the Department of War. And as a further consideration for "said cession, the United States do hereby agree to pay to the "State of Georgia, whatever balance may be found due by the "Creek Nation to the citizens of said State, whenever the same "shall be ascertained, in conformity with the reference made by "the commissioners of Georgia and the chiefs, head-men and war- "riors of the Creek Nation, to be paid in five annual installments, "without interest, provided the same shall not exceed the sum of "two hundred and fifty thousand dollars; the commissioners of "Georgia executing to the Creek Nation a full and final relinquish- "ment of all the claims of the citizens of Georgia against the Creek "Nation, for property taken or destroyed prior to the act of Con- "gress, of one thousand eight hundred and two, regulating the "intercourse with the Indian tribes."

The fifth article merely provides for running the boundaries of the several reservations. It was duly signed and witnessed, and bears date on the eighth of January, 1821.

Gopher John, Seminole Interpreter

Deeming the treaty not sufficiently explicit in its terms, the commissioners on the part of Georgia, entered into a further agreement with the Indians, which reads as follows :

" Whereas at a conference, opened and held at the Indian " Spring, in the Creek Nation, the citizens of Georgia, by the " aforesaid commissioners, have represented that they have claims " to a large amount against the said Creek Nation of Indians : " Now, in order to adjust and bring the same to a speedy and final " settlement, it is hereby agreed by the aforesaid commissioners, and " the chiefs, head-men and warriors of the said Nation, that all the " talks had upon the subject of these claims, at this place, together " with all claims on either side, of whatever nature or kind, prior " to the act of Congress of one thousand eight hundred and two, " regulating the intercourse with the Indian tribes, with the docu- " ments in support of them, shall be referred to the decision of the " President of the United States, by him to be decided upon, " adjusted, liquidated and settled, in such manner and under such " rules, regulations and restrictions as he shall prescribe : Provided, " however, if it should meet the views of the President of the Uni- " ted States, it is the wish of the contracting parties, that the liqui- " dation and settlement of the aforesaid claims shall be made in the " State of Georgia, at such place as he may deem most convenient " for the parties interested ; and the decision and award thus made " and rendered, shall be binding and obligatory upon the contract- " ing parties."

There was also an assignment of the title, or right of property claimed, executed to the United States by the Commissioners of Georgia, which is in the following language :

" Whereas a treaty, or convention, has this day been made and " entered into, by and between the United States and the Creek " Nation, by the provisions of which the United States have agreed " to pay, and the commissioners of the State of Georgia have " agreed to accept, for and on behalf of the citizens of the State of " Georgia having claims against the Creek Nation, prior to the

" year one thousand eight hundred and two, the sum of two hun-
" dred and fifty thousand dollars :

" Now know all men by these presents, that we, the undersigned,
" commissioners of the State of Georgia, for and in consideration
" of the aforesaid sum of two hundred and fifty thousand dollars,
" secured by the said treaty, or convention, to be paid to the State
" of Georgia, for the discharge of all bona fide and liquidated
" claims which the citizens of the said State may establish against
" the Creek Nation, do, by these presents, release, exonerate and
" discharge the said Creek Nation from all and every claim and
" claims, of whatever description, nature or kind the same may be,
" which the citizens of Georgia now have, or may have had, prior
" to the year one thousand eight hundred and two, against the said
" Nation. And we do hereby *assign, transfer and set over unto the*
" *United States, for the use and benefit of the said Creek Nation,*
" for the consideration hereinbefore expressed, all the right, title
" and interest of the citizens of the said State to all claims, debts,
" damages, and property of every description and denomination,
" which the citizens of the said State have or had, prior to the year
" one thousand eight hundred and two, as aforesaid, against the
" said Creek Nation."

It were useless for the historian to criticise the language of these
several instruments. The " claims" mentioned in them, and referred to the President, were mostly for slaves who left their
masters during the Revolution, and prior to 1802; at least such
was the construction given to the treaty, the agreement and
assignment by the parties; and we cannot, at this day, assert that
they did not understand their own compacts.

The Creeks were to receive two hundred thousand dollars in
cash; and the United States agreed to pay to Georgia her claims,
provided they did not exceed *two hundred and fifty thousand dollars*. The amount due to Georgia was to be ascertained by the
President, and paid by the United States. The third, and a very
important point, was the *assignment* to the United States, for the

benefit of the Creek Indians, of the interest vested in the claimants to the *property* and *persons* claimed — the *United States to hold such interest in trust* for the Creek Indians.

By this arrangement, our Government became owners of the Exiles referred to, *in trust for the benefit of the Creeks*, according to the construction which the Indians, the authorities of the United States and those of Georgia, placed upon the assignment, the agreement and treaty. This important point, if borne in mind, will aid the reader in understanding the subsequent action of the Federal authorities in relation to this subject.

1822.] In pursuance of this treaty, the President promptly appointed a commissioner to ascertain the amounts due the several claimants. But great difficulties had to be encountered. The claims commenced in 1775 and extended down to 1802, and it was extremely difficult to obtain evidence of facts which transpired so long prior to the examination. Sufficient proof was produced, however, to satisfy the commissioner that ninety-two slaves had, within the periods mentioned, left their masters, in Georgia, and fled to the Indians; and the estimated value of slaves and other property lost to the owners in this manner, amounted to one hundred and nine thousand dollars.[1]

1823.] This amount of money was duly appropriated by Congress. So far as we are informed, no member of the House of Representatives, or of the Senate, appears to have entertained doubts as to the propriety of this governmental slave-dealing. The whole negotiation and arrangement had been conducted and managed by Southern men, and Northern statesmen quietly submitted. Thus, after a struggle of thirty-eight years, the Slaveholders of Georgia, by the aid of our Federal Government, obtained compensation for the loss of their fugitive bondmen.

(1) Vide Report of Commissioner on this subject; also, the Report of Wm. Wirt, Attorney General of the United States, to whom the President referred the subject. "Opinions of the Attorney General," 1822. Mr. Wirt states the price paid for these slaves was from two to three times their real value.

After the distribution of the amount found due to the claimants, there yet remained in the hands of the President one hundred and forty-one thousand dollars, being the remainder of the two hundred and fifty thousand appropriated by the treaty to secure the payment of these claims. This money apparently belonged to the Indians. The claimants for slaves could not have any title to it, for they had expressly stipulated, that the award of the commissioner should be *conclusive* upon the parties. The claimants, by that award, received full compensation for their loss ; yet they next demanded of the President the hundred and forty-one thousand dollars which remained in his hands. Notwithstanding the commissioners on the part of Georgia expressly agreed to abide by the award, and had assigned all interest in the property and *in the persons* residing with the Indians, to the United States, and had received their money in full, under the treaty ; yet they desired to get the remainder, which was considerably larger than the amount awarded them by the commissioner.

CHAPTER VI.

FURTHER EFFORTS TO ENSLAVE THE EXILES.

Indians and Exiles on the Appalachicola River — Other Exiles at Withlacoochee, St. John's, Cypress Swamp, Wahoo Swamp — Indians in various parts of Territory — Difficulty of the subject — President's Message — Committee of Congress — Interrogations — Mr. Penieres' Answer — General Jackson's Answer — He relies on Force — United States recognize the Florida Indians as an Independent Band — Willing to treat with them — Difficulties — Instructions to Commissioners — Treaty of Camp Moultrie — Reservations — Covenants on part of United States — Covenants on part of the Seminoles — Congress makes no objection — Effect of Treaty — Its Objects — Election of the younger Adams — His Policy — Indian Agent, Colonel Humphreys — William P. Duval's Instructions — Claimants complain of the Agent — Commissioner of Indian Affairs reproves him — His Letter — Reply — Difficulty of Agent — Dangers which threaten the Exiles — Colored Man seized and enslaved — Indians Protest — Colonel Brooke's Advice — United States Judge expresses his Opinion — Effect on Exiles — Mrs. Cook's Slave — Demand for Negroes — Suggestions of Agent — Practice of Government — Treaty of Payne's Landing — Its Stipulations — Abram — His Character — Chiefs become Suspicious — Delegations sent West — Executive Designs — Supplemental Treaty— Major Phagan— Petition of the People of Florida — Indorsement thereon — Treaties approved by Senate — Creeks remonstrate — Payment of $141,000 to Slave Claimants — Supineness of Northern Statesmen — Creeks demand Exiles as Slaves — Georgians kidnap Exiles — Their Danger — They dissuade from Emigration — Their Warriors — Wiley Thompson's Statement — General Clinch's Interest — Colonel Eaton's Views — General Cass's Reply — His Address to Indians — He authorizes Slave Trade — Effects of such License — Agent and others Remonstrate — He replies —Agent rejoins — Exiles prepare for War.

AFTER the close of the war of 1818, many of the Seminole Indians took possession of the deserted plantations and villages along the Appalachicola River, whose owners had fallen in the massacre of Blount's Fort, in 1816; and some of the Exiles united in reoccupying the lands which had been reduced to cultivation by their murdered brethren. Some six or eight small bands of Indians thus became resident along that river. The fertile bottom lands,

(69)

near that stream, constituted the most valuable portion of Florida, so far as agriculture was concerned. These towns afforded convenient resting places for fugitive slaves, while fleeing from their masters in Georgia, Alabama, Tennessee and Louisiana, to the interior portions of Florida.

The United States, nor the slaveholders of the States named, could with any propriety whatever hold the Creek Indians responsible for the many refugees, who were now almost daily increasing the number of fugitives located far in the interior of Florida; and the difficulties attending the holding of slaves increased in exact proportion as the slaveholding settlements extended towards these locations; while the greater portion of the Exiles were taking up their residence farther in the interior of the territory, upon the Withlacoochee, the St. John's, the Big Cypress Swamp, the Islands in the Great Wahoo Swamp, and places far retired from civilization. The Seminole Indians were scattered extensively over different portions of the country; and although the United States now owned the unoccupied lands, it was difficult to determine upon any course of policy by which the difficulties, so long existing, could be terminated.

1822.] The subject was alluded to by the President in his Annual Message to Congress (Dec. 3), and a select committee was appointed to take that portion of it into consideration. The committee propounded interrogatories to various officers of government, who were supposed capable of giving useful information in regard to the subject.[1]

In answer to these interrogatories, Mr. Penieres, Sub-Agent for the Florida Indians, replied, stating the number of Indians at more than five thousand, while the number of slaves which they held were estimated at only forty. These he declared to be far more intelligent than the slaves resident among the white people, and possessing great influence over their Indian masters. He alluded to the Exiles in the following language: "It will be

(1) Vide Reports of Committee XVIIth Congress, 2d Session, No. 195.

"difficult (says he) to form a prudent determination with respect
"to the 'maroon negroes,' (Exiles), who live among the Indians,
"on the other side of the little mountain of Latchiouc. They fear
"being again made slaves, under the American Government, and
"will omit nothing to increase or keep alive mistrust among the
"Indians, whom they, in fact, govern. If it should become ne-
"cessary to use force with them, it is to be feared that the Indians
"will take their part. It will, however, be necessary to remove
"from the Floridas this group of freebooters, among whom runa-
"way negroes will always find a refuge. It will, perhaps, be pos-
"sible to have them received at St. Domingo, or to furnish them
"means of withdrawing from the United States!"

This gentleman appears to have had more knowledge of the
Exiles, than was possessed by the officers of the United States,
generally, who supposed that each negro must have a legitimate
master. He appears, also, to have had sufficient humanity to suggest the plan of their *removal*, rather than their enslavement.

In answer to the interrogatories of this committee, General
Jackson proposed to compel the Seminoles to *reünite with the
Creeks*, by leaving Florida and returning to the Creek country;
and closed his recommendation by saying, "this must be done, or
"the frontier will be much weakened by the Indian settlements,
"and be a perpetual harbor for our slaves. These *runaway*
"*slaves, spoken of by Mr. Penieres*, MUST BE REMOVED from the
"Floridas, or scenes of murder and confusion will exist."[1]

This suggestion of General Jackson for the removal of the
Seminoles, both Indians and negroes, bears date September second,
1822, and is the first suggestion, of that precise character, of
which we have knowledge. General Jackson was a warrior, and
had more faith in the bayonet than in moral truths. He trusted
much to physical power, but had little confidence in kindness, or in

(1) Vide Am. State Papers, Vol. VI, pages 411, 412. It will be observed that General
Jackson discarded the term "*maroon*," used by Penieres, as that, in Jamaica, signifies
"*free negroes* of the mountains," who once fled from service, but have maintained their
liberty so long that they cannot be identified, and are therefore admitted to be free.

justice or moral suasion. He was an officer of great popularity, however, and it is not unlikely that his views had greater weight with those who followed him in official life, than their intrinsic merits entitled them to. It is certain that his policy of removing the Indians and Exiles from Florida, was subsequently adopted by him while President, and has continued to be the cherished object with most of his successors in that office.

The controversy between the State of Georgia and the Creeks had been settled at Indian Springs. In the treaty entered into at that place, the United States had held the Creek Nation responsible for the action of the Seminoles, under the plea that they were a part of the Creek Nation. Having obtained two hundred and fifty thousand dollars from the Creeks in this way, to satisfy the slave claimants of Georgia, the Executive now suddenly became satisfied that the Seminoles were a distinct and independent tribe, and he prepared to treat with them as such. Commissioners were appointed for that purpose, and efforts made to collect their chiefs, warriors and principal men, in order to carry out this object.

Suspicious of the objects which prompted this proposal, the Indians were unwilling to meet the commissioners. Runners were sent to the different bands, and eventually some thirty or forty were collected. These were declared by the commissioners to represent 1823.] a majority of the Seminole tribe, and (Sept. 18) they proceeded to form the treaty of "Camp Moultrie." The letter of instructions, from the Secretary of War, was specific on one point only. The commissioners were directed to so arrange the treaty as to constrain the Indians to settle within the territory south of Tampa Bay, excluded from the coast on all sides by a strip of country at least fifteen miles in width. This would have taken from them their most fertile lands on the Suwanee River, the Appalachicola River, and in the vicinity of the Mickasukie Lake. Some six chiefs, who had taken possession of the plantations which had been opened and cultivated by the Exiles murdered at "Blount's Fort," refused to sign the treaty. They were, however, prevailed upon to agree to the treaty, when it had been so modified as to give them each a reservation of fertile lands, to meet their own necessities.

By agreeing to these stipulations, the commissioners obtained their signatures to the treaty — the United States guaranteeing to the Indians peaceable possession of the country and reservations assigned them. They also covenanted to "*take the Florida In-*" *dians under their care and patronage, and* AFFORD THEM PRO-" TECTION AGAINST ALL PERSONS WHATSOEVER," and to "*restrain*" *and prevent all white persons* from hunting, settling, or other-" wise *intruding*, upon said lands." They also agreed to pay the Indians six thousand dollars in cattle and hogs, furnish them with provisions to support them one year, and pay them five thousand dollars annually for twenty years. But one great object of the treaty was embraced in the seventh Article, which was expressed in the following language :

" The chiefs and warriors aforesaid, for themselves and tribes,
" stipulate to be active and vigilant in preventing the retreating
" to, or passing through, the district, or country assigned them, of
" any absconding slave, or fugitives from justice ; and they further
" agree *to use all necessary exertions to apprehend and deliver*
" *the same to the agent,* who shall receive orders to compensate
" them agreeably to the trouble and expense incurred."

It is worthy of note, that the commissioners, acting under instructions of the Secretary of War, now assured the Seminoles that they had been a separate and independent tribe more than a century ; while other commissioners, acting under instructions from the same Secretary, only twenty months previously, insisted that the Seminoles were, at that time, a part of the Creek tribe ; and on that assumed fact, the Creeks were held responsible for the value of such slaves as left their masters during the Revolution and prior to 1802, and took up their residence with the Seminoles. But these contradictory positions appeared to be necessary to sustain the slave interest.

It may be remarked that from the signing of this treaty, there was no longer any controversy between our Government and the Creeks in relation to fugitive slaves. That quarrel was transferred to the Seminoles; and now, after thirty-four years have passed away, and many millions of treasure have been expended, and thousands of human lives sacrificed, at the moment of writing these incidents, our army is actively employed in carrying on the contest which arose, and for more than the third of a century has been almost constantly maintained, for the recapture and return of these people; and although our members of Congress from the free States had witnessed the long and expensive contest, and the vast sacrifice of blood and treasure, which had been squandered in efforts to regain possession of the Exiles; yet we do not find any objection to have been raised or protest uttered against this new treaty, in either branch of our National Legislature. Indeed, so far as we have information on the subject, the appropriations for carrying it into effect were cheerfully made, without objection.

This compact drew still more closely the meshes of the federal power around the Exiles. The United States now held what is called in slaveholding parlance the "legal title" to their bones and sinews, their blood and muscle, while the Creek Indians were vested with the entire beneficial interest in them. But neither the United States nor the Creek Indians had been able to reduce them to possession. The white settlements were, however, gradually extending, and the territory of the Seminoles was diminishing in proportion; and it was easy to foresee the difficulties with which they were soon to be surrounded.

By the treaty, many of their cultivated fields, and most of the villages, which they had recently defended with so much bravery, were given up to the whites, and those who had so long occupied them, were compelled to retire still further into the interior, and commence new improvements. A few Exiles remained with the chiefs who held reservations upon the Appalachicola. Those who remained, however, were persons who had become connected by marriage with the Indians belonging to those small bands, from whom they were unwilling to separate.

To this treaty some writers have traced the causes which produced the recent "Florida War." They attribute to its stipulations that vast sacrifice of treasure, and of national reputation, which has rendered that territory distinguished in history. With that war, our present history is connected only so far as the Exiles were concerned in its prosecution; but it would appear difficult for any historian to overlook the important fact that obtaining possession of fugitive slaves constituted the moving consideration for this treaty, and the primary cause of both the first and second Seminole wars.

1824.] Most of this year was occupied in removing the Indians to their new territory. They also suffered severely for the want of food, and the attention of both Indians and officers of Government appears to have been occupied with these subjects.

In the autumn, Mr. Adams was elected President. But his policy was in part unfavorable to the Exiles. Removals from office under his administration were limited. If an officer were removed, it was not until after it had been ascertained that just cause existed for the removal. This policy continued nearly every man in office who had been connected with the Indian Department under the former Administration. Colonel Gad Humphreys had been appointed Agent for the Seminoles as early as 1822. He was a resident of Florida, and a slaveholder, deeply interested in maintaining the institution; but so far as his official acts have come before the public, he appears to have performed his duty with a good degree of humanity. Indeed, such were his efforts in behalf of justice to the oppressed, that he became obnoxious to Southern men, and was eventually removed from office on that account. William P. Duval was also continued in the office of Governor, and ex-officio Superintendent of Indian Affairs for the Territory of Florida. He was also a slaveholder, and resident of the territory; but even Southern men found little cause to complain of his devotion to liberty or justice. He, and many other officers, appear to

have supposed the first important duty imposed on them, consisted
in lending an efficient support to those claims for slaves which
were constantly pressed upon them by unprincipled white men.

Early as the twenty-fifth of January, Governor Duval, acting
Superintendent of Indian Affairs for the Territory, wrote Colonel
Humphreys, giving him general directions in regard to the course
which he should pursue in all cases where fugitive slaves were
claimed. "On the subject (said he) of runaway slaves among
"the Indians, within the control of your agency, it will be proper
"in all cases, where *you believe* the owners can identify the slaves,
"to have them taken, and delivered over to the Marshal of East
"Florida, at St. Augustine, so that the Federal Judge may inquire
"into the claim of the party, and determine the right of property.
"But in all cases where the same slave is claimed by a white
"person and an Indian, *if you believe* the Indian has an equitable
"claim to the slave, you are directed not to surrender the slave,
"except by the order of the Hon. Joseph L. Smith, Federal Judge
"residing at St. Augustine; and in that case, you will attend
"before him, and defend the right of the Indian, *if you believe* he
"has right on his side."

In all these cases, the slave or colored man, whether bond or
free, was to be treated in the same manner as a brute. He was
permitted to say nothing upon the subject of his own right to
liberty. His voice was silenced amidst the despotism with which
he was surrounded. No law was consulted. The *belief* of a
slaveholding Agent decided the fate of the person claimed. Those
who claimed to own their fellow men, would always find persons to
testify to their claims, and it was in vain for an Indian to attempt
litigation with a slaveholding white man before a slaveholding
Judge.[1]

The Exiles were not the property of the Indians in any sense.

---

(1) It is an interesting fact, that the doctrine recently avowed by the Supreme Court
of the United States, that "*black men have no rights which white men are bound to respect*,"
was recognized and practiced upon in Florida, more than thirty years since, by the
officers of Government.

The Indians did not claim to own them. Under the rule prescribed, if a white man could get one of the Exiles within his power, he could at any time prove some circumstance that would entitle him to claim *some* negro; when he proved this, the law of Florida presumed every colored man to be a slave, unless he could prove his freedom. This, no Exile could do; and, when seized, they were uniformly consigned to bondage. The only safety for the Exile was, to entirely avoid the whites, who were not permitted to enter the territory except upon the written permit of some officer.

The slave-catchers, therefore, had recourse to the practice of describing certain black persons, in the Indian country, as their slaves, and demanding that the Agent should have them seized and delivered to him. But the Agent, knowing these claims to be merely fictitious in some instances, paid no attention to them. The claimants, intent on obtaining wealth by catching negroes, and selling them as slaves, complained of the Agent to the Commissioner of Indian Affairs, who, on the eighth of February (1827), wrote the Agent, reproving him for his remissness in failing to capture and return fugitive slaves, saying: " Frequent complaints have " been made to the Department, respecting slaves claimed by the " citizens of Florida, which are in possession of the Indians; all " which have been acted on here, in issuing such orders to you as " it was expected would be promptly obeyed; * * * and that " these proceedings would be followed by the proper reports to the " Department. *Nothing satisfactory has been received.*"

1826.] Thus the Indian Bureau, at Washington, took upon itself the responsibility of deciding particular cases, upon the *ex parte* testimony which the claimants presented; and the commissioner concluded his letter by a peremptory order to Colonel Humphreys, directing him to capture and deliver over two slaves, said to be the property of a Mrs. Cook.

To this order the Agent replied in the language of dignified rebuke. After stating that one of the slaves had been captured

by the Indians, and given up, he says: " but they will not, I ap-
" prehend, consent further to risk their lives in a service which has
" always been a thankless one, and has recently proved so to one
" of their most respected chiefs, who was killed in an attempt to
" arrest a runaway slave." [1]

The love of liberty is universal. We honor the individual who
gives high evidence of his attachment to this fundamental right,
with which God has endowed all men, and we applaud him who
manfully defends his liberty, whether it be a Washington with
honors clustering upon his brow, or the more humble individual
who defends his liberty in Florida, by slaying the man who attempts
to deprive him of it. But these views were not recognized by the
agents of our Government.

While the Department at Washington supposed the Agent to
have neglected his duty, the Superintendent of Indian Affairs for
the territory supposed the Agent had been quite too faithful to
1827.] the slaveholders. On the twentieth of March he wrote
Colonel Humphreys, saying, " *Many slaves belonging to*
" *the Indians* ARE NOW IN POSSESSION OF THE WHITE PEOPLE.
" These slaves cannot be obtained for their Indian owners without
" a lawsuit ;" and he then directed the Agent to submit the claim,
in all cases where there was an Indian claimant, to the chiefs for
decision.

In these contests between barbarians and savages, concerning the
rights which they claimed to the bodies of their fellow men, the
Exiles had no voice. They well understood that the rapacity of
the slave claimants was unbounded and inexorable ; they therefore
endeavored to avoid all contact with the whites, and to preserve
their freedom by affording the piratical slave-catchers no opportunity to lay hands on them.

These demands for negroes alleged to be among the Indians,
continued to excite the people of Florida and to perplex the officers

---

(1) Vide Executive Documents, No. 271, 2d Session XXVth Congress.

of Government, threatening the most serious results,[1] and continually enhancing the dangers of the Exiles.

The troops at Fort King were called on to aid in the arrest of fugitive slaves; but their efforts merely excited the ridicule and contempt of both Indians and negroes. These circumstances becoming known to the slaves of Florida, naturally excited them to discontent; and while their masters were engaged in efforts to arrest negroes to whom they had no claim, their own servants in whom they had reposed every confidence, suddenly disappeared and became lost among the Exiles of the interior. The white people became irritated under these vexations. Their indignation against the Indians was unbounded. The Agent, Colonel Humphreys, gave a vivid description of their barbarity, in a letter to the Commissioner of Indian Affairs.[2] But remonstrances with the Indian Department appeared to have no effect. Peremptory orders for the arrest and delivery of slaves continued to reach the Agent. These orders he *could not carry into effect*, as he could command no force adequate to the **arrest of the fugitives.**

1828.] Governor Duval began to regard the Agent as remiss in his efforts, and so reported him to the War Department. Some of the most wealthy Seminoles had purchased slaves of the white people, and for many years, perhaps we may say for generations, had been slaveholders. They held their slaves in a state between that of servitude and freedom; the slave usually living with his own family and occupying his time as he pleased, paying his master annually a small stipend in corn and other vegetables. This class of slaves regarded servitude among the whites with the greatest degree of horror.

The owners of fugitive slaves, or men who pretended to have lost slaves, when able, would seize and hold those belonging to the Indians. The Indians being ignorant of legal proceedings, were unable to obtain compensation from those who thus robbed them

---

(1) Captain Sprague, of the United States Army, so states, in his History of the War.
(2) Vide Letter of the Agent, dated sixth of March, 1827.

of what the slaveholders termed *property*. This practice became so common that, on the seventeenth of April, many of the chiefs and warriors assembled at the Agency, and made their protest to the Agent, declaring that " many of their negroes, horses, cattle, " etc., were in the hands of the white people, for which they were " unable to obtain compensation." Contrary to the treaty of Camp Moultrie, white men were at that time in the Indian country searching for slaves, and the chiefs demanded of the Agent the reason why the white people thus violated the treaty to rob the Indians? The Agent could only reply, that the white men were there by permission given them by the *Secretary of War*.[1]

So flagrant were these outrages upon the Indians and negroes, that Colonel Brooke, of the United States Army, at that time commanding in Florida, took upon himself the responsibility of addressing the Agent, advising him not to deliver negroes to the white men, unless their " *claims were made clear and satisfactory.*"[2] The District Judge of the United States for the Territory, also wrote Colonel Humphreys, giving his construction of the rules adopted by the Indian Bureau. He thought, in no case, should a negro be delivered up, where the Indians claimed him, until proofs had been made and title established before judicial authority.[3]

No law was looked to as the rule by which officers of Government were to be controlled in their official duties. The opinion, the judgment, of the individual constituted his rule of action. During the nineteenth century, perhaps no despotism has existed among civilized nations more unlimited, or more unscrupulous, than that exercised in Florida, from 1823 to 1843.

This state of affairs determined the Exiles *not to be arrested by white men*. Thus, when Governor Duval ordered a compensation for a slave claimed by Mrs. Cook, to be retained from their annui-

---

(1) Vide Minutes of Talk held at Seminole Agency, with Treskal, Mathla, and other Chiefs. Ex. Doc. 271, 1st Sess. XXIVth Congress.

(2) Vide Letter of Col. Brooke to Col. Humphreys, 6 May, 1828, contained in the above cited Document.

(3) Vide Letter of Judge Smith, May 10, 1828, contained in same Document.

ties, the chiefs held a talk with the Agent, and assured him that the "*man was born among the Seminoles, and had never been out of the nation.*"[1]

These demands for negroes increased in number; and the whites became more and more rapacious, and the Indians more and more indignant, until hostilities appeared inevitable. The Agent, from long association with the Indians and his knowledge of facts, naturally sympathised with them. He assembled a number of the chiefs at the Agency, and suggested to them the absolute necessity of submitting to the white people; and for the purpose of avoiding further difficulties, advised them to emigrate west of the Mississippi, or, rather, to send a delegation to examine the country; and, as an inducement, offered to accompany their chiefs and warriors on such a tour. To this proposition a few of them consented, and the Agent notified the Department of the fact.[2]

It was easy to see that, under the existing state of affairs, hostilities could not long be avoided. Up to the period of which we are speaking, the action of our Government had been dictated by those who sought to uphold and encourage Slavery; nor could it be expected that this long-established policy would be suddenly changed, unless such change were peremptorily demanded by the people.

There was apparently but one course to be pursued under this policy — that was the removal of the Indians from Florida. This plan had been recommended by General Jackson ten years previously, and he now being President, had an opportunity of carrying out his proposed policy. To effect this purpose, it would be necessary to negotiate a treaty by which the Indians should consent to abandon Florida and remove west of the Mississippi.

It had long been the policy of those who administered the Government, to select Southern men to act in all offices in which the institution of slavery was likely to be called in question. From the

(1) Vide Statement of John Hick, 15 August, 1828. Ex. Doc. 271, before quoted.
(2) Vide Letter of Gad Humphreys, Oct. 20, 1828. It probably was the first time the proposition was submitted to the Seminoles.

time General Washington sent Colonel Willett to ascertain facts in regard to the controversy between the State of Georgia and the Creek Indians, in 1789, to the period of which we are now speaking, no Northern man was appointed to any office which required his personal attention to the situation of the Exiles.[1]

1832.]   In accordance with this practice, General Cass, acting as Secretary of War, appointed Colonel James Gadsden, of South Carolina, to negotiate the treaty of Payne's Landing. By the preamble of this treaty, the Seminoles stipulated that eight of their principal chiefs should visit the Western country, "*accompanied by their faithful interpreter, Abraham,*" (an Exile, and a man of great repute among both Exiles and Indians,) and should they be satisfied with the character of the country, and of the favorable disposition of the Creeks to reünite with the Seminoles as one people, they would, in such case, agree to the stipulations subsequently contained in said treaty.

The first article merely makes an exchange, by the Seminoles, of lands in Florida for an equal extent of territory, west of the Mississippi, adjoining the Creek Nation.

The second article provides compensation for the improvements, and specifically stipulates, that Abraham and Cudjoe (two Exiles who acted as interpreters) should receive, each, two hundred dollars.

The third provides for the distribution of blankets and frocks among them.

The fourth article provides for certain annuities, etc.

The fifth merely stipulates the manner in which the personal property of the Seminoles shall be disposed of in Florida, and the same articles supplied them in their new homes at the West.

The sixth is in the following language : "The Seminoles, being "anxious to be relieved from the repeated vexatious demands for "slaves and other property, alleged to have been stolen and de-

_____

(1) Even Mr. Adams, when President, continued in office those men who had been placed there by his predecessors.

" stroyed by them, so. that they may remove to their new homes
" unembarrassed, the United States stipulate to have the same
" properly investigated, and to liquidate such as may be satisfac-
" torily established, provided the amount does not exceed fourteen
" thousand dollars."

The seventh article stipulates that a portion of the Indians
should remove in 1833, and the remainder in 1834.

Two leading features of this treaty attract the attention of the
reader. The first is the removal of the Seminoles; second, their
reunion with the Creeks. The Creeks, having paid the slaveholders of Georgia for their loss of Exiles, had permitted the subject to
rest in silence, and, so far as we are informed, no formal claim had
yet been asserted by the Creeks to seize and hold the Exiles as
slaves; but it is evident that the negotiators of this treaty intended
to place the Seminoles, when settled in their western homes, within
the power, and under the jurisdiction, of the Creeks. Yet it was
well known that, from the time of their separation, in 1750, up to
the signing of this treaty, they had disagreed and, at times, had
been in open war with each other. General Cass, the Secretary of
War, as well as the President, must have known that McIntosh,
the principal chief of the Creeks, had accompanied Colonel Clinch,
with five hundred warriors, when he invaded Florida for the purpose of massacreing the Exiles at " Blount's Fort," in 1816; that
the Creeks shared in that massacre, and had publicly tortured and
murdered one Indian and one negro, whom they styled chiefs. It
is difficult to believe that any man could expect them to live together in peace, with the recollection of those scenes resting on the
mind; nor has any explanation yet been given, nor reason assigned,
for the anxiety of our officers to place the Seminoles within the
power of the Creeks, except a desire to enslave the Exiles.

Abraham, who acted as interpreter, had been born among the
Seminoles. His parents had fled from Georgia, and died in their
forest-home. He appears to have been a man of unusual influence
with his more savage friends; and although he insisted on emigra-

ting to the West, in opposition to many of his brethren, yet he has
to this day maintained a high reputation among his people. Cudjoe
was less known, and, subsequently, was less conspicuous than
Abraham; indeed, we know but little of him. But the experience of Abraham, nor the learning of Cudjoe, could detect that vague
use of language which was subsequently seized upon for justifying
the fraud perpetrated under this treaty.

In the preamble, it was stipulated that the Seminoles were to
send six of their confidential chiefs to view the western country;
and if *they* were satisfied with the country, etc. The Seminoles
supposed the pronoun *they* had relation to the Tribe; while General
Jackson construed it to refer to the chiefs sent West. If they were
satisfied, he held the Tribe bound to emigrate at all events; and
his efforts were, therefore, directed to satisfying the chiefs who went
to view the country.

But the leading men of the Seminoles became suspicious of the
design of the Creeks to enslave the Exiles, before their delegation
left Florida, and publicly expressed their suspicion.[1]

The President appears to have determined on securing the
emigration of the Indians at all hazards and at any sacrifice. For
that purpose he appointed commissioners to go west and obtain
from the Seminole delegation, while yet in the western country,
and absent from the tribe, an acknowledgment that the country
was suitable for a residence, and that the Creeks were anxious to
unite with them as one people. This was to be obtained before
the Seminole delegation should return to Florida, or make report
to their nation, or give the Tribe an opportunity to judge or act
upon the subject.

1833.]   His object was accomplished (March 28). The commissioners obtained an "*additional treaty*," signed by the
Seminole delegation sent West, without any authority from their Nation to enter into any stipulation; nor had the commissioners, on the
part of the United States, authority to form any treaty whatever: yet

---

(1) Vide Sprague's History of the Florida War.

this additional treaty, as it was called, after reciting some of the stipulations contained in that of Payne's Landing, declares "that " the chiefs sent to examine the country are well satisfied with it;" and then stipulates, " that the Seminole Indians shall emigrate to " it so soon as the United States shall make the necessary prepara- " tions." There was also another provision in this additional treaty of vast importance to the Exiles; it designated and assigned to the Seminoles a certain tract of country, giving its metes and bounds, to the " *separate* use of the Seminoles forever."

Their agent, Major Phagan, appears to have been willing and capable of performing his part in this diplomatic intrigue. We have no knowledge of the means used to obtain this additional treaty, nor the bribery by which it was secured; but it is known that the chiefs, before they went West, expressed their dislike of reuniting with the Creeks; that when they returned, they denied having agreed to settle under Creek jurisdiction; it is also certain that the additional treaty stipulates that the Seminoles shall have their lands *separate* from the Creeks.

When they returned, their agent, Major Phagan, represented them as having stipulated for the positive removal of the Seminoles. The chiefs denied it, and insisted they had understood their author- ity as extending only to an examination of the country, and to report the result to the Nation. They requested that the chiefs, head-men and warriors be assembled to hear their report, and to express their own determination. But the agent refused to call such council, and assured them that their homes and heritage were already sold, and that nothing now remained for them to do but to prepare for removal.

The people of Alachua County, Florida, feeling indignant at the determination of the Seminoles to remain in that Territory, addressed a protest to the President of the United States, declaring that the Seminoles did *not capture and return* the fugitive slaves who fled to the Indian country, according to their stipulations in the treaty of Camp Moultrie, but rather afforded protection to them. They further stated that while the Seminoles remained in the country no slaveholder could enjoy his property in peace. This protest was signed by ninety of the principal citizens of said county, and forwarded to the President.

This statement aroused the ire of the President, who at once indorsed on the back of the petition an order to the Secretary of War to "inquire into the alleged facts, and if found to be true, to "direct the Seminoles to *prepare to remove West and join the* "*Creeks.*" The order was characteristic of the author. He waited not for the approval or ratification of any treaty; with him the whole depended upon the alleged fact of the Seminoles failing to bring in fugitive slaves — not upon treaty, nor upon the ratification of treaties.[1]

1834.]   The Senate of the United States was subsequently called on by the President to approve the treaty after the lapse of nearly two years from its date. This was done, and the President by his proclamation immediately declared it in force. It was said by public officers, then in Florida, that had the Seminole delegation been permitted to give an unbiased opinion to their people, there would not have been a man in the Nation willing to migrate.[2]

The whole Nation became indignant at this treatment, and such was the feeling against the agent that he deemed it prudent to retire from the agency. General Wiley Thompson was appointed to succeed him. General Clinch was appointed to the command of the troops, and every preparation was made to insure the speedy removal of the Indians and Exiles west of the Mississippi.

In the meantime, the Creeks learning that a tract of country was, by the additional treaty, agreed to be set off to the separate use of the Seminoles, saw clearly the influence which Abraham had exercised in the matter, and, fearing their own designs for obtaining slaves would be defeated through their principal chiefs, addressed a

(1) Vide Documents relating to the Florida War, 1st Session, XXIVth Congress.
(2) Vide Sprague's History of the Florida War.

protest to the Hon. Lewis Cass, then Secretary of War, remonstrating against the policy of giving the Seminoles a *separate* country.

These chiefs were sagacious men, who had attained distinction with the Creeks by their manifestation of superior intelligence. Two of them, Rolley McIntosh and Chilley McIntosh, sons of a Scotch trader who lived with the Indians, had been educated, and were regarded as among the able politicians of the day. They, together with "Toshatchee Mieco" and "Lewis," urged the propriety of uniting the two tribes as one people, without any separate organization. The next day they addressed another letter to Secretary Cass, giving additional reasons and arguments why the Seminoles should not have separate lands.[1]

The President had already adopted the policy of compelling the Seminoles to unite under one government with the Creeks: and this stipulation for *separate* lands was introduced into the "ad-"ditional treaty," by commissioners who were not fully informed of the President's views. This compact, entered into at Fort Gibson, erroneously called an "additional treaty," was known to be void : neither the Seminole chiefs nor the United States commissioners had authority to negotiate any treaty whatever ; and this stipulation, for holding separate lands by the Seminoles, appears to have been totally disregarded by the Executive, as will more fully appear hereafter.

Another circumstance had induced the Creeks to remain silent in regard to the Exiles. By the treaty of Indian Spring, they had placed at the President's disposal $250,000, out of which the slaveholders of Georgia were to be paid for slaves and property lost prior to 1802. The commissioners appointed to make the examination found but $109,000 due the claimants under this stipulation, leaving in the hands of the President $141,000 belonging to the Creeks. This, however, was claimed by the slaveholders, in addition to the amount allowed by the treaty. To obtain this money the slaveholders sent their petition to Congress.

(1) Vide Ex. Doc. 271, XXIVth Congress, 1st Session, pages 43 and 44.

The subject was referred to a committee, of which Mr. Gilmer, of Georgia, was Chairman. The committee made a very elaborate report, setting forth that the claimants had an equitable right to this money as an indemnity *"for the loss of the offspring which the " Exiles would have borne to their masters had they remained in " bondage,"* and it is among the inexplicable transactions of that day, that the bill passed, giving the money to those claimants without the uttering of a protest, or the statement of an objection, by any Northern representative or senator.

The Creeks now having paid the full amount stipulated in the treaty, and being robbed of the $141,000, to compensate the slaveholders for children who had never been born, were excited to madness. They believed themselves to hold the beneficial interest in the bodies of the Exiles, and determined to obtain possession of them.[1] They immediately sent a delegation to the Seminoles to demand possession of the Exiles as their slaves.

While the Creeks were thus demanding possession of the refugees, the Executive of the United States and his officers were endeavoring to compel them to go West, where the Creeks could, without opposition, lay hands upon them and enslave them.

The six Seminole chiefs holding reservations upon the Appalachicola River owned some slaves, and with those slaves some of the Exiles had intermarried. Each chief, by the terms of the treaty of Camp Moultrie, was permitted to name the *men* who

---

(1) The Author, while serving in Congress in 1847-8 was, by the Speaker, placed upon the committee of Indian Affairs. While serving on that committee, the Creek Indians applied for the return of this money which had belonged to them, but had been wrongfully paid over by Congress to the slaveholders of Georgia, some fourteen years previously. The case was referred to the Author, as sub-committee, who reported that the money, in justice, in equity, and in law, belonged to the Indians; that its payment to the slaveholders was unjust and wrong, and that it ought to be paid to the Indians. The report was confirmed, and the money paid to the Indians. The justice of the cause was so obvious that it met with no opposition, and by the vote of both Houses it now stands acknowledged and declared that this sum of $141,000 was taken from the pockets of the laboring men of our Nation, and paid to those slaveholders for *imaginary slave children who were never born;* nor have we been able to learn that an objection was raised, or protest uttered, by any Northern member of Congress.

were to reside with him, and such chief became responsible for the conduct of the persons thus named ; while the United States stipulated to "afford the chiefs and their people *protection against* "*all persons whatsoever.*"

The white settlements had extended to the vicinity of these reservations, and the Exiles and Seminole slaves living on them were more immediately exposed to the rapacity of the whites than were those in the interior of the territory.

1835.] The mania for obtaining slaves by piratical violence, seems to have reached a point almost incredible to the people of the free States. E-con-chattimico was one of the chiefs whose reservation lay on the west side of the river. He had long been highly respected by the whites. He owned some twenty slaves, who were residing with him in a state of partial freedom — paying him an annual stipend of provisions for their time, and holding such property as they could acquire. Connected with these slaves, and with some of the Indians on the Reservation, were about an equal number of Exiles, who had never known slavery, but whose ancestors, in former generations, had toiled in bondage. Unwilling to separate from their intimate friends and connexions, they had, as stated in a former chapter, come here to occupy, with E-con-chattimico and his friends, one of the extensive plantations which had been occupied by their brethren who fell at Blount's Fort, in 1816. The chief had named them as his friends, and a record of the fact had been deposited in the office of the Commissioner of Indian Affairs ; and for their conduct E-con-chattimico was responsible, under the treaty of " Camp Moultrie ;" while, by the same instrument, the faith of the nation had been solemnly pledged " to protect them *against all persons whatsoever.*" '

The piratical slave-dealers of Georgia looked upon these people, both Exiles and slaves, with strong desire to possess them. One of these fiends in human shape, named Milton, residing in Columbus, Georgia, professed to have purchased them from a Creek

Indian. The claim was presented to the Commissioner of Indian Affairs, and by him referred to Judge Cameron, of the United States District Court in Florida, for examination.

The chief being a man of influence and respected by the whites, found friends to espouse his cause. The claimant began to doubt his success under such circumstances, and proposed to withdraw his claim; but so flagrant was its fraudulent character, that Judge Cameron felt it his duty to report upon it, showing it to be void.[1] This report was duly transmitted to the proper department at Washington, and the Old Chief, with his people, once more reposed in apparent security.

It has been alleged, that men who so far paralyze their own moral sensibilities as to rob their fellow-men of their labor, their liberty, their manhood, and hold them in degrading bondage, can not entertain any clear conceptions of right and wrong. However this may be, it is certain that men who deal in slaves, are ever regarded, even by slaveholders, as destitute of moral sentiment.

In this case, Milton, finding that Judge Cameron had reported the claim to be fraudulent and void, professed to sell his interest in these people to certain other slaveholders, of Columbus. These men provided themselves with chains, and fetters, and bloodhounds, and all the paraphernalia of regular slave-dealers upon the African coast, and descending the river in a steamboat, intended to surprise their victims before any notice should be given of their approach. But some friendly white, who had learned the intentions of the pirates, had whispered to the aged chief the danger which threatened his people. They were soon armed, and prepared to defend themselves or die in the attempt. The desperadoes landed upon the Reservation; but finding the people armed, and ready to receive them in a becoming manner, they retired into the country and alarmed the settlers, by proclaiming that E-con-chattimico had armed his people and was about to make war upon the whites. The news flew in all directions; troops were mustered into service;

(1) Vide Opinion of Judge Cameron, pages 35 and 36 of Doc. 271, last quoted.

an army was organized and marched to the Reservation, and the proper officer sent, with a white flag, to demand the object and intentions of the chief, in arming his people. The old man was most indignant that his honor should be impugned in such manner. He fully explained the cause which induced his people to convene, and assume a hostile attitude towards those who had come to rob them of their liberty.

The officers, who sympathized with the pirates, were sustained by military force. They assured the old man that no persons should be allowed to injure him or his people; that the country was alarmed, and the public mind could only be pacified by a surrender of his arms and ammunition. To this proposition he was constrained to yield. They took his arms and ammunition, and left him defenseless. They remained undisturbed, however, during the night; but the next morning the slave-hunters returned, fully armed. They seized every negro residing upon the Reservation, including both Exiles and the slaves of E-con-chattimico, and, fastening the manacles upon their limbs, hurried them off to Georgia, where they were sold into interminable bondage.[*][1] They, and their ancestors, had enjoyed a hundred years of freedom; but they were suddenly precipitated into all the sufferings and sorrows of slavery, and now toil in chains, or have departed to that land where slavery is unknown.

E-con-chattimico petitioned Congress for indemnity, but obtained no redress. Neither the President, nor the Secretary of War, manifested any interest in maintaining our most solemn treaty obligations with the Indians, or attempted any redress for their violation. Disheartened and broken down in spirits, E-con-chattimico yielded

[*] NOTE.—When the author, in 1841, denounced this transaction, in the House of Representatives, and spoke of these slave-catchers as *Pirates*, Hon. Mark A. Cooper, of Georgia, became indignant at the denunciation;—said he was well acquainted with the men who seized and enslaved these people; that they were *honorable men*, and that he took them by the hand almost daily while at home.

(1) The statement of these facts may be found in Ex Document, 1st Sess. XXIVth Congress.

to General Jackson's orders, emigrated to the western country, and spent the remainder of his days in poverty and want.

Nor were the piracies of the white people confined to the crime of kidnapping Exiles. They robbed the Indians and Exiles of horses, cattle and money.

A chief named Blunt also held a reservation on the river, under the treaty of Camp Moultrie. He had some friends among the Exiles who preferred to occupy, with him, one of the plantations left destitute by the murder of the people at "Blount's Fort," in 1816. He too had named his friends and become responsible for their conduct, and relied upon the pledged faith of the nation to protect them.

Some desperadoes, said to have come from Georgia, entered his plantation, robbed him of a large amount of money, and carried away all the negroes living on the Reserve.

Another chief named Walker, also residing on a reservation, with some slaves and Exiles, discovered that a notorious slave-catcher from Georgia, named Douglass, and some associates, were hanging around his plantation, with the apparent intention of capturing and enslaving the colored people. Warned by the outrage committed upon E-con-chattimico and his people, both Indians and negroes collected together, armed themselves, and determined to resist any violence that should be offered them.

When the piratical Georgians approached, they fired upon them. Finding the people armed and determined to resist, the man-stealers retreated and disappeared. Feeling they were in danger, Walker wrote the Agent of the Seminoles, calling for protection, according to the stipulations of the treaty of Camp Moultrie. In his letter he says, "Are the free negroes (Exiles), and negroes " belonging to this town (slaves), to be *stolen away publicly* in " the face of law and justice—carried off and sold to fill the pockets " of those worse than land pirates?"

This appeal was in vain. The Agent paid no attention to it. The kidnappers were vigilant and watchful, and when their victims supposed themselves safe, they stole upon them, seized them, and hurried them off to the interior of Alabama, and sold them into slavery.

The scenes so often witnessed upon the slave coast of Africa became common in Florida; while Georgia, and Alabama, and Florida, afforded a class of men in no respect superior in morals to those outlaws and pirates who pursue the foreign slave trade.

The dangers threatening the Exiles now became imminent. They saw clearly they were to be enslaved, or compelled to resort to arms in defense of their liberties. Their entire influence was exercised to prevent emigration, as they feared that would subject them to Creek jurisdiction and enslavement.

These objections were made known to the Department at Washington by the Agent of the Seminoles, Wiley Thompson, who, in plain and unmistakable language, informed the Commissioner of Indian Affairs, that the principal objection to removing West which operated upon the minds of the Seminoles arose from the claim of the Creeks to those people who had fled from Georgia prior to 1802, and extending back to the commencement of the Revolutionary War. He assured the Department, that if the Seminoles were compelled to remove West, *these descendants of the Exiles would be enslaved by the Creeks*, and if they remained in Florida, they would be enslaved by the whites. He told the Department in plain language, that many of those negroes who had been born and raised among the Indians had been enslaved by the people of Florida and of Georgia, and were then held in bondage.[1]

Among other officers who espoused the cause of humanity at that period, so interesting to the Exiles, was the veteran General Clinch. He was a man of great probity of character. One of the most gallant officers in the service was at the time in actual command of the troops in Florida. He had long been acquainted with the Indians, and no man perhaps better understood the character of the Exiles. He had twenty years before commanded the troops at the massacre

(1) Vide Ex. Doc., 1st Sess. XXIVth Congress, page 104.

of "Blount's Fort," and well understood the persecutions to which the Exiles had been subjected. In strong language, he pointed out the wrong about to be perpetrated upon them, as well as upon the Seminoles. He informed the Secretary of War, in direct and posi tive language, that if the Seminoles and their "negro allies" were sent West, the *negroes would be enslaved by the Creeks.*[1]

Hon. John H. Eaton, Governor of Florida, a warm personal and political friend of the President, in whom it was believed the Exec utive reposed great confidence, also wrote the department, delineating the wrongs about to be perpetrated upon these colored people, who for several generations had resided with the Seminoles.

These and other officers of Government united in the opinion, that these "*negroes,*" as they were generally called, exerted a con- trolling influence over the Indians, and that it would be in vain to attempt the removal of the Indians under these circumstances.

To these remonstrances, the Hon. Secretary of War, General Cass, replied, with apparent determination to remove the Indians at any expense of blood, of treasure, and of national reputation. The appeals made to the justice of our Government were stigmatized " as the promptings of a *false philanthropy;*" and our agents and officers were directed to inform the Seminoles, in peremptory lan guage, that they must emigrate to the western country.

Laboring under the delusion that official station would add a con trolling influence to his language, General Cass transmitted to the Indian Agent a speech, addressed to the Seminoles and their allies, in which he endeavored to persuade them to emigrate and join the Creeks, and subject themselves to Creek authority. The Seminoles and their friends listened to the speech with that respectful atten- tion which would be expected from men who knew their lives and liberties were in danger.

It was at one of these consultations, in the presence of their Agent, that "Osceola," at that time a young warrior, attracted attention by saying, "*this is the only treaty I will ever make with*

---

(1) Vide his letter at length in the Document last quoted.

"*the whites;*" at the same time drawing his knife and striking it forcibly into the table before him.[1]

It was at this period that abandoned white men conceived the plan of buying negroes from Seminoles while in a state of intoxication, and selling them to the white people. If they could get an Indian drunk, they could of course obtain from him a bill of sale of any negro they pleased, whether the Indian had any title to him or not. This plan of separating the Seminoles from their colored friends, it was thought would conduce to their removal.

Applications to enter the Indian Territory for the purpose of purchasing slaves were referred by the Secretary of War to the Commissioner of Indian Affairs, and by the latter officer to the Attorney General Felix Grundy, who gravely reported, that he " saw no good " reason why the white people should not be permitted to buy slaves " of the Indians;" and the President having considered the matter, ordered permission to be granted for that purpose.

Officers who were in Florida saw at once that this policy would kindle the smothered indignation of the Indians and Exiles into a flame. The Agent of the Seminoles, refusing to obey the orders thus given, remonstrated against the policy in a letter addressed to the head of the Department, in which he says : " The remark in " your letter that it is not presumed the condition of these negroes " (the Exiles) would be worse than that of others in the same sec- " tion of country is true ; yet you will agree that the same remark " would apply to *you, to me, or to any other individual of the* " *United States,* as we should, if subjected to slavery, be in the " precise condition of other slaves."

So general and so great was the indignation excited by this order for establishing a commerce in human flesh with drunken Seminoles, that it was soon after countermanded ; yet the immediate emigration of the Indians was urged with increased earnestness, although the Department of War was informed by nearly every officer in the military and Indian service of Florida, that they could not be in-

(1) Vide Sprague's Florida War.

duced to emigrate, so long as the Exiles should be regarded as in danger of being subjected to Creek authority.

But the stern decree had gone forth that " the Indians should prepare to emigrate West and *join the Creeks ;*'' and the necessary preparations were hurried forward both in the Military and Civil Departments of Government. The Exiles and Seminoles saw clearly the terrible alternative to which they were soon to be driven, and they turned their attention to active preparations for the conflict. Their crops were carefully secured ; their cattle driven far into the interior ; and their women and children removed from the frontier to places of safety. They omitted no opportunity of securing powder and lead ; and while associating with the white people, they manifested a bold contempt and dislike for them, which gave gloomy forebodings of the future.

CHAPTER VII.

COMMENCEMENT OF THE SECOND SEMINOLE WAR.

THE number of Exiles at the commencement of the Second Seminole War, has been variously estimated. Probably their whole number, including women and children, was not less than twelve hundred. To these may be added the slaves belonging to the Seminoles, estimated at two hundred, making a population of fourteen hundred blacks. Most of the slaves lived with the Exiles, separate and apart from their masters, paying a certain quantity of vegetables annually, for the partial freedom which they enjoyed. There were many half-breeds, however, some of whom resided with the Indians, and others were located with the Exiles.

The Spanish population called the Exiles "Maroons," after a class of free negroes who inhabit the mountains of Cuba, Jamaica, and other West Indian islands. Indeed, some of the Maroons of

7   (97)

Cuba appear to have found their way to Florida,[1] and many of the Exiles passed from that Territory to the West India Islands. Many officers of Government appear to have known or cared little for these people, while others manifested much intelligence and humanity in regard to them. We have already noticed the efforts of Mr. Thompson, the Indian Agent, of Colonel Clinch, and of Colonel Eaton, in behalf of the Exiles, who had long resided in Florida.

During the summer, the Indians committed various depredations upon the white people, such as stealing horses and killing cattle ; but the first open hostilities occurred on the twenty-eighth of December, when two important and bloody tragedies took place, which left the country no longer in doubt as to the actual existence of war.

A young and gallant warrior, named Osceola, was the principal actor in one of these scenes. He was the son of an Indian trader, a white man, named Powell. His mother was the daughter of a Seminole chief.

He had recently married a woman said to have been beautiful. She was the daughter of a chief who had married one of the Exiles ; but as all colored people by slaveholding laws are said to follow the condition of the mother, she was called an African slave. Osceola was proud of his ancestry. He hated slavery, and those who practiced the holding of slaves, with a bitterness that is but little understood by those who have never witnessed its revolting crimes.

He visited Fort King, in company with his wife and a few friends, for the purpose of trading. Mr. Thompson, the Agent, was present, and, while engaged in business, the wife of Osceola was seized as a slave. Evidently having negro blood in her veins, the law pronounced her a slave ; and, as no other person could show title to her, the pirate who had got possession of her body, was supposed of course to be her owner.

(1) Lieutenat Reynolds, while conducting the first party of emigrants West, in 1841, found among the Exiles persons who possessed so much Spanish blood, that he offered to leave them at New Orleans, and some of them accepted the offer. He left them in that city, and they probably now pass for Spaniards.

Osceola became frantic with rage, but was instantly seized and placed in irons, while his wife was hurried away to slaveholding pollution.[1] He remained six days in irons, when, General Thompson says, he became penitent, and was released.

From the moment when this outrage was committed, the Florida War may be regarded as commenced. Osceola swore vengeance upon Thompson, and those who assisted in the perpetration of this indignity upon himself, as well as upon his wife, and upon our common humanity.

The Exiles endeavored to stimulate the Indians to deeds of valor. In general council, they decreed that the first Seminole who should make any movement preparatory to emigration, should suffer death. Charley E. Mathler, a respected chief, soon after fell a victim to this decree. Osceola commanded the party who slew him. He had sold a portion of his cattle to the whites, for which he had received pay in gold. This money was found upon his person when he fell. Osceola forbade any one touching the gold, saying it was the price of the red man's blood, and with his own hands he scattered it in different directions as far as he was able to throw it.

But his chief object appeared to have been the death of General Thompson. Other Indians and Exiles were preparing for other important operations; but Osceola seemed intent, his whole soul was absorbed, in devising some plan by which he could safely reach Mr. Thompson, who was the object of his vengeance. He, or some of his friends, kept constant watch on the movements of Thompson, who was unconscious of the danger to which he was exposed. Osceola, steady to his purpose, refused to be diverted from this

(1) Vide account of this transaction by M. M. Cohen, given in the Quarterly Anti-Slavery Magazine, vol. II, page 419. Mr. Thompson, the Agent, in his letter to the Commissioner of Indian Affairs, bearing date soon after, says: " Powell used such language, that I was constrained to order him into irons." Mr. Sprague, in his history of the Florida War, reiterates the statement of Mr. Thompson. But neither Sprague, nor Thompson, nor any other person who was present, it is believed, has ever denied the relation which Mr. Cohen has given.

favorite object. Thompson was at Fort King, and there were but few troops to protect that fortress. But Indians seldom attempt an escalade, and Osceola sought an opportunity to take it by surprise. With some twenty followers, he lay secreted near the fort for days and weeks, determined to find some opportunity to enter by the open gate, when the troops should be off their guard.

Near the close of December, a runner brought him information that Major Dade, with his command, was to leave Fort Brooke on the twenty-fifth of that month, and that those who intended to share in the attack upon that regiment, must be at the great "Wahoo Swamp," by the evening of the twenty-seventh. This had no effect whatever upon Osceola. No circumstance could withdraw him from the bloody purpose which filled his soul.

On the twenty-eighth, in the afternoon, as he and his followers lay near the road leading from the fort to the house of the sutler, which was nearly a mile distant, they saw Mr. Thompson and a friend approaching. That gentleman and his companions had dined, and, on taking their cigars, he and Lieut. Smith, of the Second Artillery, had sallied forth for a walk, and to enjoy conversation by themselves.

At a signal given by Osceola, the Indians fired. Thompson fell, pierced by fourteen balls; Smith received about as many.[1] The shrill war-whoop followed the sound of the rifles, and alarmed the people at the fort. The Indians immediately scalped their victims, and then hastened to the house, where Mr. Rogers, the sutler, and two clerks, were at dinner. These three persons were instantly massacred and scalped. The Indians took as many valuable goods as they could carry, and set fire to the building. The smoke gave notice to those in the fort of the fate that had befallen the sutler and his clerks. But the condition in which the commandant found his troops, forbade his sending out any considerable force to ascertain the fate of Thompson and his companion. Near nightfall, a few daring spirits proceeded up the road to the hommock, and brought

---

(1) Sprague's History of the Florida War.

the bodies to the fort; but Osceola and his followers had hastened their flight, not from fear of the troops, but with the hope of joining their companions at Wahoo in time to engage in scenes of more general interest.

General Clinch had foreseen that hostilities were unavoidable, and, as early as the fifteenth of November, had sought to increase the number of troops at Fort King by such reinforcements as could be spared from other stations. For this purpose, he ordered Major Dade, then at Fort Brooke, near Tampa Bay, to prepare his command for a march to Fort King. The distance was one hundred and thirty miles, through an unsettled forest, much diversified with swamps, lakes and hommocks. No officer nor soldier could be found who was acquainted with the route, and a guide was indispensable : yet men competent to the discharge of so important a trust were rarely to be found, for the lives of the regiment might depend upon the intelligence and fidelity of their conductor.

At this point in our history, even before the commencement of general hostilities, we are led to the acquaintance of one of the most romantic characters who bore part in the stirring scenes of that day. On making inquiry for a suitable guide, the attention of Major Dade was directed to a colored man named Louis. He was the slave of one of the old and respectable Spanish families, named Pacheco, who resided in the vicinity of Fort Brooke. Major Dade applied to the master, Antonio Pacheco, for information concerning his slave, and was assured that Louis, then near thirty years of age, was one of the most *faithful, intelligent,* and *trustworthy* men he had ever known. He had also been well bred, was polite, accomplished, and learned. He read, wrote, and spoke, with facility, the Spanish, French, and English languages, and spoke the Indian, and was perfectly familiar with the route to Fort King, having frequently traveled it.

Pleased with the character and appearance of Louis, Major Dade entered into an agreement with the master for his services in conducting the troops through the forest to Fort King, at the rate of twenty-five dollars per month, and stated the time at which the service was to commence. The contract was made in the presence of Louis, who listened attentively to the whole arrangement, to which he of course gave his own consent.

Louis Pacheco was too enlightened to smother the better sympathies of the human heart. He was well informed, and understood the efforts that were making to reënslave his brethren, the Exiles. With many of them he had long been acquainted ; he had witnessed the persecutions to which they had been subjected, the outrages heaped upon them, and now saw clearly the intention to subject them to slavery among the Creeks. He had spent his own life thus far in servitude, and, although his condition was regarded with envy by the plantation servants around him, he yet sighed for freedom.

Blessed with an intellect of no ordinary mould, he reflected deeply upon his condition, and determined upon his course. Hostilities had not yet commenced, and he was in the daily habit of conversing with Indians, and often with Exiles. He was well acquainted with the character of each, and knew the men to whom he could communicate important information with safety. To a few of the Exiles, men of integrity and boldness, he imparted the facts that Dade, with his troops, would leave Fort Brooke about the twenty-fifth of December, for Fort King, and that he, Louis, was to act as their guide ; that he would conduct them by the trail leading near the Great Wahoo Swamp, and pointed out the proper place for an attack.[1]

This information was soon made known to the leading and active Exiles, and to a few of the Seminole chiefs and warriors. The Exiles, conscious that the war was to be waged on their account, were anxious to give their friends some suitable manifestation of their prowess. They desired as many of the Exiles capable of bearing arms as could assemble at a certain point in the Great Wahoo Swamp, to meet them there as early as the twenty-seventh of De

(1) Vide Testimony accompanying Pacheco's Petition to Congress for indemnity.

cember, armed, and prepared to commence the war by a proper demonstration of their gallantry.

Information was sent to Osceola and his followers, inviting them to be present. They were lying secreted near Fort King, too intent upon the death of Thompson to turn their eyes for a moment from their victim. However, many other chiefs and warriors assembled at the time and place designated, in order to witness what they supposed would be the first scene in the great drama about to be acted. Their spies detached for that purpose, arrived at their rendezvous almost hourly, bringing information of the commencement of Dade's march, the number of men forming his battalion, and their places of encampment each night.

In the evening of the twenty-seventh, their patrols brought word that Dade and his men had arrived within three miles of the point at which they intended to attack them. Of course every preparation was now made for placing themselves in ambush at an early hour, along the trail in which it was expected the troops would pass. The scouts reported that precisely one hundred and ten men constituted the force which they expected to encounter, and the official report fully confirms the accuracy of their intelligence. The Exiles looked to the coming day with great intensity of feeling. More than two hundred years since, their ancestors had been piratically seized in their own country, and forcibly torn from their friends — from the land of their nativity. For a time they submitted to degrading bondage ; but more than a century had elapsed since they fled from South Carolina, and found an asylum under Spanish law in the wilds of Florida. There their fathers and mothers had been buried. They had often visited their graves, and mourned over the sad fate to which their race appeared to be doomed. For fifty years they had been subjected to almost constant persecution at the hands of our Government. The blood of their fathers, brothers and friends, massacred at " Blount's Fourt," was yet unavenged. They had seen individuals from among them piratically seized and enslaved. Their friends, residing with E-con-chattimico and with

Walker, had been openly and flagrantly kidnapped, and sold into interminable servitude, where they were then sighing and moaning in degrading bondage. In looking forward, they read their intended doom, clearly written in the slave codes of Florida and the adjoining States, which could only be avoided by their most determined resistance. If they behaved worthy of men in their condition, their influence with their savage allies would be confirmed, and they would be able to control their action on subsequent occasions. Every consideration, therefore, tended to nerve them to the work of death which lay before them.

In the meantime, their victims were reposing at only four or five miles distant in conscious security. Their encampment had been selected according to military science. The men and officers were encamped in scientific order. Their guards were placed, their patrols sent out, and every precaution taken to prevent surprise. They had seen service, and cheerfully encountered its hardships, privations and dangers, but had no suspicion of the fate that awaited them on the coming day.

At early dawn, the men were paraded, the roll called, and the order for regulating the day's march given. They were then dismissed for breakfast, and at eight o'clock, resumed their march, and proceeded on their way in the full expectation of reaching their destination by the evening of that day.

But the insidious foe had been equally vigilant. They had left their island encampment with the first light of the morning, and each had taken his position along the trail in which the troops were expected to march, but at some thirty or forty yards distant. Each man was hidden by a tree, which was to be his fortress during the expected action. A few rods on the other side of the trail lay a pond of water, whose placid surface reflected the glittering rays of the morning sun. All was peaceful and quiet as the breath of summer.

Unsuspicious of the hidden death which beset their pathway, the troops entered this defile, and passed along until their rear had come within the range of the enemies' rifles, when, at a given signal, each warrior fired, while his victim was in full view and unprotected. One-half of that ill-fated band, including the gallant Dade, fell at the first fire. The remainder were thrown into disorder. The officers endeavored to rally them into line ; but their enemy was unseen, and ere they could return an effective shot, a second discharge from the hidden foe laid one-half their remaining force prostrate in death. The survivors retreated a short distance toward their encampment of the previous night, and, while most of the Exiles and Indians were engaged in scalping the dead and tomahawking those who were disabled, they formed a hasty breastwork of logs for their defense. They were, however, soon invested by the enemy, and the few who had taken shelter behind their rude defenses were overcome and massacred by the Exiles, who conversed with them in English, and then dispatched them.[1] Only two individuals beside Louis, the guide, made their escape. Their gallant commander, his officers and soldiers, whose hearts had beat high with expectation in the morning, at evening lay prostrate in death ; and as the sable victors relaxed from their bloody work, they congratulated each other on having revenged the death of those who, twenty years previously, had fallen at the massacre of " Blount's Fort." The loss of the allied forces was — three killed and five wounded.

After burying their own dead, they returned to the island in the swamp long before nightfall. To this point, they brought the spoils of victory, which were deemed important for carrying on the war. Night had scarcely closed around them, however, when Osceola and his followers arrived from Fort King, bringing intelligence of the death of Thompson and Lieutenant Smith, together with the sutler and his two clerks. There, too, was Louis, the guide to Dade's command. He was now *free!* He engaged in conversation with his sable friends. Well knowing the time and place at which the attack was to be made, he had professed necessity for stopping by

---

(1) Vide Statement of Tustenuggee, a Seminole Chief, who was present, and whose account of this massacre is given in Sprague's History of the Florida War.

the way-side before entering the defile ; thus separating himself from the troops and from danger. Soon as the first fire showed him the precise position of his friends, he joined them ; and swearing eternal hostility to all who enslave their fellow men, lent his own efforts in carrying forward the work of death, until the last individual of that doomed regiment sunk beneath their tomahawks.

The massacre of the unfortunate Dade and his companions, and the murder of Thompson and his friends, at Fort King, occurred on the same day, and constituted the opening scenes of the second Seminole War.

1847.]   We bespeak the indulgence of the reader, while we digress from the chronological narration of events which followed consecutively upon this opening of the second Seminole War, in order to give a short sketch of some incidents which occurred in Congress, and were connected with the employment of Louis, and his subsequent service with the enemy.

Twelve years after the massacre of Dade's command, Antonio Pacheco presented his petition to Congress, setting forth that he had been the owner of a valuable slave named Louis ; that he hired him as guide to Major Dade to conduct his command from " Fort Brooke " to " Fort King ;" that at the time of Dade's defeat, Louis had been *captured by the Indians*, and by them had been subsequently surrendered to Major General Jessup, and by that officer sent to the Indian country, west of the Mississippi, whereby he became lost to his owner, who, therefore, prayed Congress to grant him full indemnity for his loss.

Among the proofs accompanying this petition was a letter from General Jessup, setting forth that, after Louis had been employed to act as guide, he had kept up a correspondence with the "Seminole negroes," informing them of the intended march of Major Dade, etc. He also represented Louis as a man of extraordinary intellect and learning, declaring that he regarded him as a *dangerous* man ; that he would have had him tried and hanged, instead of sending him West, if he had found leisure to attend to it ; that from prudential motives he had sent him to the Indian country; and stated that he was worth a *thousand dollars.*

The case was most interesting in its character. Louis was probably the most dangerous enemy of the United States at that time in Florida. With his intelligence, he must have felt an inveterate hostility to the Government and the people, who robbed him of his most sacred right to liberty. Probably his former master and family were in greater danger from his vengeance than any other persons. He had surrendered to General Jessup as prisoner of war with arms in his hands; had been treated — very properly treated — as a prisoner of war : therefore, the master called on the people of the nation to pay him a thousand dollars for protecting him, his family, friends and nation from the fury of his own slave ; and General Jessup and many Northern Representatives exerted their personal and political influence to sustain the claim.

The petition and accompanying papers were referred to the committee on Military Affairs, a majority of whom were known to be favorable to the interests of slavery. At the head of it was the Hon. Armisted Burt, of South Carolina, a man of intelligence and influence. He appeared devoted to the interests of the "peculiar institution."

1848.] Having examined the case, he presented it to the consideration of the committee, and a majority at once agreed to sustain a bill giving to the owner a fair compensation for the loss of his slave. The Chairman agreed to draw up a report sustaining the bill, and present it to the committee the next morning.

Hon. John Dickey, of Beaver County, Pennsylvania, now deceased, was also a member of the committee. He boarded at the same house with the author of this narrative. While at tea that evening, Mr. Dickey remarked, that his committee were about to report a bill to pay for this slave, and said, if he were familiar with the subject, he would draw up a minority report against the bill. A gentleman sitting at the table remarked, that other gentlemen, who were familiar with the subject, would doubtless feel willing to lend him any aid in their power. All however agreed, that an evening was too short a time to draw up a suitable report on so important a question; yet it was known that slaveholders controlled the action of the House, and they showed no courtesy to those opposed to the " peculiar institution," and would of course grant no time to draw up a minority report. After tea, Mr. Dickey and another gentleman retired to a room by themselves, and before sunrise the next morning, had completed the report, which now appears among the House Documents, Thirtieth Congress, first session, numbered 187, filling sixteen heavy octavo pages of printed matter. At ten o'clock the committee met, and, having listened to the report of their Chairman, they were called on to hear that of Mr. Dickey, which took distinct and unmistakable grounds against the right of men to hold their fellow-beings as *property*, under the Federal Constitution. This case furnishes the first instance in which the records of the nation show a minority report from any committee *against* slavery. Mr. Dickey, having taken his position, stood firmly upon the doctrines he had avowed in his report; and the other members of the committee took their choice between the report of Mr. Burt and that of Mr. Dickey.

General Dudley Marvin, of New York, General James Wilson, of New Hampshire, and Hon. David Fisher, of Ohio, signed the report of Mr. Dickey; while the four Democratic members, all of whom resided in the slave States, signed that of Mr. Burt. So far as the committee were concerned, the five Democratic members assumed the position now occupied by that party, to wit, that under our Federal Constitution, man may hold, sell and transfer human beings as property; while the four Whig members based their action upon the doctrine now occupied by the Republican party — that, under our Federal Constitution, men cannot be transformed into brutes; nor can one man hold *property* in another.

The reports of the majority and minority were printed, and attracted attention among the members; but the bill did not come up for discussion until the next session. On the twenty-third of the following December, the committee of the whole House, in passing through its calendar of private claims, reached this case. Mr. Dickey led off in a short, but well-arranged argument, sustaining his report. His remarks were so well directed and so pertinent, that, near the close of his speech, Mr. Burt called him to order, for *discussing the subject of slavery.* Upon the conclusion of Mr. Dickey's remarks, General Wilson of New Hampshire obtained the floor, and the House adjourned.

The bill did not come up again for discussion until the twenty-ninth. Before going into committee on that day, Mr. Rockwell, of Connecticut, Chairman of the committee on Claims, offered a resolution closing debate on this bill at half-past one o'clock, allowing but one hour and a quarter for the discussion of this important question, which now agitates the whole Union ; but it was regarded at that time as meritorious in any member to prevent agitation of the subject of slavery, and the resolution passed with little opposition. When the House resolved itself into committee of the whole, Mr. Wilson, of New Hampshire, delivered his views, sustaining the report of the minority of the committee ; making the question distinctly to depend upon the right of men to hold property in men, under the Federal Constitution.

Mr. Brown, of Mississippi, followed in a few remarks, taking strong ground in favor of the principle, that slaves are *property*, to the same extent that horses and cattle are property. Mr. Cabel, of Florida, followed in a few words to the same point. Here the time for closing the debate arrived ; but Mr. Burt, having reported the bill, held the right to speak one hour, under the rules, in reply to those who opposed its passage. He had evidently expected the bill would pass without serious opposition, and had become somewhat excited by the difficulties with which he had to contend ; confident however of final success, he at once declared the only question to be, that of *property in human flesh.* Many Northern men were unwilling to meet this bald question. Mr. Collamer, of Vermont, interrupted Mr. Burt, inquiring, if there were not other questions of law involved? Burt replied, with some degree of arrogance, that he would "leave no other loop-hole for gentlemen to escape." This supercilious bearing of Mr. Burt greatly delighted some Northern members, while it appeared greatly to embarrass others; but his speech was the last, and, there being no opportunity for reply, every thing gave promise of a triumphant victory to the slaveholders.

After the conclusion of this speech, the vote was taken in committee, where no record was kept, and stood for the bill *seventy*, against it *forty-four* — the majority being even greater than the slaveholders expected. The bill was then reported to the House, and Mr. Crowell, of Ohio, moved to lay it on the table, and called for the yeas and nays; and the recorded vote stood, ayes *sixty-six*, noes *eighty-five* — being a majority of nineteen in favor of the claim. The bill was then ordered to a third reading without division.

Soon as this result was announced, the Author moved a reconsideration of this vote. The reconsideration being a privileged question, he held the floor, and was proceeding to deliver his views, but gave way for an adjournment.

1849.] On the sixth of January, the bill again came up in the regular order of business, and Mr. Giddings concluded his remarks. He endeavored to meet the arrogance of Mr. Burt, clearly and as fully as his abilities would permit. He accepted the challenge thrown out by that member, that he would leave no other loop-hole for gentlemen to escape, than by meeting the question of *property in human flesh*. To this point he directed his remarks, attempting to show the doctrine of Mr. Burt to be opposed to the Declaration of Independence, to the Constitution of the United States, to civilization, to the dictates of our common humanity.[1] When he concluded his remarks, he withdrew his motion to reconsider, in order to test the sense of the House on the passage of the bill, which would be the next question in order.

(1) These Speeches may be found in the Congressional Globe, 2d Sess. XXXth Congress,

As the roll was called, and the votes given, the result became doubtful, and much interest was manifested in all parts of the hall. The bill and discussion had been thrust upon the House by slaveholders : its whole merits were based upon the most vital principles of slavery. The question of property in human flesh, constitutes one of the essential elements of the institution, without which it could not survive one hour. The slave power had not for many years been defeated on any proposition touching slavery, and it appeared painful for those interested in that institution to have their influence doubted.

The Clerk (a deputy) was engaged a long time in counting the votes, and ascertaining the result. He was a slaveholder, and appeared perplexed ; some members, even before he made report of the vote, expressed doubts of his accuracy. At length he passed his report to the Chair. The Speaker, Mr. Winthrop of Massachusetts, casting his eye upon the figures, rose from his seat, and announced the vote — "ayes *ninety,* noes *eighty-nine,*" and then remarking that the rules of the House made it his duty to vote in all cases when such vote would *change the result,* began to give his reasons for the vote he was about to record, and as he proceeded it became evident that he was *opposed to the bill.* The Clerk then handed him another paper, and the Speaker, after reading it, announced that the Clerk had mistaken the vote, and without saying more, announced — "ayes *ninety-one,* noes *eighty-nine,*" and declared the bill "*passed.*"

The interest had now become intense in all parts of the hall. It was perfectly natural that men should be suspicious of the Clerk. Mr. Dickey, in particular, had taken a deep interest in the question. He was sitting near the Author, and expressed freely the opinion, that the Clerk had reported the vote incorrectly. So strong was this belief, that he went to the Clerk, and demanded a copy of the record giving the ayes and noes. The Clerk promised to give it soon. Dickey waited a short time, and renewed his call on the Clerk, who again promised. Dickey, after waiting a proper time, went to the Clerk's table, and took the record of yeas and nays, and brought it to the seat of the Author, and requested his assistance in counting the vote. They counted and *re*-counted several times, but were unable to make the vote other than " *eighty-nine* ayes, and *eighty-nine* noes "—showing a tie vote ; which, without the Speaker's vote, would have defeated the bill. Dickey returned the record to the Clerk, and then called the attention of the House and the Speaker to the fact, that the Clerk had inaccurately reported the vote. The Speaker replied, if an error had occurred, the proper time to correct it would be the next morning, on reading the Journal, when a motion to correct the entry would be in order, in preference to any other business.

On looking over the list, it was subsequently discovered, that the vote of Hon. John W. Farrelly of Crawford county, Pennsylvania, was not recorded. This added intensity to the interest already felt on the subject.

The next meeting of the House was on Monday, when the Speaker recited the facts as they occurred on Saturday, and declared that, on a more careful examination, it was found that the vote stood—"ayes *eighty-nine*, noes *eighty nine*."

Mr. Farelly inquired, if his vote was recorded ? The Speaker informed him it was not, but that it was his right to have it recorded, if he had actually voted on the passage of the bill. That gentleman declared that he had voted *no*, on the passage of the bill, and the vote being recorded, the Speaker declared the result to be " *ayes eighty-nine, noes* NINETY," and then announced the bill " *lost !* "

The friends of freedom were greatly cheered, from the consideration, that party ties had not been strong enough to control members on this important vote. Of the twenty-one members from Ohio, only Mr. Ritchey of Perry, Mr. Cummins of Tuscarawas, and Mr. Taylor of Ross, voted with the slaveholders ; while such Democrats as Messrs. Faran, Fries, Kennon, Lamb, Miller, Morris, Sawyer and Starkweather voted against the doctrine that men and women

As-se-he-ho-lar. (known as Osceola, or Powell.)

may be held and treated as property. Indeed, there were but few Representatives from the free States willing to recognize that doctrine. No member from New Hampshire, Massachusetts, Rhode Island, Connecticut, Vermont, Michigan, Wisconsin or Iowa voted for it. From Maine, Messrs. Clapp, Clarke and Williams; from New York, Messrs. Birdsal, McClay, Murphy, Necoll and Tallmadge; from Pennsylvania, Messrs. Brady, Bridges, Brodhead, Charles Brown, C. J. Ingersol, Levin and Job Mann; from Indiana, Messrs. Dunn, R. W. Thompson and Wick; and from Illinois, Messrs. McClernand and Richardson voted to pay Pacheco a thousand dollars, because General Jessup sent a most dangerous enemy out of Florida.

Mr Burt, and the friends of slavery generally, appeared irritated by defeat. They had driven their Northern allies to revolt. The more they reflected upon the subject, the more important the issue appeared. They had caused great agitation, while professing to deprecate all discussion in regard to slavery. If slaves were not *property* under the Federal Constitution, they must be regarded as *persons.* If the civilized world looked upon them as persons, those who held them in bondage must of course be considered as oppressors of mankind, and could have no claim to the title of Democrats or of Christians. In every point of view, the result appeared disastrous to the slave power.

It was under these circumstances, that the Hon. William Sawyer of Ohio, was induced to move a reconsideration of the vote by which the bill was lost. From the fact that none but those voting in the negative could by the rules of the House move a reconsideration, and that he subsequently voted against his own motion, it is probable he made it from personal kindness to those who supported the bill. On this motion, a long discussion subsequently arose, which did not terminate until the nineteenth of January, when the motion to reconsider prevailed, and on the final passage of the bill the vote stood—ayes 101, noes 95. So the bill was passed by the House of Representatives, and the struggle in that body terminated.

8

But the bill was never brought up for discussion in the Senate, and the claim was never more moved in either House of Congress. The question of property in human flesh, however, continued to be discussed by the people, and in Congress, until it has become one of the great issues on which political parties now base their action.

NOTE.—The life of this slave Louis is perhaps the most romantic of any man now living. Born and reared a slave, he found means to cultivate his intellect — was fond of reading; and while gentlemen in the House of Representatives were engaged in discussing the value of his bones and sinews, he could probably speak and write more languages with ease and facility than any member of that body. In revenge for the oppression to which he was subjected, he conceived the purpose of sacrificing a regiment of white men, who were en gaged in the support of slavery. This object effected, he asserted his own natural right to freedom, joined his brethren, and made bloody war upon the enemies of liberty. For two years, ho was the steady companion of Coacoochee, or, as he was afterwads called, " Wild Cat," who subsequently became the most warlike chief in Florida. They traversed the forests of that territory together, wading through swamps and everglades, groping their way through hommocks, and gliding over prairies. They bivouacked together; suffered heat and cold, hunger and thirst, together. For two years, they stood shoulder to shoulder in every battle; shared their victories and defeats together; and when General Jessup had pledged the faith of the nation that all Indians who would surrender should be protected in the enjoyment of their slaves, Wild Cat appeared at head quarters, followed by Louis, whom he claimed as his *property*, under slaveholding law, as he said he had *captured* him at the time of Dade's defeat. The ruse took. General Jessup, being a slaveholder, and believing that slaves, like horses and cattle, were the subjects of capture, immediately sent Louis with other black warriors to Fort Pike, near New Orleans, and thence with the first emigrating party of Seminoles to the western country, where he was three years subse-quently joined by Coacoochee, and these friends, again united, became intimate, sharing together the fortunes which awaited them, of which we shall speak in due time.

CHAPTER VIII.

HOSTILITIES CONTINUED.

THE night after the massacre of Dade and his companions was spent in exultation by the allies. Osceola and his friends brought with them from the sutler's store various goods, with which they decorated their persons; while the numerous scalps taken from the heads of their enemies, were displayed as trophies of victory. They had also found among the stores with which Major Dade's party were provided, sufficient rum and whisky to intoxicate most of them, and their rejoicings and felicitations continued, for hours, amid the darkness of night.

It was a late hour in the morning when they awoke from the stupor occasioned by severe labors of the previous day, and the night's debauch. Before they had refreshed themselves with the morning's meal, their scouts arrived, bringing intelligence that troops were advancing towards the Withlacoochee, in pursuit of Indians and Exiles. General Clinch had been lying at Fort Drane. He clearly saw the evidence of approaching hostilities; and, although wholly unconscious of the danger which had threatened Major Dade, had felt it his duty to raise such forces as he could command, and advance into the Indian country as far as the Withlacoochee. He gathered about two hundred Regulars, from the 1st, 2d and 3d Artillery, and, with some four hundred Florida volunteers, under General C. K. Call, had nearly reached the Withlacoochee before the captors of Dade were informed of his approach.

About two hundred warriors, fifty of whom were Exiles, volunteered to meet this army, of three times their own number, under the command of one of the most able and gallant officers at that time in the service of the United States.

Osceola and Halpatter-Tustenuggee commanded the allies. They hastened to the crossing of the Withlacoochee, and there lay awaiting the approach of General Clinch. Here the water was not more than two feet in depth, and they entertained no doubt that the advancing forces would seek this place for the purpose of fording the stream. Here they waited until the morning of the thirtieth, when they learned that General Clinch, with his two hundred Regulars, had already passed the stream some two miles below. He had effected his passage by the aid of a bark canoe, which carried only eight men at a time.

Having attained a position on the south side of the river with his Regulars, General Clinch was ready for battle; although the four hundred volunteers were yet on the north side of the stream. The Indians and Exiles immediately engaged these veteran troops, although sustained by a heavy force of volunteers, who were yet on the opposite side of the river. At twelve o'clock, on the thirtieth of December, the contending forces engaged, and a severe and deadly conflict followed.

As Osceola now for the first time engaged in battle, he felt anxious to distinguish himself by his intrepidity. His voice was heard on every part of the field, urging on his troops to deeds of daring. Undaunted by the shrill war-whoop, and the constant report of Indian rifles and the whistling balls around him, General Clinch charged his enemy. The allies fell back, and he continually advanced until he drove them from the thick hommock into the open forest. The gallant general coolly passed along the lines during the action encouraging his men, and stimulating them to effort by his presence and bravery. A ball passed through his cap and another through the sleeve of his coat, to which he paid no attention, but continued to encourage his men.

The Exiles also displayed unusual gallantry. Feelings which had descended from father to son through several generations, had been recently inflamed to the highest degree of indignant hatred. Conscious that they were contending for their homes, their firesides, their families, their liberties, they fought with desperation, and their aim was fatal. Unfortunately, Osceola was wounded and disabled early in the contest, and it was said that the Indians did not exhibit that undaunted firmness on the field that was manifested by their more dusky allies. They suffered less than our troops. Two negroes and one Indian were killed, and three negroes and two Indians wounded—the loss of the Exiles being twice as great as that of the Indians, although they numbered but one-fourth of the allied force.

The battle continued an hour and twenty minutes. During this time, the regular troops under Colonel Clinch were subjected to a brisk fire, and their loss was severe. Eight men were killed and forty wounded, of whom about one-third died of their wounds. Several officers were also wounded. The militia consulted their own safety by refusing to expose themselves to the fire of the enemy; while the regular troops lost, in killed and wounded, nearly one-fourth of their number. The allies drew off, leaving Colonel Clinch in possession of the field; but the victory had been won at great expense of blood; and the determined coolness and gallantry of the veteran officer who commanded our forces, saved them from a total defeat.

The blows thus far had fallen most heavily upon our own troops. It became evident, that the carrying out of General Jackson's policy, of removing the Exiles and Indians from Florida, in order to encourage and sustain slavery, was to be attended with great sacrifice of blood and treasure. But while the Government and people were looking at these unexpected exhibitions of firmness and love of liberty, on the part of the allied forces, other scenes were presented to their view. The fugitive slaves who had recently left their masters in Florida and joined the Exiles, were stimulated with that hatred which slavery alone can engender in the human breast. They thirsted for revenge upon those who had held them in bondage ; who had scourged and tortured them. They were acquainted with the location of the small settlements throughout the Territory. Uniting with the more daring spirits among the Indians and Exiles, they proceeded rapidly and stealthily from plantation to plantation, burning buildings, destroying property, and scattering devastation throughout the border settlements ; at times murdering whole families, killing and scalping such individuals as fell in their way.

Men who had urged on the war with the hope of seizing and enslaving the maroons of the interior, now saw their own plantations laid waste, and in frequent instances mourned the loss of wives and children, instead of rejoicing over captured slaves, whom they had intended to acquire by piratical force. Farms, and the smaller villages on the frontier, were abandoned to the enemy ; and the inhabitants fled to the larger villages, where they banded together for mutual defense. The citizens of Florida who had petitioned General Jackson for the forcible removal of the Indians, because they failed to capture and return slaves, were now compelled to flee, with their families, before the infuriated servants who had left them subsequently to the signing of that petition. Driven from their homes — their property destroyed, their servants fled — many families, who but a few months previously had been regarded as wealthy, were now suffering from the want of bread.[1]

The whole scene was calculated to impress statesmen and people with that religious philosophy which teaches, that every violation of justice or of moral principle, is, by the immutable law of the Creator, inseparably connected with an appropriate penalty. All that the Exiles or Indians had ever asked or desired of the American Government, was to leave them to themselves; to permit them to remain as they were, as they had been for many generations.

The war on our part had not been commenced for the attainment of any high or noble purpose. No desire to elevate mankind, or confer benefits upon our race, had guided our national policy in commencing the war. Our national influence and military power had been put forth to reënslave our fellow men; to transform immortal beings into chattels, and make them the property of slaveholders; to oppose the rights of human nature; and the legitimate fruits of this policy were gathered in a plentiful harvest of crime, bloodshed and individual suffering.

The great body of the people were ignorant as to the real causes of the war. General Jackson had been popular as a military officer, and was not less so as President of the United States. With his political friends his will was law. The opposing political party were comparatively few in numbers. They feared his power; and no member of either Senate or House of Representatives appeared willing to expose the great moral crimes which the Government was committing against humanity. Hence Congress granted whatever supplies were demanded for carrying on this piratical war, and enabling the President to slay those who refused to be enslaved.

General Cass, a statesman with whose character the present generation is familiar, was Secretary of War. On him devolved the duty of controlling the movements of the army. Unfortunately for him and for mankind, he appears to have regarded moral and politi-

(1) Sprague's History of the War.

cal duties as separate and distinct in their character. He evidently believed that no moral turpitude was attached to movements of the army, and the outrages committed upon the Indians and Exiles, in order to compel them to emigrate to the western country. He ordered Major General Scott to the field, as Commanding General of the army in Florida (Jan. 20), with authority to call on the Governors of South Carolina, Georgia and Alabama for such troops as he should deem necessary. General Eustis, commanding at Charleston, South Carolina, was directed to repair at once to Florida with such forces as were stationed in that city and Savannah, and to accept the services of such number of volunteers as he might deem necessary under the circumstances.

1836.]

Major General Gaines, commanding the western military department, holding his head quarters at New Orleans, hearing of the sad fate of Major Dade and his regiment, embarked at once with a brigade of eleven hundred men, and reached " Fort Brooke " on the tenth of January. On the thirteenth, he took up his line of march for " Fort King," and on the nineteenth, encamped upon the same ground which Major Dade had occupied on the night of the twenty-seventh of December. The next day they took possession of the field of massacre, and buried the bodies of those who had fallen in that unfortunate conflict. He then proceeded to Fort King, where he arrived on the twenty-second. Leaving Fort King on the twenty-fifth, he took a more westerly route back toward Fort Brooke.

On the twenty-seventh, as he was seeking a place at which to cross the Withlacoochee, the allied forces opened a fire upon his advanced guard from the opposite bank. The firing increased as other forces were brought into action, and continued for more than two hours, ceasing with the nightfall.

There were resident at different points upon the Withlacoochee many families of Exiles. Their commander was named " Ino," of whom General Jessup speaks in respectful terms. He is said to have been their principal counselor, and one of the most important chiefs among the Exiles. He, and such of his men as could be collected, hastily joined the allied forces already in the field, and shared in the dangers of that and of several following days. Both parties bivouacked upon the field, on the different sides of the river, and at daylight the next morning every man had his arms in readiness for renewing the conflict.

At sunrise, General Gaines moved down the river three miles, where he expected to find a suitable ford ; but on reaching it, the Indians and Exiles opened a brisk fire upon his men. Lieutenant Izard of the dragoons, endeavoring to rally his men to ascertain the possibility of fording the stream, fell by a shot from the opposite bank.

Finding it impossible to ford the river, attempts were made to construct rafts ; but the fire upon the men employed was so galling that they were ordered back out of the range of the enemies' shot. During these movements, the Exiles, understanding the English language, kept up a conversation with the whites on the opposite side of the river, and tauntingly defied them. General Gaines was too well acquainted with the Indian mode of warfare to attempt a retreat, under the circumstances with which he was surrounded. He at once dispatched an express to General Clinch, who was at Fort Drane, directing that officer to repair as soon as possible to his relief with such troops as he could at the moment bring with him. General Gaines soon after retired with his forces into a pine barren, half a mile from the river, threw up a breastwork of logs for the protection of his men, and awaited reinforcements.

The allied forces were estimated by General Gaines at fifteen hundred, though subsequent reports show they did not exceed five hundred Indians and two hundred negroes. He was immediately invested in his fortified camp, but he coolly awaited the arrival of General Clinch. As the enemy crossed the river in large forces, and became more bold in their advances toward the breastwork, their fire became more annoying. In a few days his provisions were nearly exhausted, and his men appeared to feel unsafe, and expressed solicitude for the arrival of General Clinch.

On the first of February, the allied forces made a vigorous attack upon the fortified camp, but they were repulsed after an hour of steady firing. On this day, General Gaines directed all the corn in the camp to be collected and dealt out to the men in equal quantities. It gave to each *one pint*. On the third, they commenced killing horses, and appropriating the flesh to sustain the lives of the men. The fire of the allied forces was kept up on the fourth and fifth, while the troops had nothing but horse flesh for food, and no tidings had yet arrived from General Clinch. At this time great enthusiasm prevailed among the allies. Their women were at the camp, a mile distant, casting balls, cooking food for the men, and doing what they could to cheer them on to victory, which they began to regard as almost certain. In the meantime, the situation of General Gaines and his army was constantly becoming more critical. His troops were depressed with a sense of their situation; while the allies were becoming hourly more enthusiastic. They had destroyed Dade's regiment; had maintained a severe battle with General Clinch in the open forest. They knew their power, and that any attempt to retreat from them would be fatal; while it would be impossible for our troops to remain much longer in camp, as their stock of horses must soon fail.

Twenty-one years had passed since General Gaines transmitted a letter to the War Department, giving the first official notice that the Exiles were collecting at " Blount's Fort " He then despised the friendless people who were seeking liberty. He had himself detailed Colonel Clinch and the regiment under his command, attended by Creek Indians, with General Jackson's orders *" to destroy the fort, and return the slaves to their rightful owners."* He then called the Exiles " outlaws," supposed them incapable of taking care of themselves, even if in full possession of their liberty. But he and his gallant army were now surrounded by them and their friends, who were killing his men whenever they exposed themselves to view. On the fifth of March, he had lost four men killed and thirty wounded.

A circumstance occurred on the night of the fifth of February, which has never been fully explained. About ten o'clock in the evening, John Cæsar, one of the Exiles residing at Micanopy, an old man and somewhat of a privileged character among both Indians and Exiles, advanced in the darkness near the camp of General Gaines, and hailed the nearest sentinel on duty. Speaking in good English, the sentinel supposed him a messenger from General Clinch; but, on learning his true character, he was inquired of as to his object. He declared that the allies were tired of fighting, and wished to come in and shake hands with General Gaines and his men. He was told to come in the morning with a white flag.

Cæsar returned to the allied camp and reported his conversation. He had spoken to our troops as if authorized, while all the chiefs and head-men denied his authority, and many were for inflicting upon him the penalty of immediate death for this unauthorized act. Osceola, now raised to the dignity of a chief, interposed to save him. He had headed the party who put to death Charley E. Mathler, a brother chief, for consenting to go West, and with his own hands had scattered the gold found on his person, declaring it to be "the price of the red man's blood:" While now a black man, one of their "allies," had committed a far greater impropriety, he interposed to save him. All agreed that their honor had been pledged, although Cæsar had no authority for his conduct.[1]

The next day some of their warriors left in disgust, after it had been determined to send in a flag of truce, according to Cæsar's agreement. But those who remained to carry out the arrangement, formed at twelve o'clock into line, some forty rods in the rear of General Gaines's camp. Three of their number, gaily dressed,

---

(1) Osceola, though a fierce and gallant warrior, entertained high notions of honor; and, although a savage, he was punctilious on those points, and finally fell a victim to the treachery of those calling themselves *civilized* men.

advanced with a white flag. Adjutant Barrow of the Louisiana Volunteers, met them. Osceola told him that he desired a talk with General Gaines.

While these arrangements were going forward, General Clinch arrived in sight of the Indians, on his way to relieve General Gaines. Seeing the enemy thus drawn up, facing the camp, he at once deployed his column, and opened a fire upon them. The allies supposing themselves to have been betrayed fled precipitately, and the forces under General Clinch united with those under General Gaines.

It is said that up to the time the allies received the fire of General Clinch, they had not lost a man. That fire killed two Indians and one negro, and wounded five others.

One of the Exiles, residing upon the Withlacoochee, who, after the compact with General Jessup in 1838, surrendered, with others, and emigrated West, stated that he assisted Osceola in counting the sticks handed in by each warrior engaged in this affair, and there were seven hundred present; and another bunch of sticks numbering one hundred had been sent by a party who expected to reach the scene of action the next day, when a general and determined attack was to have been made. But their forces disbanded upon the arrival of General Clinch, and they separated to their different homes.

The officers under General Gaines charged the allies with bad faith, intending to massacre them under pretense of treating with them; while the allies charged our troops with a treacherous effort to shoot them while their flag of truce was floating over them, and they engaged in peaceful negotiation.

General Gaines proceeded to Fort Brooke, and thence returned to New Orleans; while General Clinch conducted his troops back to Fort Drane.

CHAPTER IX.

HOSTILITIES CONTINUED.

General disappointment in regard to the continuance of the War — Its Difficulties — Feelings of the People of Florida — Letter of their Delegate in Congress — Letter of General Jessup to F. P. Blair — President Jackson's order in regard to it — Secretary of War orders General Scott to Washington, and General Jessup to take command — General Call in temporary command of the Army— Court of Inquiry—Osceola attacks Micanopy—Major Heilman's gallant Defense — General Jessup meets General Call at Talahasse —Refuses to assume Command — Major Pearce's Expedition to Fort Drane — Meets Osceola with an equal force — Severe Contest — Major Pearce retires to Micanopy— General Jessup's contract with Creeks — Its Character — Resumes barbarous practice of Enslaving Prisoners — General Call's Expedition to Withlacoochee — Its Failure — Further attempts to destroy Stores on that River —Armstrong's Battle — Another severe Battle — Another Expedition to Withlacoochee — Its Failure — Skill and Valor of the Exiles and Indians — Loss of Creeks — They become Disheartened.

WHEN General Scott took command of the army in Florida, the Administration and the country confidently expected that he would bring the war to an immediate close. There was but little known of the combined strength, or the determined purpose, of the Seminoles and Exiles. They were regarded as few in number, and were supposed to be fighting without any very definite purpose. The difficulties of collecting an army in that territory, procuring supplies and arranging a campaign, were great ; and the most effective mode for penetrating the strongholds of the allied forces could only be ascertained by experience.

The inhabitants of Florida had urged on the war. They held

(125)

their enemy in great contempt. They were slaveholders, accustomed to look upon the negro as an inferior being, possessed of very limited reasoning powers, and devoid of the nobler sentiments which adorn the human character. They do not appear to have supposed the African capable of noble aspirations, or of manly effort. They were also accustomed to look upon the Indians with about the same degree of contempt. Regarding the war as commenced and prosecuted for their own benefit, they felt authorized in some degree to dictate the manner in which it should be conducted.

General Scott, bred to the profession of arms, and conscious of that self-respect which was due to an officer of his rank, paid but little attention to their attempts at interference with his official duties. This was regarded as offensive, and the delegate in Congress from that Territory demanded his withdrawal from the command.

General Jessup, at that time in command of the army in Georgia, operating against the Creek Indians, in order to compel them to emigrate West, also wrote a letter (June 20), addressed to a private citizen of Washington City,[1] criticising General Scott's policy. This letter was placed in the hands of President Jackson, who, after reading it, indorsed upon it as follows :

"Referred to the Secretary of War, that he forthwith order General Scott to this place, in order that an inquiry may be had into "the unaccountable delays in prosecuting the Creek war, and the "failure of the campaign in Florida. Let General Jessup assume "the command.[2]

                                                    A. J."

It is very evident that General Jackson, when speaking of the "*unaccountable delays*" of a few months, had little expectation that under the direction of his most favorite officer the war would continue during his life, and that he would leave another generation involved in hostilities, for the purpose of enslaving persons whom he had ordered to be "returned to their masters" twenty years pre-

(1) Francis P. Blair, who is yet living, (1858.)
(2) Vide Ex. Doc., 2d Sess. XXVth Congress, No. 78, pages 558-9.

viously. But it is also apparent that neither the President, nor Congress, nor the officers of the army, had any just conceptions of that love of liberty which nerved the Exiles to effort, and stimulated them to encounter every hardship and privation, and suffering and danger, rather than be delivered over to degrading bondage.

Congress, participating in the general astonishment at the failure of our arms to conquer a handful of Indians and negroes, adopted a resolution, calling on the President for information touching that subject. In answer to this resolution, General Cass, Secretary of War, transmitted voluminous papers to Congress, which may be found in the Executive Documents of the second session, Twenty-fourth Congress, from which much of our information is derived.

The Secretary of War issued the order for General Scott to retire, and another for General Jessup to assume the command.

A court of inquiry was duly convened for the purpose of ascertaining the cause of delay under General Scott.[1]

Several months now passed without any important incident to mark the progress of hostilities. As the summer approached and the sickly season commenced, General Scott left Florida, and the command of the army, for the time, devolved on General C. K. Call. The allied forces seemed to have retired to the interior, and were supposed to be engaged in raising corn and other provisions, for their support during the coming winter, and all appeared quiet.

Osceola, after the death of Thompson at Fort King, had become a master-spirit among the Seminoles. He had conducted bravely during the battle with General Clinch, and equally so in the several conflicts with General Gaines, and had been raised to the dignity of a chief. He now conceived, and executed, one of the boldest movements ever made by savages against a fortified post manned by regular troops.

On the ninth of June, with three hundred warriors, some sixty

---

(1) His vindication before the court was triumphant, and he was honorably acquitted from all censure.

of whom were negroes, he attacked the stockade at Micanopy, garrisoned by an equal force of disciplined troops, under the command of Major Heilman. The assault was maintained with determined obstinacy for an hour and a half, the assailants boldly facing the artillery, which was brought to bear upon them; and when they left the scene of action, they carried away their dead and wounded.

Although this attack proved unsuccessful, it gave the country to understand, in some degree, the character of the enemy with whom our Government was contending.

Major Heilman, in his report, regrets the severe wound of Capt. Lee; but says nothing of his other loss, or that of the allies, either in killed or wounded He himself died soon after, from excessive fatigue during the action.

Soon after this attack the allies became again active, making their appearance at various points on the frontier, again spreading devastation wherever they went.

Major General Jessup continued in Georgia, engaged in constrain ing the Creeks to emigrate. In this he was very successful, and for that reason was ordered to take command of the army in Florida. With this view he repaired to Tallahasse, where he met General Call, who laid before him a plan, which he had conceived, for an expedition to Withlacoochee. General Jessup, not having received his instructions for prosecuting the campaign, refused to assume the command at that time, leaving General Call to carry out his contemplated movement.

General Clinch owned a plantation some twenty miles northwesterly of Fort King. During the early part of the season he had encamped there with his troops, and planted sugar-cane, and other crops; and, being occupied as a military post, he gave it the name of "Fort Drane."

In consequence of the constant depredations committed by the enemy, he was directed to fall back to an Indian town called "Micanopy," which thereby became an outpost. He left Fort Drane in July, when his crops were growing luxuriantly; and

Osceola, being in the vicinity with about a hundred followers, consisting of Indians and Exiles, took possession of this plantation, and occupied it with apparent pride, at having driven its veteran owner back farther towards the settlements.

On the twelfth of August, Major Pearce, being in command at Micanopy, left that station, with one piece of artillery and one hundred and ten regular troops, for the purpose of attacking the allies at Fort Drane. He reached the plantation, situated eight miles from Micanopy, at sunrise, and commenced the attack. Osceola and his followers fell back to a hommock, where they made a stand. The number of men engaged were about equal; Major Pearce and Osceola were known as gallant warriors; of course, the battle was warm and well contested.

After an engagement of an hour and a quarter, Major Pearce fell back; and the allied forces showing no disposition to follow him into the open fields, he retreated to Micanopy, leaving them in possession of the field of battle. Major Pearce's loss was reported to be one killed and sixteen wounded.

Before leaving Alabama, John A. Campbell, aid to General Jessup, acting under direction of that officer, entered into a written contract with certain Creek chiefs and warriors. Being somewhat extraordinary in its character, and rendered still more so by the construction given to it by the Administration and the Indians, it is deemed worthy of being inserted. The following is the language of the instrument:

"The State of Alabama, Tallapoosa County.

" This contract, entered into between the United States of
" America on the first part, and the Creek tribe of Indians on the
" other part, Witnesseth: That upon the consideration hereafter
" mentioned, the party of the first part agrees to advance to the
" party of the second part the sum of thirty-one thousand nine hun-
" dred dollars, to be applied to the payment of the debts due by
" the Creek Nation of Indians. And the party of the second part

9

" hereby covenants, and agrees to furnish from their tribe, the
" number of from six hundred to one thousand men, for service
" against the Seminoles, to be continued in service until the same
" shall be conquered ; they to receive the pay and emoluments,
" and equipments, of soldiers in the army of the United States,
" and such *plunder as they may take from the Seminoles.*"

" And the party of the second part releases, transfers and
" assigns to the party of the first part, all their right, title, claim,
" interest and demand in and to the annuity granted by the party
" of the first part to the party of the second part, for the year
" 1837. In witness whereof, I, John A. Campbell, on the part
" of the United States, do hereby set my hand and affix my seal,
" the 28th of August, 1836.
                                    "JOHN A. CAMPBELL, [L. S.]

" In witness whereof, we, the Chiefs and Head-men of said
" tribe, on the behalf of said Nation, do hereby set our hands and
" affix our seals, the 28th of August, 1836.
                    " HYPOTHLE YOHOLA, his ✕ mark,   [L. S.]
                    " LITTLE DOCTOR, his ✕ mark,   [L. S.]
                    " TUCKABATCHEE MICO, his ✕ mark, [L S.]
                    " YELCO HAYO, his ✕ mark,   [L. S.]
"Attest: EDWARD HAWICK,
          BARENT DUBOIS."

The real character of this contract will at once be seen when the
reader shall be reminded, that the laws of the United States had,
in the most specific manner, prescribed the amount to be paid each
man who should enter the military service of the Government,
and the manner and time of payment ; nor had there been any act
passed enabling General Jessup, or the Secretary of War, or the
President, to employ any other persons in the army except those
enlisted in the ordinary mode ; yet this contract was duly approved
by the War Department, at that time under the direction of General Cass. That provision which gives to the Creek warriors such
plunder as they might capture, has been denounced as "*piratical;*"
and we are constrained to admit there is some degree of propriety

in this denunciation, when we find that General Jessup, by whose orders it was framed, and General Cass, Secretary of War, who approved it, and the Creek Warriors who signed it, all understood that the Creeks were to *hold as slaves all the negroes they might capture*, while engaged in the service of the United States. It was this construction which subsequently involved the War Department in difficulties, from which it has never been able to extricate itself.

The barbarous practice of enslaving prisoners captured in war, had been repudiated by all Christian nations for more than two hundred years. The civilization of the sixteenth century had brought that atrocious practice into disrepute, which was now resorted to and renewed in the nineteenth, by this American Republic, so boastful of its refinement and Christianity. While the laws of the United States provided for an ignominious punishment of those who seize the stupid heathen of Africa and enslave them, our nation was taxing its resources, employing our army and paying out its funds, to employ heathen allies to capture and enslave a people who for generations had been free.

On the nineteenth of September, General Armstrong, with a brigade of twelve hundred Tennessee militia, was ordered to Suwanee "Old Town." Here he was met by a detachment of two hundred Creek warriors, under Major Brown, and a battalion of Florida militia, under Colonel Warren; and with this formidable army, Governor Call moved upon Withlacoochee. On coming near the stream he encamped.

During the darkness of night the allies fired upon his troops, and kept them in a state of alarm. In the morning it was found that the *river had suddenly risen*, which rendered it difficult for the troops to cross; and this gallant army returned to Fort Drane for supplies without firing a gun or seeing an enemy, leaving the allies in peaceful possession of the country.

But the Indians and Exiles now found themselves almost daily threatened in their own fastnesses. Along the Withlacoochee were many small villages and plantations occupied almost exclusively by Exiles. Large crops of corn and other vegetables had been raised there during the season, and it was known that stores of provisions were located upon various islands surrounded by the swamps lying along that river, and in the great morass called the "Wahoo Swamp;" while it was equally known that many families of the Exiles were residing in that vicinity. It was therefore deemed important to destroy those villages and obtain the supplies which they contained.

General Armstrong, with five hundred mounted men, while marching toward these villages on the fourteenth of November, encountered a strong force consisting of Indians and Exiles. The conflict was spirited. In forty minutes, eleven of Armstrong's men fell before the deadly aim of the allies. He, however, drove them from the field, but they took with them their dead and wounded. This fact with savages is regarded the only test of success in battle : they never acknowledge defeat while they hold possession of their dead and wounded.

But the time drew near when they were constrained to acknowledge a *defeat*. On the eighteenth of November, a regiment of Tennesseeans, consisting of about five hundred, encountered a body of the enemy whose numbers are not given by any officer or historian whom we have consulted. They were posted in a hommock. The Tennesseeans were the assailing party. The battle continued more than two hours, when the allies fled, leaving upon the field twenty-five Indians and Africans slain in battle ; while the loss of the assailants was still larger. This was the best contested battle which occurred during the campaign of 1836, and the first in which the allies left their dead in possession of our troops.

This defeat appears to have taught the allies to be cautious, and stimulated a desire to wipe out the impression which their defeat was calculated to make upon the public mind.

General Call having formed a junction with Major Pearce of the regular service, with nearly three hundred regular troops under his command, making in all more than one thousand men, entered the great Wahoo Swamp on the twenty-first of November. Their intention was to obtain the provisions supposed to be deposited in the villages situated upon the islands in that extensive morass. But they were attacked soon after entering the swamp. The fire at first was principally concentrated upon the Creek Indians, the mercenary troops employed by General Jessup. Major Pearce hastened to their relief. The fire then became general. The men were in a swamp which was nearly covered with water, and much of it with a thick underbrush. After maintaining the battle for a time, the Indians fell back, crossed the river, and formed upon its bank, each man protected by a log or tree. The river was turbid and appeared difficult to pass. As our troops approached it, the fire upon them was severe. Captain Moniac, of the Creek warriors, was killed while examining the stream to ascertain if it could be forded. Others were wounded. The allied force appeared determined to make their final stand upon this stream. Behind them were their wives and children, their provisions, their homes and firesides.

General Call and his troops now obtained an opportunity of fighting the enemy; a privilege which he had long sought, though he embraced it under disadvantageous circumstances. Our troops had great inducements to advance, but the dangers corresponded with the advantages to be gained.[1] General Call, however, concluded to withdraw; and after sustaining a heavy loss he retreated and left the allies in possession of the field. They very correctly, feeling that their success depended greatly upon the position they had taken, did not pursue General Call, who, with his whole force, retired to Volusi to recruit. His loss was fifteen killed and thirty wounded.

It is certain the allies manifested great skill in selecting their place

(1) Sprague, in his History of the Florida War, says there were *two hundred negro warriors* in this battle; that their women and children were a short distance in their rear, mounted on their ponies, and ready to flee, if their husbands, brothers and fathers had been compelled to retreat.

of attack, and the position for their final stand. Their success greatly encouraged them, and the gallantry displayed by the Exiles served to increase their influence with the Indians.

The Creek warriors had shown themselves very efficient in this expedition, but they suffered severely; and at no subsequent period did they maintain their former character as warriors. They had been greatly stimulated in this conflict with the expectation of capturing women and children, whom they expected to seize and sell as slaves. But so far as that object was concerned, their warriors who fell in this battle died ingloriously, and the result discouraged the survivors.

CHAPTER X.

THE WAR CONTINUED — PEACE DECLARED.

General Jessup assumes command of the Army — Number of Troops in the Field — His Advantages — His energetic Policy — Orders Crawford to the Withlacoochee — Capture of fifty two Women and Children — They are held as *plunder* by the Creeks — Wild Cat and Louis attack Fort Mellon — Severe Battle — Allies retire with their dead and wounded — Death of Captain Mellon — Our loss in killed and wounded — Caulfield's Expedition to A-ha-popka Lake — Capture of nine Women and Children — Expedition to Big Cypress Swamp — Capture of twenty-five Women and Children — General Jessup seeks Negotiation — Abram and Alligator meet him preparatory to a more general Council — Several Chiefs agree upon terms of Capitulation — Difficulty in regard to Exiles — Jessup yields — Express Stipulation for their Safety — Indians and Exiles come into Tampa Bay — Are Registered for Emigration — General Jessup discharges Militia and Volunteers — Transports prepared — He declares the War at an end, and asks to be relieved from active duty.

On the eighth of December, 1836, Major General Jessup joined General Call at Volusi, and relieved that officer from the further command of the army in Florida. He had now eight thousand troops in the field well provided in all the material of war. They were in fine spirits, and he was in all respects prepared to push the campaign with energy. He had all the advantages which experience of the previous campaign had furnished, and endeavored to profit by it. He was careful to order no large body of troops, nor any artillery, into the uninhabited portions of the country. He employed only light troops for such purposes. His first attention was directed to the settlements of Exiles on the Withlacoochee who had up to that time defied our army. They had been the

object of frequent attacks, and the scene of as frequent defeats.
He directed a battalion of mounted men under Major Crawford, accompanied by two battalions of Creek Indians, to make a
sudden descent upon those villages. But the allies had removed
their provisions, and most of the people had abandoned the settlements. A few only were left. The warriors fled to the swamps;
and the troops seized and secured fifty-two women and children.
These were the first prisoners captured during the war; and General Jessup made a formal report of this important victory. It was
a victory over defenseless women and helpless children, obtained by
the aid of Creek Indians, who claimed both women and children as
plunder under their contract. But this victory stimulated the allies
to strike in retaliation for the injury thus inflicted upon non-combatants.

1837.] Fort Mellon, on the south side of a small body of water
called Lake Monroe, some thirty miles west of the Atlantic,
was supposed by the allies to be in a weak condition, and they determined to surprise it. Preparatory to this, however, they sent spies
to examine and report the condition of the troops at that station.
Their report being favorable, " Wild Cat," acting in conjunction
with Louis, the slave of Pacheco, who, it will be recollected, concerted the massacre of Major Dade, made their arrangements for an
assault. With a force of two hundred and fifty warriors the allies
invested this fort, which they supposed to be garrisoned by not more
than one hundred men. Unfortunately for the assailants, however,
other troops arrived after the Indian spies had left the vicinity of the
fort, and the allied forces unexpectedly met superior numbers protected by defenses which are always regarded as safe against savage
foes. The attack was made with great determination, and continued
for three hours, when the assailants retired without leaving either
dead or wounded upon the field.

Lieutenant Colonel Faning commanded our troops, numbering
some three hundred men. A steamboat was lying in the lake, near
the fort, having a field-piece on board. This was also brought to

bear upon the left wing of the allied forces, so as to completely drive them from that part of the field.

Captain Mellon, who had entered the military service of the United States in 1812, fell early in the action. Midshipman McLaughlin and seventeen others were wounded; some of them mortally.

It may well be doubted, whether history furnishes an instance in which savage troops have beset a superior number of disciplined forces in a fortified position with such daring and obstinacy as that which was manifested at Fort Mellon.

There was a small settlement of Exiles and Indians upon the south side of A-ha-popka Lake, situated about the twenty-eighth degree of north latitude, and nearly equi-distant between the Atlantic and the Gulf of Mexico. On the twenty-second of January, Lieutenant Colonel Caulfield with his regiment was ordered to visit that settlement, attended by the Creek Indians. A sub-chief of the Seminoles, named Osuchee, with his band of warriors, hastened to the defense of their friends, as soon as they ascertained the object of our troops; but they were unable to resist the large force under Caulfield. Osuchee and three warriors were killed; and nine Exiles, all of them women and children, were taken prisoners.

All the disposable forces under General Jessup were now put into active employ. With the main body of the army he penetrated far into the Indian territory. His report, dated at Fort Armstrong, February seventh, after stating the commencement of his march, says, " On approaching the Thla-pac-hatchee, on the morn-" ing of the twenty-seventh ultimo, the numerous herds of cattle " feeding on the prairies, and the numerous recent trails in various " directions, indicated the presence of the enemy." He goes on to say : " On the twenty-eighth, the army moved forward, and occu-" pied a strong position on ' Ta-hop-ka-liga' Lake, *where several* " *hundred head of cattle were obtained.*" These immense herds of cattle show to some extent the means of subsistence which the allies possessed. The commander of our army, however, proceeds to state that " the enemy was found on the Hatchee-lustee, in and

" near the great Cypress Swamp, and gallantly attacked. Lieutenant
" Chambers of the Alabama Volunteers, by a rapid charge, suc-
" ceeded in capturing the horses and baggage of the enemy, with
" twenty-five Indians and negroes, principally women and children."
This language was novel in the military reports of our officers. A
charge made by a body of armed troops upon horses, women and
children, is termed by the commanding General " *gallant.*"

The next day one of the prisoners was directed to return to the
two principal chiefs, Abraham, with whom the reader is already acquainted, and Alligator, who commanded the Indians, with a message of peace, desiring them to meet the commanding General in
council.

Abraham was, perhaps, the most experienced and best informed
chief in the allied forces. He had lived at Micanopy ; and his
familiar acquaintance with the treaty of Payne's Landing, and the
supplemental treaty entered into at the West, qualified him to exert
a powerful influence with the Exiles.[1] The Indians, also, appear
to have held him in the highest respect.

Alligator was an active warrior and chief. He was a bold leader ;
but was supposed to be much under the influence of Micanopy, a
chief somewhat advanced in years, said to be very corpulent, and
too indolent to be otherwise than pacific in his desires. It is related of him, that he was actually carried, by the younger and more
enthusiastic warriors, into battle on one occasion, in the early part
of the war. It is not unlikely that both Abraham and Alligator
were influenced in some degree by Micanopy to visit General Jessup, and make arrangements to hold a conference with him, at Fort
Dade, on the eighteenth of February.

Lieut. Colonel Henderson, of the United States Marines, serving
on land, also made a very successful excursion into the Indian

---

(1) General Jessup was undoubtedly somewhat ignorant as to the history of the Exiles.
Speaking of Abraham, that officer says : " He is married to the wife of the former chief of
the Nation ; is a good soldier, and an *intrepid leader.* He *is the negro chief,* and the most
cunning and intelligent negro we have here ; *he claims to be free.*"

Country, with a pretty large force of mounted men and friendly Indians. In his report, he states the capture "of twenty-three "negroes, young and old; over a hundred ponies, with packs on "about fifty of them; together with all their clothes, blankets, and "other baggage." In this expedition, his loss was two men killed and five wounded.

On the first of March, the troops under the command of Major General Jessup had captured one hundred and nine women and children of the Exiles, and some fifteen belonging to the Indians. The fortunes of war now bore hard upon those friendless and persecuted people; but not a warrior had fallen into the hands of our troops. It is a remarkable fact, that in all the conflicts which had occurred, no Seminole Indian nor negro warrior had surrendered, even to superior numbers. They had fought gallantly, they had died freely; but they preferred death to that slavery which they knew would follow a surrender.

General Jessup now ordered the cessation of hostilities, in the hope of getting the Indian and negro chiefs to assemble in council, in order to negotiate for their emigration West. After his interview with Abraham and Alligator, he appears to have felt confident of success. The Exiles and Indians also began to feel that it would soon be necessary for them to plant corn, potatoes and pumpkins, for their support during the coming season. Every effort was made by General Jessup to acquaint the different chiefs with this arrangement, and to induce them to come in, or send by some subchief or warrior an expression of their willingness to emigrate to the western country.

Agreeably to these arrangements, a few of their principal men met General Jessup at Fort Dade, near the Withlacoochee, on the sixth of March. Only five chiefs were present, either in person or by proxy. The principal chiefs in attendance were Halatoochie and Jumper.

But the former difficulty was again encountered, at the very commencement of the negotiation. The Indians would enter upon no arrangement that did not guarantee to the Exiles equal protection and safety as it did to the Indians. Such stipulation would constitute an abandonment of the objects for which the war had been commenced and prosecuted; but, after sixteen months occupied in hostilities, and the expenditure of much blood and treasure, this question lay directly across the path of peace. But the Indians were firm. Not one of the Exiles, except Abraham, now dared trust himself within the power of our troops; yet Abraham's influence was powerful with the Indians.

General Jessup yielded. The articles of capitulation were drawn up and considered. The fifth reads as follows: — " Major General " Jessup, in behalf of the United States, agrees that the Seminoles " and *their allies, who come in and emigrate West, shall be secure* " *in their lives and property;* that their negroes, their bona fide " property, shall also accompany them West;[1] and that their cattle " and ponies shall be paid for by the United States."

The language of this article could not be misunderstood. The black men then residing with the Indians, in the Indian Country, who were acting with them, and fighting our troops by the side of the Seminoles, were their " *allies;* " and to show that the capitulation was not a surrender of *property*, they were careful to have the compact expressly state, that their own " *negroes*, their bona fide *property*" (for many Seminoles owned slaves), should accompany them; and that their cattle and ponies, which would become the *property* of the captors by virtue of an ordinary surrender, under their ideas of warfare, were to be paid for by the United States. There was no room left for cavil or dispute on these points;[2] nor could it be supposed that Abraham, with his experience and shrewdness, would leave such an important point doubtful.

Under these articles, the Exiles were to enjoy that security for

(1) General Jessup *subsequently* reported his determination to *separate the negroes, or Exiles, from the Indians* He therefore stipulated for *their safety*, and, at the same time, agreed that the *slaves* of the Indians should accompany their owners, and not be separated from them. These facts will appear as we proceed in our history.

(2) Vide these articles at length, Ex. Doc. 225, 3d Sess. XXVth Congress.

which they had contended during a century and a half. It was for this that their ancestors left South Carolina, Georgia, Alabama and Florida; to attain it, they were willing to leave the graves of their fathers — the country in which they had lived during many generations. Abraham now entered upon the work of inducing all his brethren, both Indians and negroes, to go to the Western Country, where they could be free from persecutions.

Those willing to emigrate, were to assemble within a district of ten miles square, marked out for that purpose, near Tampa Bay. Many of the Indian chiefs visited that station; spoke encouragingly of the prospect; that the whole Nation would emigrate at no distant day. Even Osceola, the most inveterate of all the Seminole chiefs, visited Fort Mellen, avowing his intention to emigrate; while Abraham made report of a like feeling among the Exiles. Twenty-six vessels, employed to transport the emigrants to New Orleans, were anchored in Tampa Bay. Hundreds of Indians and negroes had reached the camp assigned to the emigrants, near "Fort Brooke." Their names were duly registered; they drew their rations, and made every preparation to go West.

General Jessup announced the war at an end, dismissed the militia and volunteers, and asked of the Department leave to retire from active duty.

CHAPTER XI.

GENERAL JESSUP OVERTHROWS HIS OWN EFFORTS IN FAVOR OF PEACE.

Mr. Van Buren's advent to the office of President — Follows the policy of his predecessor — General Jessup's stipulation in favor of the Exiles — Sustained by precedent, and by National Law — Not contrary to General Jackson's object in commencing the War — Citizens of Florida protest — Compact ratified by War Department — General Jessup for a time endeavors to carry out Articles of Capitulation — Begins to yield — Promises to make arrangements with Chiefs to deliver up Slaves who had left their Masters during the War — Then declared he had done so — No such Compact found by the Author — Subsequent history shows that he had made such arrangement, by parol, with Co-Hadjo only — He also uses army to seize and return Exiles claimed by citizens of Florida — Revokes Order No. 79 — Indians and Exiles take alarm — Flee to their fastnesses — General Jessup acknowledges *all is lost* — The War renewed.

On the fourth of March, Mr. Van Buren assumed the duties of President of the United States, and General Jackson retired to private life. Belonging to the same political party to which General Jackson had attached himself, Mr. Van Buren was not expected to make any particular change in the administration of the Government. Indeed so popular had General Jackson been, that it would have required great boldness in his successor to attempt any very obvious change in our national policy; and so far as the Florida war was concerned, there was none whatever.

It was therefore fortunate that, under the administration of General Jackson, the existence of the Exiles, as a distinct people, had been acknowledged. In the articles of capitulation, they were again recognized as the "allies" of the Indians. In entering into this stipulation, General Jessup went no farther than his legitimate

(142)

powers extended. The peace of the country in that region was entrusted to his judgment, under the direction of the President. If necessary to secure peace, he had the undoubted right to send every slave, of whatever description, from the Territory of Florida; and it would appear, that no doubt whatever could arise as to his authority to transport to the Western Country, all who were engaged in actual hostilities against our nation, and that too without stopping to inquire whether one portion of the people were, or were not, claimed as property by the people of Florida. General Jackson had set a noble example on this subject which was well worthy of imitation. When New Orleans was threatened by the British, in 1814, he proclaimed marshal law — ordered men into service without inquiring whether they were slaves or freemen. Many of them were slaves, and on the day of battle were emancipated by being captured or killed by the enemy. The same powers had been exercised by our officers almost constantly during the Revolution. It is a principle understood by all intelligent men, that when war exists, peace may be obtained by the emancipation of all the slaves held by individuals, if necessary.[1]

These articles of capitulation were duly transmitted to the War Department, and were regularly approved by the Executive. It would appear impossible that General Jessup, or any other person, could either misapprehend or fail to understand this stipulation, which was in no respect modified by other covenants.

But this solemn covenant was in direct conflict with the views and feelings of the slaveholders in Florida and the adjoining States. They understood the war to have been commenced for the purpose of reënslaving the Exiles. These articles of capitulation constituted

(1) General Jessup at all times practiced upon this principle. When "Louis," the guide who planned the defeat and massacre of Major Dade, became a prisoner and Wild Cat claimed to have captured him, General Jessup disregarded the claim of Pacheco, the owner, and sent the negro West; and, in other instances, he kept those known to have been slaves as guides, and, at a proper time, sent them to the Western Country, as freemen. He even bribed negroes to act as guides to his army by promising them liberty, and carried out such arrangement.

not only an abandonment of that policy, but actually operated as an emancipation of all the slaves who, having fled from service in Florida, Georgia and Alabama, had joined the Seminoles and taken up arms against their oppressors. The slaveholders were indignant at this stipulation, nor did they fail to express their indignation.

A few gentlemen of distinction, who, with their families, had been driven from the Territory, were residing at Charleston, South Carolina. Having learned the character of the capitulation from private sources, without waiting for its publication, they at once addressed the Secretary of War, stating they had casually learned from a gentleman who was present, that a treaty of peace had been concluded with the Seminole Indians which contained " no " stipulation for *indemnity, on the part of the Indians, for* " *such property of the inhabitants as had been captured by said* " *Indians,* and destroyed. Nor (say they) is it, we are told, " exacted from them that they should even *make restitution of* " *such stolen and other property, to wit,* NEGROES, *etc., as they* " *now have in possession,* or as has been invited into their country " and allowed refuge from its owners. We respectfully conceive, " that the termination of the war on such terms, anxiously as we " desire peace, would be a sacrifice of the national dignity, and an " absolute and clear triumph on the part of the Indians, who cannot " fail to view the proposition made to them, to close hostilities, fol- " lowed up by a treaty permitting to them such extraordinary terms, " as a virtual suing for peace on the part of the United States, and " evidencing a want of confidence in their ability to conclude the " war through the means of their belligerent and physical strength."[1]

But the most singular portion of this memorial is the reference to the treaty of Camp Moultrie, by which the Indians agreed to arrest and return fugitives; and the memorialists insisted that unless the Indians be compelled to perform this stipulation the owners " *may never regain their slaves.*"

---

(1) Vide this Memorial at length, Ex. Doc. 225, 3d Sess. XXVth Congress.

The gentlemen who thus attempted to control the action of our National Government appear to have forgotten that the treaty of Camp Moultrie had been abrogated by that of Payne's Landing, which our Government was now professing to enforce. By this latter treaty, the Indians agreed to pay seven thousand dollars as an indemnity for all slaves then in their territory. This was accepted as a full indemnity, and the slaves then resident with the Indians became free in law.

This memorial, though written at Charleston, South Carolina, bears date only twelve days later than the articles of capitulation, entered into at "Fort Dade in Florida." Of this movement of the slaveholders, General Jessup appears not to have been informed at the time; nor is there any doubt that he then intended to carry out this solemn compact in good faith. On the nineteenth of March, we find his aid-de-camp Colonel Chambers, by order of General Jessup, writing Lieutenant Colonel Harney, stationed at Fort Mellon, directing him not to permit the friendly Indians (the Creeks) to pass into the country occupied by the Seminoles, and to distinctly inform the Creeks they "*must make no more captures of property;*" and if they had made any since the signing of the treaty, (meaning the capitulation,) Harney was directed to take a list of such captures.

But the first serious difficulty suggested to General Jessup, in carrying out his stipulations with the "*allies,*" appears to have been a letter from Major Thomas Child, commanding at Fort Armstrong, informing him that a "Colonel Dill," a citizen of Florida, was at that post, wishing to pass into the Indian country for the purpose of reclaiming certain negroes which he professed to have owned, but who were then supposed to have fled to the Seminoles.

In reply to this note Colonel Chambers said : " I am *instructed* " *by the commanding General* to say, that ' Colonel Dill,' the person " whom you report having detained at Fort Armstrong, must not " be permitted to pass, *but be required to return from whence he* " *came with all convenient dispatch.* Hereafter, no person, not in

10

" the employment of the Government, or express rider, must be
" allowed to pass your post. The necessity of this order, and the
" strict enforcement of it, arise from the necessity, that, if persons
" come forward to urge their claims to negroes, it will evidently
" prevent the negroes from coming in ; and if they do not come in,
" the commanding General is decidedly of opinion that the Indians
" themselves will be greatly delayed, if not entirely prevented, from
" compliance with the terms of capitulation."

The termination of the war had been regarded as certain by the
commanding officer, and by him so reported. The first article in
the capitulation, provided for the cessation of hostilities. But they
were renewed soon after, and the Indians and Exiles charged with
a breach of faith, both by General Jessup and by the Executive.
And it becomes important to the truth of history, that facts should
be stated. The articles of capitulation pledged the faith of the
nation for the safety of both persons and property of the " Seminoles *and their allies*." Those " allies " could have been no other
people than the black men who were with them contending against
a common foe. It is also evident that Abraham and the Exiles who
came in for the purpose of emigrating so understood it. It is
equally certain that the people of Florida who memorialized the
Secretary of War so understood it ; and we need only read the letters and orders of General Jessup to learn that he surely so understood it ; and the whole conduct of the Indians shows that they put
the same construction upon it. While, therefore, justice should be
done to General Jessup, we should be careful to do no injustice to
either the Seminoles or the Exiles. As further evidence of General Jessup's good faith at the time, we quote an extract from a letter, bearing date six days later than the one last referred to. It
was addressed to Lieutenant Colonel Miller, commanding at Tampa
Bay, and is dated March twenty-seventh, 1837. It is signed by
General Jessup himself, who says : " I have also been informed
" that Mr. Cooley's business at Tampa Bay is to *look after negroes*.
" If that be so, he must be sent away ; a trifling circumstance

"would *light up the war again. Any inteference with the ne-*
" *groes which would produce alarm on their part would inevita-*
" *bly deprive us of all the advantages we have gained.* I sympa-
" thize with Mr. Cooley in his afflictions and losses ; but responsible
" as I am for the peace of the country, *I cannot and will not per-*
" *mit that peace to be jeopardized by his imprudence.*"

But these demands for slaves increased. The slaveholders were
indignant at the loss of slaves, and it soon became apparent that
the stipulation of safety to the "allies" of the Seminoles was *un-
popular* in Florida.

On the twenty-ninth of March, General Jessup wrote Colonel
Warner, of the Florida Militia, saying, "There is no disposition on
" the part of the great body of the Indians to renew hostilities ; and
" they will, I am sure, faithfully fulfill their engagements, if the
" inhabitants of Florida be prudent : but any attempt to seize their
" negroes, or other property, would be followed by an instant resort
" to arms. *I have some hopes of inducing both Indians and In-*
" *dian negroes* to unite in bringing in the *negroes taken from the*
" *citizens during the war.*"

In this letter, General Jessup begins to modify his former position. He still entertains no fear of the Indians, if *their* negroes or
other property be not interfered with, and suggests the hope that he
may effect an arrangement with the Indians and Indian negroes to
bring in (that is, to surrender up,) the negroes *taken during the
war.* This letter gives the first evidence, which we find on record,
of General Jessup's intention to modify or disregard the solemn
compact he had made, or to make another with the Indians and Indian negroes by which they should betray those who had fled to
them during the war.

But that he did make some arrangement of that character with
the chiefs, we are led to infer from a letter bearing date May fifth,
1837, addressed to General Jessup by the Commissioner of Indian
Affairs, informing him that his articles of capitulation with the Seminoles had been submitted to the Secretary of War, "*together with*

"*his letters of the first and fifteenth of April, and had been ap-*
"*proved;*" and the writer then adds : " In relation to the negroes
" captured by the Seminoles and to be *surrendered,* I am directed
" to say, that your arrangement for having them delivered to offi-
" cers of posts on the St. John's River, *is approved.*" [1]

This letter also directs General Jessup to keep a registry of all
negroes delivered to citizens, showing their names, age, sex, etc.

A general order, dated Tampa Bay, April fifth, and numbered
seventy-nine, announces first, "The commanding General has reason
" to believe that the interference of unprincipled white men with
" the *negro property of the Seminole Indians* will prevent their
" emigration, and lead to a renewal of the war.   Responsible as he
" is for the peace and security of the country, he will not permit
" such interference under any pretense whatsoever.   And he there-
" fore orders that no white man, not in the service of the United
" States, be allowed to enter any part of the territory, between the
" St. John's and the Gulf of Mexico, south of Fort Drane."

On the eighth of April, General Jessup wrote Colonel Harney,
saying, " I have made an arrangement with the chiefs *to-day* to
" surrender the negroes of white men, particularly those taken du-
" ring the war."

With what particular chiefs this arrangement was made, or what
were the terms of the arrangement, the Author has not learned ; yet,
as we shall see hereafter, he represented it to have been made at
" Fort King " with *Co-Hadjo*, an unimportant chief, and then
attempted to hold the Seminole Nation responsible for Co-Hadjo's
promise.   But under these circumstances, the reader will ask what
consideration was paid Co-Hadjo to bribe him to enter into such a
contract?   That chief and General Jessup and General Cass, Secretary of War, must have known he possessed no power to bind

---

(1) All these communications may be found at length in the Fifth Vol. Ex. Doc., 3d Session XXVth Congress. But these arrangements made with the chiefs are supposed to
have rested entirely in parole. No copy of any such agreement has been found by the
Author, who is fully of opinion that it does not exist in any authentic form.

the Seminole Nation, nor to surrender those persons to slavery. It will long remain a subject of inquiry. Why did the War Department sanction this violation of the solemn articles of capitulation, which these officers termed a *treaty*, and which certainly possessed all the solemnity and binding force of a treaty?

There is also an inexplicable obscurity attending this subject. General Jessup wrote Colonel Harney, on the eighth of April, that he had *that day* made the arrangement, etc.; while the Secretary of War states that he had learned of this arrangement by General Jessup's *two* letters, dated the first and fifteenth of April. One of these letters appears to bear date seven days before, and the other seven days after, the day on which he declares the arrangement was made. The withholding of such fact seven days from the War Department would be as incompatible with military duty as the giving it seven days before its existence, is irreconcilable with the common perceptions of mankind.

In several instances, General Jessup had foretold that a renewal of the war would follow any attempt to deliver up negroes to the claimants in Florida, and it would appear that he must have expected that result; but he communicated to the commandants of nearly all the different posts, that he had made arrangements *with the chiefs* for returning slaves *captured during the war*. But, up to the twenty-sixth of April, he steadily insisted that no obligation rested upon the Indians to bring in runaway negroes who had fled to them before the war.

On the twenty-sixth, he wrote Colonel Brown, of St. Augustine, saying: — "I have made arrangements with the Indians for the " delivery of the negroes *captured during the war*. They are to " be delivered, if they can be taken without delaying the Indians " in their movements, at the posts on the St. John's. The Indians " are not bound to surrender runaway negroes. *They must, and* " *shall, give up those taken during the war:* at all events, they " shall not take them out of the country. Further than that, I " shall not interfere."

But while relating facts on this subject, we should be unfaithful to the truth of history were we to omit the letter which this officer wrote, on the following day, to Hon. J. L. Smith, a citizen of Florida. This letter, bearing date at Tampa Bay on the twenty-seventh of April, 1837, says:

"I received, yesterday, your letter of the eighteenth, with a list "of the slaves which you claim. Ansel is the only one of the "three who has been taken. I have him employed, at one of the "interior posts, as an interpreter. *The negroes generally have* "*taken the alarm,* and but few of them come in; and those who "remain out, prevent the Indians from coming. But for the pre-"mature attempts of some citizens of Florida to obtain possession "of their slaves, a majority of those taken by the Indians during "the war, as well as those who absconded previous to it, would "have been secured before this time. More than thirty negro men "were in and near my camp, when some of the citizens, who had "lost negroes, came to demand them. The Indian-negroes imme-"diately disappeared, and have not been heard of since."

It is believed that, in the conducting of this second Seminole war, no act of any public officer will hereafter appear more inexplicable than the conduct of General Jessup, in regard to this stipulation in favor of the Exiles. No person can suppose there was any doubt in regard to the original design of this stipulation. *He at first appears determined to carry it out in good faith;* this was before he learned the complaint of the slaveholders of Florida, made to the Secretary of War. He next expressed his intention to make an arrangement with the chiefs to surrender negroes captured during the war — *as though the chiefs were authorized to consign* "their allies" *to slavery.* He next says he had made such an arrangement, but fails to say with whom. At length it comes out, in the future history, that he alleges it to have been made with Co-Hadjo, an obscure chief, in no way a party to the capitulation, or connected with it. And finally, in this letter to Judge Smith, he intimates that he would have *betrayed* many of those allies to slavery, if the people of the Territory had been quiet.

Our present duty, however, is to record facts, without asking attention to the intended treachery or fraud of individuals; but this avowed intention of entrapping the negroes by inducing them to come in under the expectation of emigrating West with their Seminole friends, and then consign them to bondage, must attract the attention and excite the wonder of Christian men. This wonder is increased by the fact, that language is constantly used by slaveholders apparently intended to mislead the Northern reader. For instance, General Jessup speaks of slaves "*captured during the war,*" as though the Indians made prisoners of slaves. This is believed to be entirely without foundation. Slaves being regarded by Southern men as *property*, incapable of thought, whenever they fled from their masters and sought an asylum with the Indians, the masters spoke of them as *captured.*

Soon as it was known that slaves were to be seized and returned, claims were preferred from all quarters. The correspondence on this subject, now in the Department of War, would of itself form a volume, if quoted at length. Spaniards sent in claims for slaves lost while the Territory was in possession of Spain, in 1802 and 1803. Claims from South Carolina, from Georgia, Alabama and Florida, and from Creek Indians, were presented to the commandants of different posts. Slaveholders evidently felt that they were to be permitted to seize such colored prisoners as they could lay their hands upon, and enslave them. They no longer waited for black prisoners to be brought to the St. John's, or other posts, but like wolves greedy for their prey, they hurried into the Indian Country, and risked their lives in order to secure victims for the slave-markets.

The Legislative Council of Florida became affected with this general mania, and in the most formal manner declared the right of masters to regain possession of their slaves, without regard to the Federal Government or its officers.

Finding General Jessup incapable of resisting the popular clamor, the claimants for slaves openly demanded a revocation of the General Order, by which they were prohibited from entering the Indian territory for the purpose of seizing slaves. A public meeting of the citizens of various parts of Florida, was held at San Augustine, and a committee appointed to remonstrate with General Jessup, and procure a rescission of his order, No. 79, prohibiting them from entering the Territory, between the St. John's River and the Gulf of Mexico, south of Fort Drane. The committee addressed him in a long, written protest, in which they declare, " the regaining of their slaves constitutes an object of scarcely less " moment than that of peace to the country." [1]

General Jessup now began to modify his order, No. 79, so as to admit citizens to enter the Territory as far south as the road leading from Withlacoochee to Volusi; and, on the first of May, so informed Major McClintock, commanding at Fort Drane. On the day following, he addressed a letter to Brig. General Armistead, directing that officer to " consider Order No. 79 so far modified, " that citizens will be permitted to visit any of the posts on the St. " John's, and to traverse or remain in any part of the country " south of Withlacoochee. There are large herds of cattle in that " part of the country which no doubt *belong to the citizens,* and by " allowing them to go into the country, they may perhaps secure a " large portion of them."

It will be recollected, that General Scott would not permit the people of Florida to interfere in the discharge of his official duties, and that they, through their representative in Congress, had demanded his removal from command of the army. They now applied directly to the Secretary of War, remonstrating against the action of General Jessup; and it is possible that officer deemed it prudent to yield to their dictation. Be that as it may, it is certain that he now lent the power of the army to carry out the wishes of the citizens. Officers and men were detailed to take black prisoners —

(1) Vide Ex. Doc. 225, 3d Sess. XXVth Congress.

who had come in and surrendered with the expectation of emigrating West — from their places of rendezvous to certain points where it would be most convenient for claimants to receive them.

On the seventeenth of April, Major Churchill, aid to General Jessup, wrote Colonel Harney, saying, "I am instructed by the "commanding General to acknowledge the receipt to-day of your "letter of the seventh instant, and to inform you that the negro "prisoners captured from the Indians, and supposed to belong to "the white people, were sent from this place, on the eleventh in- "stant, to Lieutenant D. H. Vinton, at St. Marks, for the purpose "of being returned to their owners. The Indians have agreed to "send all slaves, *taken from white people during the war*, to Fort "Mellon and Volusi; and runners are now employed in the inte- "rior on that service." On the same day, information was given to William De Payster, that seven of the number sent to Volusi probably belonged to him. On the same day also, "A. Forrester" was informed of the fact, that those slaves "had been sent to St. "Marks, and that six of the number probably belonged to him."

Other plans were devised for securing slaves, as we are informed by a letter from General Jessup to E. K. Call, Governor of Flori- da, dated eighteenth of April, 1837, in which he says: "If the "citizens of the territory be prudent, the war may be considered at "an end; but any attempt to interfere with the *Indian negroes,* or "to *arrest* any of the chiefs or warriors as *debtors* or *criminals,* "would cause an immediate resort to arms. The negroes control "their masters; and have heard of the act of your legislative coun- "cil. Thirty or more of the Indian negro men were near my camp "on the Withlacoochee in March last; but the arrival of two or "three citizens of Florida, said to be in search of negroes, caused "them to disperse, and I doubt whether they will come in again; "at all events the emigration will be delayed a month I apprehend "in consequence of this alarm among the negroes."

The emigration of those Indians who had come in to Fort Brooke, and registered themselves as ready for emigration, was delayed in consequence of the difficulty of collecting those who were expected; and General Jessup began to see the effects which his violation of the articles of capitulation had wrought on the minds of both Indians and negroes. Indeed, he had in plain and distinct language repeatedly affirmed that the negroes *controlled the Indians;* that any interference with the negroes would cause a resort to arms; yet he himself subsequently ordered negroes to be sought out, separated from their friends, and delivered over to slavery.

The ships were yet lying in the harbor. About seven hundred Indians were encamped ready for emigration, and had been waiting for others to join them. Impatient at delay and disappointment, on the twenty-fifth of May, he wrote Colonel Harney, as follows:

"If you see Powell (Osceola) again, I wish you to tell him that "I intend to send exploring and surveying parties into every part "of the country during the summer, and that I shall send out and "*take all the negroes who belong to the white people*, and he must "not allow the Indians or Indian negroes to mix with them. Tell "him I am sending to Cuba for bloodhounds to trail them, and *I* "*intend to hang every one of them who does not come in.*"

This intention to reënslave the Exiles who had recently taken up their residence with the Seminoles became known, and created general alarm. Many of the blacks, who had come in for the purpose of emigrating, became alarmed and fled; and General Jessup, doubtful whether more could be obtained by peaceful means, seized about ninety Exiles who were confined within the pickets at Tampa Bay, on the second of June, and at once ordered them to New Orleans, under the charge of Lieutenant G. H. Trevitt, of the United States Marines.

This struck the Indians and Exiles with astonishment. The chiefs, warriors and families, numbering some seven hundred, who had collected at Tampa Bay for the purpose of emigrating to the western country, thinking themselves betrayed, now fled to their former fastnesses, far in the interior, and once more determined to defend their liberties or die in the attempt. A few, however, were secured at other posts, and sent to New Orleans, where they were delivered over to Quarter-Master Clark, and confined at "Fort Pike."

On the fourteenth of June, General Jessup, writing General Gadsden of South Carolina, says: *"All is lost,* and principally, I " fear, *by the influence of the'negroes* — the people who were the " subject of our correspondence. * * * I *seized,* and sent off " to New Orleans, about ninety Indian negroes, and I have about " seventeen here. I have captured ninety, the property of citizens; " all of whom have been sent to St. Marks and St. Augustine, ex- " cept four at this place, twelve at Fort Mellon, and six who died."

General Jessup now saw that both Seminole Indians and negroes had clear conceptions of justice and honor. That his efforts to deliver over negroes to slavery had defeated the entire object of the articles of capitulation of the eighteenth of March. The Indians had fled. The negroes, except those who were imprisoned, had fled. The twenty-six vessels, collected at Tampa Bay to transport them to New Orleans, were yet idle; and, to use his own words, " *all was lost!* "

Abraham, acting for his brethren while West, in 1833, had caused the article to be inserted in the supplemental treaty, giving the Seminoles a separate country for their settlement.

In forming the articles of capitulation with general Jessup, he again exhibited his capacity for negotiation; obtaining the insertion of an article which, if carried out, would have proved a triumphant vindication of their cause. But from this second manifestation of his powers for negotiation, the Government of the United States found it necessary to recede, in order to maintain its designs of enslaving the Exiles.

CHAPTER XII.

THE RENEWAL AND PROSECUTION OF THE WAR.

By the articles of capitulation, entered into on the sixth of March (1837), the second Seminole War had been terminated. General Jessup so regarded it, and so declared it. The Exiles and Indians so regarded it, and some eight hundred came in under it and registered their names for emigration, in good faith. The people of Florida regarded it in that light, and remonstrated against it. They declared it a treaty of peace; but complained of its terms, for the reason that it gave up the slaves whom they claimed to own.

Learning this dissatisfaction to exist among the slaveholders of Florida, General Jessup expressed, in his correspondence, an intention of making an *arrangement* with the chiefs, by which the slaves belonging to the *citizens of Florida*, captured during the war, should be given up. Why those claimed by the citizens of Florida should be given up, and those escaped from Georgia and Alabama remain free, he has failed to show! Why those who escaped, or, as he expresses it, were captured during the war, should be returned, and those who escaped or had been captured the day previous to the commencement of hostilities, should not be returned, he has not explained; but he soon announced, that he had made an arrangement with the chiefs to deliver up these persons; and at once set the army at work to restore them. This restoration of slaves, of itself, constituted a renewal of the war. It had caused the first Seminole war, in 1816: it had caused this second Seminole war, and General Jessup was himself conscious that such interference with the Exiles would induce a renewal of hostilities. That class of Exiles was numerous; they constituted a portion of the "allies" for whose safety he had solemnly pledged the faith of Government.

It were useless for the friends of the then existing Administration to say, that General Jessup made an arrangement with the Indian chiefs for delivering up these people. The Exiles were the persons interested in their own safety, for which they had fought. No chiefs had authority to sell them, or to deliver them over to interminable bondage. But the reader will inquire, with what particular chiefs was this arrangement made? When, and where was it made? What were its terms? The only answers, so far as we are informed, are to be found in the interrogatories propounded to Osceola and other chiefs, when they were captured, at Fort Peyton, on the twenty-first of October following. General Jessup's first written interrogatory was, " Are they (the " chiefs) prepared to deliver up the negroes taken from the citizens? " Why have they not surrendered them already, as *promised by* " *Co-Hadjo, at Fort King?*" Here he merely claimed a promise from Co-Hadjo, an obscure chief, who was not a party to the capitulation — did not sign it, and, so far as we are informed, was not present when it was entered into.

But, to show that no obligation whatever rested on the chiefs in this matter, his next interrogatories were, "Have the chiefs of the "Nation held a Council in relation to the subjects of the talk at "Fort King? What chiefs attended that Council, and what was "their decision?" These questions seem to admit, that Co-Hadjo had merely promised to lay the subject before the chiefs in Council; and here we find the reasons, on the part of General Jessup, for not laying the arrangement before the people: yet, under these circumstances, that officer charges bad faith upon the Indians and Exiles, in renewing the war. The Exiles possessed no means of informing the American people, and other nations, as to these facts, or of maintaining their honor against this charge of having violated their plighted faith.

In renewing hostilities, General Jessup appears to have fully determined on carrying out the designs of General Jackson, in 1816, when he directed General Gaines to "destroy the fort, and *return the slaves to their owners.*" From this time forward, he lent his energies, and the power of the army, to the object of capturing and returning slaves. He also deemed it necessary to change the mode of prosecuting the war, and to make it a series of forays for the capture and enslavement of the Exiles.

He had, the previous year, entered into a contract with the Creek Indians, by which he stipulated to pay them a large pecuniary compensation, and to allow them to hold all the plunder (negroes) whom they might capture, as *property.* He now evidently believed that such inducements, held out to the Florida militia, would have an effect to stimulate them to greater effort.

On the eleventh of June, he wrote Colonel Warren, saying, "There is no obligation to spare the property of the Indians; they "have not spared that of the citizens. Their *negroes,* cattle and "horses, as well as other property which they possess, will belong "to the corps by which they are captured."

The same orders were communicated to the Commandants of other posts, and to the militia from other States; and the system by which the *negroes and other property* were to be distributed among the captors, was prescribed in a letter to Colonel Heilman, declaring the field officers entitled to *three shares*, the company officers to receive *two shares*, and the non-commissioned officers and soldiers *one share each.*

These arrangements were, of course, all duly certified to the War Department, and approved, and thereby became acts of the Administration. The letters of General Jessup, written during the summer and autumn of 1837, to Colonel Crowell, at Fort Mitchell, Alabama; to Colonel Mills, of Newmansville, Florida; to Thomas Craghill, Esq., of Alabama; to Captain David S. Walker, Captain Bonneville and Captain Armstrong;[1] all show, conclusively, that the war was to be conducted by the organization of slave-catching forays, in which the troops were expected to penetrate the Indian Country for the purpose of capturing negroes.

During the sickly season no active operations against the allies could be carried on, and the time was occupied in preparing for the more vigorous prosecution of hostilities, so soon as the unhealthy months should be passed. In order to carry out these forays, the Indians residing west of the Mississippi were applied to for assistance. The Choctaws and Delawares furnished many individuals whose low moral development did not prevent their engaging in the proposed piratical expeditions, for seizing and enslaving their fellow-men; but of the precise number of individuals thus furnished, we have no authentic information. The Cherokees however appear to have rejected a proposition which, to them, appeared incompatible with the civilization of that tribe; they evidently felt deep sympathy for their brethren, the Seminoles, as well as for the Exiles. They agreed to furnish a delegation who should, in a friendly manner, visit the Seminoles, state to them the condition of the Western Country, and advise them in good faith to emigrate.

At that period John Ross was acting as principal chief of the Cherokee Nation. He was the son of a wealthy white man, who

---

(1) These Letters may be found in Ex. Doc. 225, 3d Sess. XXVth Congress.

had long been engaged as an Indian trader. His mother was a Cherokee. Ross had been educated; had seen the advantages of civilization, and of Christianity, and was at the time, and had long been engaged, in promoting civilization among his own people. It will readily be supposed, that the feelings of such a man would revolt at a proposition for his people to engage in the capture and enslavement of any portion of the human family. The correspondence between Ross and the Secretary of War is interesting, and its perusal would well compensate the curious reader.[1]

This delegation from the Cherokees consisted of some twelve of their most influential men. They bore with them an address from Ross, written with great ability and sincerity. Among other things, he assured the Seminoles that they might confide in the justice and honor of the United States.[2] This address was directed to Micanopy, Osceola and Wild Cat, the three most powerful and warlike chiefs among the Seminoles.

The Creek warriors had engaged to serve until the Seminoles were conquered; but after the death of Captain Moniac, and their other friends who fell in the Great Wahoo Swamp, they had shown a disposition rather to *avoid danger* than to *catch negroes;* and it was deemed proper to discharge them. But difficulties intervened in regard to the division of the negroes claimed to have been captured by them, while acting in concert with our troops. Some ninety negroes had been captured, in whose bones and muscles, blood and sinews, seven hundred Creek warriors claimed an interest; while the Tennesseans, and other troops, had been in the field acting with the Creeks at the time of capture; and the Creeks could, in equity, claim only a pro rata interest. General Jessup however met the difficulty with promptness, and, to put an end to all future strife and discontent, he issued the following:

(1) This Correspondence may be found in the 8th vol. Ex. Doc., 2d Sess. XXVth Cong., No. 285.

(2) Of this declaration he had subsequent cause to repent, and most eloquently he expressed his mortification, in a letter to the Secretary of War. Vide his Letter of Jan. 2, 1838, in the Document last quoted.

"ORDER No. 175. TAMPA BAY, Sept. 6, 1837.

" 1. The Seminole negroes captured by the army, will be taken
" on account of Government and held subject to the *orders of the*
" *Secretary of War.*

" 2. The sum of eight thousand dollars will be paid to the Creek
" chiefs and warriors by whom they were captured, or who were
" present at their capture, in full for their claims; the amount to
" be apportioned among the battalions in proportion to the numbers
" respectively taken by each, viz: To the first battalion, five thou-
" sand seven hundred dollars; to the second battalion, two thou-
" sand dollars; and to the spy battalion, three hundred dollars.

" 3. To induce the Creeks to take alive, and not destroy, the
" negroes of citizens who had been captured by the Seminoles, a
" reward was promised them for all they should secure. They
" have captured and secured thirty-five, who have been returned to
" their owners. *The owners have paid nothing*, but the promise
" to the Indians must be fulfilled. The sum of twenty dollars will
" be allowed them for each, from the public funds.

" 4. Lieutenant Frederick Searle is charged with the execution
" *of this order. He will cause accounts to be made, in the name*
" of the United States, and receipts taken from the Indians in full,
" for all claims to the negroes, both of the Seminoles and citizens.
" Lieutenant Searle will call on the Commanding General for funds
" to enable him to comply with this order.

" 5. Until further orders, the Seminole negroes will remain at
" Fort Pike, Louisiana, in charge of the Assistant Quarter-Master
" at New Orleans, and in custody of the Commanding Officer of
" the post. They will be fed and clothed at the public expense."

This order was reported to the Secretary of War, and on the
seventh of October was approved and became the act of the Executive; and the people of the nation became the actual owners of
these ninety slaves, so far as the Executive could bind them to the
ownership of human flesh.

11

Such was, undoubtedly, the view of General Jessup, who, on the fourteenth of September, wrote the Commissioner of Indian Affairs, saying, "The Seminole negro prisoners are now the *property of* "*the public.* I have promised Abraham the freedom of his family, "if he prove faithful *to us ;* and I shall surely hang him if he be "not faithful."[1]

This refinement in cruelty by which the life and liberty of a man and his family is held out as a bribe to induce him to prove traitor to his own kindred and nation, or to be hanged, and his family enslaved in case of refusal, appears worthy a place in the history of our Government, in order that our successors may have a correct idea of its administration. The intention to enslave Abraham's wife, who was an Indian woman and had been the wife of the former chief of the *nation*, and now the wife of the principal chief of the Exiles, exhibits a total disregard of the feelings and sympathies of the human heart, as well as of the prejudices and condition of both Exiles and Seminoles. These Exiles were at Fort Pike, near New Orleans, where we will leave them for the present, to pursue our narrative of events which were transpiring in Florida.

On the ninth of September, General Jessup wrote Lieutenant Searle, as follows : "You will muster the Creek regiment out of "service, and honorably discharge them. Then you will proceed "to New Orleans, and obtain funds to pay the Creeks for the cap-"tured negroes. The chiefs and warriors who were actually in the "field at the time of the capture of negroes are alone to receive any "part of the sum allowed. Those who remained in camp and did "not march are to receive nothing.

"You will examine the prisoners at 'Fort Pike,' (the ninety "Exiles,) and cause an accurate description to be taken of them, "specifying their names, ages, height, sex, and such other particu-"lars as you may deem important. They must all be comfortably "clothed, at the public expense, immediately, by the Assistant

---

(1) These facts may all be found officially recorded in Ex. Doc. 78, 2d Sess. XXVth Congress, and Ex. Doc. 225, 3d Sess. XXVth Congress.

" Quarter-Master at New Orleans, who will keep them properly " clad."

It would appear that some difficulty arose with the Choctaw and Delaware warriors, who had expected to receive higher wages than the law allowed for serving in the army. Such had been done with the Creeks, and undoubtedly had been promised the Choctaws and Delawares. To quiet these discontents, General Jessup wrote Colonel Davenport, on the seventh of November, saying, " I regret " the circumstance to which you refer. The importance of fulfill- " ing all our engagements with the Indians with the most scrupu- " lous good faith, is unquestionable. To dismiss them now, might " not only cost us another campaign, but may cause us difficulties " on our western border. We must retain them at all hazards. I " wish you to assure them, that *our laws* do not authorize the pay- " ment of the sum *stipulated;* but that the enemy has a large " property, consisting of ponies, cattle and *negroes*, and that I will " pay them for all the cattle they take, and they will be paid *fifty* " *dollars for every negro.* * * * Represent to them also, that " our country is just, and if they will serve well, I will take their " chiefs to Washington, and represent their case to the Great Coun- " cil (Congress), and I have no doubt they will get all that has " been promised them." He also wrote Captain Armstrong of the Choctaw agency, and Captain Bonneville, commanding the Choc-taw warriors, encouraging the Indians to faithful effort in order to obtain negroes.

Some of the Georgia volunteers appeared anxious to know defi-nitely the terms on which they were to expose their lives in these slave-catching forays; and a letter was addressed to Brigadier Gen-eral C. H. Nelson, commanding the Georgia volunteers, by J. A. Chambers, aid to General Jessup, saying, " We have not the order " book with us at this moment; but the General directs me to say, " that all Indian property captured belongs to the capturers."

On the same day, General Hernandez of the Florida militia, found means to secure King Phillip, an aged chief, who lived some distance south of San Augustine, with eleven others of his tribe. It may be regarded as somewhat unfortunate, that history has failed to give us the particulars of this capture. The subsequent conduct of General Hernandez may lead the reader to look back upon this incident of the war with some desire to know the manner of King Phillip's capture; to understand whether it was peaceful or hostile; and whether any, and how many, white men, and how many Indians and Exiles, fell in the conflict? But we must pass over these particulars, as we have no authentic account concerning them. General Jessup, when called on to report to the Secretary of War as to violations of the flag of truce, merely remarks, incidentally, that King Phillip and his companions were captured by General Hernandez.

Phillip had long been regarded as a chief of influence among the Seminoles. Finding himself a prisoner, he became anxious to see, and converse with, some of his friends; and General Hernandez, at his request, gave permission for one of the prisoners to carry this talk to his family, inviting them to come and visit him in his captivity. The message was faithfully delivered to his oldest son, already known to the reader as "Wild Cat." He had been an active warrior at the massacre of Dade's battalion; had been subsequently elevated to the dignity of a chief; had visited General Jessup, under the articles of capitulation of March, 1837, and at that time delivered up "Louis" as his slave, demanding his transportation West under those articles; and when he learned the intention of General Jessup to deliver up a portion of the Exiles to slavery, he left Fort Brooke, and again swearing vengeance upon the enslavers of mankind, became one of the most active warriors in the Seminole Nation.

The Cherokee Delegation had reached the Indian country. The address of John Ross was directed to Wild Cat and Osceola, as two of the principal Seminole chiefs. They were together, and received the talk of Ross, the Cherokee chief, assuring them of the integrity and honor of the United States. After due consideration, it was determined that Wild Cat should comply with the filial obligations due to his aged father, bearing with him the peace token of Osceola, consisting of a neatly wrought bead pipe, together with a beautiful white plume, to be presented to General Hernandez, as the assurance of Osceola's pacific desires. Co-Hadjo, another chief, bore a similar message and emblems.

These were received by General Hernandez, who communicated immediate information thereof to General Jessup. They were propositions for negotiating a peace, forwarded at the special request and advice of the Cherokee Delegation, who were active in their efforts to stop the effusion of blood, and restore harmony between our nation and the Seminoles. By direction of General Jessup, Hernandez returned various presents to Osceola by Co-Hadjo, saying, that General Jessup and himself would be glad to hold a conference with them. The same assurances and presents were given to Wild Cat, who also became the messenger between General Jessup and General Hernandez on the one hand, and his brethren on the other. With the hope of effecting an arrangement beneficial to his friends and to mankind, Wild Cat left San Augustine with the promise to return in ten days.

Punctual to the day, he returned with the very satisfactory assurance, that Osceola, and one hundred Indians and as many Exiles, were on their way toward San Augustine, for the purpose of entering upon negotiations. With the intention of hastening their arrival, and manifesting an earnest desire for peace, General Hernandez proceeded, with Wild Cat and other friendly Seminoles, to meet the advancing chiefs, some twenty miles south-west of San Augustine, at a place called "Pelican Creek." Here he learned that Osceola would join them at evening. General Hernandez left a quantity of provisions with them, and, desiring them to select their encampment for the next day (Oct. 22) somewhere near Fort Peyton, at which place he would meet them with a proper escort, left them, and returned to San Augustine. They accordingly encamped the next day near Fort Peyton, situated seven miles south-west from

San Augustine. They approached their encampment with great formality : Osceola and other chiefs bearing white flags, expecting to meet a suitable escort under General Hernandez, with the well-understood intentions of entering upon diplomatic negotiations with that grave dignity for which the Indian is so much distinguished. These flags were kept flying in their encampment through the night and the next morning.

At ten o'clock (Oct. 23), General Hernandez, accompanied by his staff and by most of General Jessup's staff, in full dress, met them as had been promised, with the apparent purpose of escorting them to head-quarters at San Augustine. After the ordinary salutations had been exchanged, instead of preparing to march, General Hernandez, from a written paper signed by General Jessup, read the following questions addressed to Osceola : " Are you prepared " at once to *deliver up the negroes taken from the citizens?* Why " have you not surrendered them already, as promised by Co-Hadjo " at Fort King? Have the chiefs of the nation held a council on " this subject ? " [1]

Osceola exhibited the most perfect astonishment at hearing these questions propounded at such a moment. He appeared, however, instantly to comprehend his situation. Turning to Co-Hadjo, he said to him in his own dialect, " You must answer; I am choked," at the same time exhibiting unusual emotion for an Indian chief.[2]

---

(1) The interrogatories were embraced in a paper, of which the following is a copy :

"MEMORANDA OF SPECIFIC QUESTIONS TO BE ADDRESSED TO OSCEOLA.

" Ascertain the object of the Indians in coming in at this time. Also their expectations. *Are they prepared to deliver up the negroes taken from the citizens, at once?* Why have they not surrendered them already, as promised by Co-Hadjo at Fort King ? Have the chiefs of the nation held a Council in relation to the talk at Fort King? What chiefs attended that Council, and what was their determination? Have the chiefs sent a messenger with the decision of the Council? Have the principal chiefs Micanopy, Jumper, Cloud and Alligator sent a messenger? and if so, what is their message? Why have not those chiefs come themselves?

"(Signed)   THOS. S. JESSUP, *Major General Commanding.*
" SAN AUGUSTINE, *August 21st,* 1837."

(2) From the first and second interrogatories, the reader will see that General Jessup was fully conscious, that the attempt to deliver over those negroes to slavery who were

At this moment, by a concerted signal, armed troops at once surrounded the whole encampment, gathered rapidly in upon the occupants, made prisoners of them, and at once disarmed them. They were then marched to San Augustine, and closely imprisoned in the ancient castle of that city. There was about an equal number of Exiles captured, at this violation of our plighted faith; they were, however, sent to Tampa Bay for safe keeping.

Wild Cat, having been made the instrument for betraying Osceola and other friends, felt great indignation at what he regarded as the perfidy practiced upon him and his brethren, and determined to escape from his imprisonment so soon as an opportunity should offer. But he was imprisoned in the Castle of San Augustine, whose gray walls, lofty turrets, battlements and Catholic chapel, must have presented to the young warrior a spectacle in striking contrast with the rude huts in which he was accustomed to lodge, in the interior of the Territory. We prefer letting him tell the story of his escape, which we copy from the works of one who was then serving in our army.[1] Said Wild Cat:

---

claimed by the citizens of Florida, had been the sole cause for renewing the war. He dictated the first and most important interrogatory propounded to Osceola — "*Are you prepared at once to deliver up the negroes taken from the citizens?*"

But the second shows an important fact which had, so far as we have information, been kept from the public: The words, "Why have they not already surrendered them, as promised by *Co-Hadjo at Fort King?*" This shows that the arrangement reported by him to have been made with the chiefs, was made with Co-Hadjo only. It will be recollected, that after the articles of capitulation, in March, when the people of Florida began to demand their negroes, General Jessup said he would endeavor to make an arrangement with the chiefs for delivering up those negroes who had been *captured during the war.* After the protest of the people of Florida had been addressed to the Secretary of War, against the peace, unless they were to get their negroes, and the public meeting held at San Augustine, which expressed the same views, he reported that *he had made such arrangement with the chiefs;* but with how many, or with which particular *chiefs,* was unknown until this interrogatory disclosed the fact, that it was made with one obscure chief only. And whether he were intoxicated, or sober, at the time he attempted to act without any authority, to consign hundreds of his fellow-beings to slavery, without their knowledge or consent, does not appear. But every reader at once propounds the question, *What were the terms of that arrangement?* If it existed, it should have been reported verbatim to the War Department, and made known to the public.

(1) Capt. Sprague, of the Regular service.

"We were in a small room, eighteen or twenty feet square. All
" the light admitted was through a hole (embrasure) about eighteen
" feet from the floor. Through this we must effect our escape, or
" remain and die with sickness. A sentinel was constantly posted
" at the door. As we looked at it from our bed, we thought it
" small, but believed that, could we get our heads through, we
" should have no further or serious difficulty. To reach the hole
" was the first object. In order to effect this, we from time to time
" cut up the forage bags allowed us to sleep on, and made them
" into ropes. The hole I could not reach when upon the shoulder
" of my companion ; but, while standing upon his shoulder, I
" worked a knife into a crevice of the stone-work as far as I could
" reach, and upon this I raised myself to the aperture, when I
" found that, with some reduction of person, I could get through
" In order to reduce ourselves as much as possible, we took medi-
" cine five days. Under the pretext of being very sick, we were
" permitted to obtain the roots we required. For some weeks we
" watched the moon, in order that, on the night of our attempt, it
" should be as dark as possible. At the proper time we com-
" menced the medicine, calculating on the entire disappearance of
" the moon.

" The keeper of this prison, on the night determined upon to
" make the effort, annoyed us by frequently coming into the room,
" and talking and singing. At first we thought of tying him and
" putting his head in a bag, so that, should he call for assistance,
" he could not be heard. We first, however, tried the experiment
" of pretending to be asleep, and, when he returned, to pay no
" regard to him. This accomplished our object. He came in and
" went immediately out ; and we could hear him snore, in the
" immediate vicinity of the door. I then took the rope we had
" secreted under our bed, and, mounting on the shoulder of my
" comrade, raised myself upon the knife worked into the crevice of
" the stone, and succeeded in reaching the embrasure. Here I
" made fast the rope, that my friend might follow me. I then

" passed through the hole a sufficient length of it to reach the
" ground upon the outside (about fifty feet), in the ditch : I had
" calculated the distance when going for roots. With much diffi-
" culty I succeeded in getting my head through, for the sharp
" stones took the skin off my breast and back. Putting my head
" through first, I was obliged to go down head foremost until my
" feet were through, fearing every moment the rope would break.
" At last, safely on the ground, I awaited with anxiety the arrival
" of my comrade. I had passed another rope through the hole,
" which. in the event of discovery, Talmeco-Hadjo was to pull, as
" a signal to me upon the outside that he was discovered, and could
" not come. As soon as I struck the ground, I took hold of the
" signal for intelligence from my friend. The night was very dark.
" Two men passed near me, talking earnestly, and I could see them
" distinctly. Soon I heard the struggle of my companion, far
" above me ; he had succeeded in getting his head through, but his
" body would come no farther. In the lowest tone of voice, I
" urged him to throw out his breath and then try ; soon after, he
" came tumbling down the whole distance. For a few moments I
" thought him dead. I dragged him to some water close by, which
" restored him ; but his leg was so lame he was unable to walk. I
" took him upon my shoulder to a scrub, near town. Daylight
" was just breaking : it was evident we must move rapidly. I
" caught a mule in the adjoining field, and, making a bridle of my
" sash, mounted my companion. The mule we used one day ; but
" fearing the whites would track us, we felt more secure on foot in
" the hommock, though moving very slowly. Thus we continued
" our journey for five days, subsisting on berries, when I joined my
" band, then assembled on the head-waters of the Tomoka River,
" near the Atlantic coast. I gave my warriors the history of my
" capture and escape, and assured them that they should be satis-
" fied my capture was no trick of my own, and that I would not
" deceive them."

While Wild Cat and his friends were imprisoned at San Augustine, the Cherokee Delegation had been actively engaged in exertions to induce other chiefs and warriors to come in, for the purpose of ascertaining what negotiations could be effected with General Jessup in favor of peace. Their objects were of the most humane character. Anxious to stop the further shedding of human blood, they had come a thousand miles upon this errand of mercy.

After great effort, Micanopy, the most important chief in the Nation, Choud, Toskogee, and Nocose Yoholo, agreed to accompany a portion of the Cherokee Delegation to General Jessup's camp, for the purpose of negotiation, or rather to ascertain whether further 'negotiation were practicable. They were accompanied by about seventy-five Indians and forty Exiles. They approached the American camp under a flag of truce, that emblem of peace, which is recognized as such by all civilized nations, and treated with respect.

They reached General Jessup's camp on the third of December, in company with a part of the Cherokee Delegation, and confided themselves to the power of the commanding officer, trusting to the honor of our nation. They were received with apparent respect and good faith, and remained in camp under the expectation of further negotiation; of which there was much said, and frequent conversations held.

After a few days spent in this way, the Seminole chiefs and warriors were unsuspectingly seized, disarmed, made prisoners, hurried on board a steamboat, and sent to San Augustine as prisoners of war.

As the Cherokees saw this violation of the flag, they were struck with astonishment, and began to remonstrate against an act which, to them, appeared an outrage upon the rules of civilized warfare, and which involved them in its guilt. Finding remonstrance of no avail, they requested permission of General Jessup to converse with the Seminoles, in order to assure them that they, the Cherokees, had acted in good faith, and were in no degree cognizant of the fraud practiced upon the Seminoles, or implicated in the discreditable violation of the flag of truce. This privilege, however, was denied them.

Feeling indignant, and conscious that the Seminoles would charge them with complicity, in this violation of faith, they next demanded that their principal chief should have an opportunity, in the presence of such officer or officers as General Jessup may appoint, to see the Seminoles, and explain to them that the Cherokees had in no respect participated in the perfidy practiced upon them. To enforce this request, they stated to General Jessup that, if the Seminoles were sent West, they would thereby become neighbors to the Cherokees, and, if they believed the Cherokee Delegation to have participated in this transaction, they would never forget it, but would thereafter be hostile to them.

General Jessup at length consented to permit the chief of the Cherokees to explain these facts to the Seminoles, in the presence of himself and officers; but would not suffer any other member of the delegation to attend him.[1]

The Seminoles were sent to San Augustine; and that portion of the Cherokees who had accompanied them to General Jessup's camp, at once refused all further efforts to restore peace, and returned to their homes; leaving, however, some four or five of their brethren in the Seminole country, who, ignorant of the occurrences just related, continued to urge other Seminoles to make peace upon such terms as they believed just—assuring them that the Americans demanded nothing more.

(1) This statement is taken entirely from the Letters of John Ross, chief of the Cherokees, to the Secretary of War. In these letters, he relates the whole transaction with great force and apparent candor, and, in the name of the Cherokee Nation, boldly arraigns the War Department for this treachery, practiced by a Christian nation towards a people called heathens. These letters may be found at length in Ex. Doc. 327, 2d Sess. XXVth Cong., vol. 8.

CHAPTER XIII.

VIGOROUS PROSECUTION OF THE WAR.

General Zachary Taylor — His character and past service — His expedition — Battle of Okechobee — His loss — Returns to Withlacoochee — Repudiates the work of catching Slaves — Exiles delivered over to bondage — Regular Troops despise such Employment — Indian prisoners indignant at the outrages perpetrated against the Exiles — Separated from Exiles — Are sent to Charleston — Exiles to Tampa Bay — Further efforts to re-enslave Exiles — General Jessup moves South — Skirmish of Loca Hatchee — Erects Fort Jupiter — Is persuaded to propose peace on basis of permitting Indians and Exiles to remain in Florida — Sends one of the Exiles to the enemy with these propositions — He returns with Hallec Hajo — Parties agree to hold Council and endeavor to form Treaty on that basis — Indians and Exiles meet for that purpose — Letter to Secretary of War — His answer — Indians and Exiles treacherously seized — Their numbers — Alligator and others surrender — Exiles sent to Fort Pike — Indians sent to Charleston.

GENERAL ZACHARY TAYLOR was in command of an efficient force 1837.] in the western part of Florida, holding his head-quarters at Tampa Bay. He had been thirty years in service; had distinguished himself in battle, and was regarded as an officer of great merit. Looking to the honor of our flag and the prestige of the service, he appears to have borne himself entirely above all efforts to prostitute the powers of the nation to the reënslavement of the Exiles. He was particularly opposed to the plan of General Jessup, directing that all negroes captured should be the slaves of the captors.[1]

It now became evident that there was hard fighting to be done. General Taylor was at all times ready for such service. It is one

---

(1) Vide letter of General Taylor to Commissioner of Indian Affairs, Ex. Doc. 225, 3d Sess. XXVth Congress.

of the imperfections of human government, that the men who conceive and direct the perpetration of great national crimes are usually
exempt from the immediate dangers which beset those who act
merely as their instruments in the consummation of transcendent
wrongs. Had General Jackson and General Cass been assured
they would have been the first individuals to meet death in their
efforts to enslave the Exiles, it is doubtful whether either of them
would have been willing to adopt a policy which should thus consign them to premature graves. Or had Mr. Van Buren, or his
Cabinet, at the time of which we are now writing, been conscious
that, in carrying on this war for slavery, they would fall victims to
their own policy, it may well be doubted whether either of them
would have laid down his life for the safety of that institution ; yet
they were evidently willing to sacrifice our military officers and
soldiers to maintain the degradation of the African race.

General Jessup had written General Taylor, that all hope of terminating the war through the agency of the Cherokees, was at an
end ; that Sam Jones and the Mickasukies had determined to
fight to the last. He, therefore, directed General Taylor to proceed, with the least possible delay, against any portion of the enemy he might hear of within striking distance. General Taylor at
once concentrated such force as he deemed necessary for the contemplated expedition. His little army was composed of regulars
and volunteers, including nearly one hundred Delaware and Shaw-
nee Indians, who had been induced to join the army under the
expectation of obtaining plunder by the capture of slaves. His
whole force amounted to nearly eleven hundred men. Conscious
that he was expected to encounter the full force of the enemy, if he
could succeed in bringing them to action, he left his artillery ;
divested his troops of all heavy baggage, and prepared, as far as
possible, for a rapid movement. With him were some of the most
valued officers in the service of Government ; men on whom he could
rely with confidence, and who were worthy to command veteran
troops. With this force, he left his encampment on the morning

of the nineteenth of December, and directed his course southeast-
wardly, in the direction where, it was said, Sam Jones and his
forces were encamped. As he advanced into the interior, he discovered signs of Indians; and, through the efforts of Captain Parks,
a half-breed chief, who commanded the Delawares and Shawnees,
he induced Jumper, and a few families of the Seminoles and some
few Exiles, to come in and emigrate under the articles of capitulation of March previous. On the twenty-second of December, being
the third day of their march, they found conclusive evidence that
they were in the vicinity of the enemies' principal force, but found
it difficult to bring them to action. That night every precaution
was taken against surprise. The necessary patrols were kept out,
sentinels doubled, and the troops slept upon their arms. They
confidently expected to engage the enemy the next day.

But the allies were cautious; they passed from swamps, through
hommocks, and over prairies, constantly keeping too far in advance
of our army to incur any danger. In this manner the whole of
that day was occupied.

At night the troops bivouacked as on the previous night. They
were in the deepest recesses of the Indian Country, surrounded by
swamps, everglades and hommocks: through these they had groped
their way for a hundred miles. Up to this time, the mounted
volunteers had managed to keep their horses with them, knowing
they might be useful in battle. But the enemy indicated an un-
willingness to encounter our troops with the advantages which the
mounted men would possess over them.

Early on the morning of the twenty-fourth, the troops were again
put in motion: the enemy keeping sufficiently in advance to be beyond the reach of musket or rifle balls. General Taylor and his
followers were in close pursuit; and as the allies left a swamp, or
hommock, or prairie, Taylor and his men entered it, hoping to bring
on a general action.

At about ten o'clock, the enemy were traced to a swamp of some
three-fourths of a mile in width, thickly covered with saw-grass, not

less than four feet in height. Through it flowed a turbid stream, whose current was scarcely perceptible, while it seemed to stretch away to the left in an endless savanna, and to the right it appeared to deepen into an impassable morass. After the proper reconnoissance, it was found that it could not be passed by horses; and on the farther side a thick hommock reached down to the very edge of the swamp.

It was now plain that the enemy intended to make a stand at this point, and give battle. Perhaps the whole territory did not furnish a more advantageous position than that now occupied by the allied forces. General Taylor saw at a glance the difficulties which lay before him. He well understood the superiority of the enemy's position, but determined to maintain the honor of the service. He did not hesitate in entering upon the conflict. His arrangements were soon made. The volunteers were directed to dismount, and act on foot. Knowing well that the battle was to be fought here if anywhere, he directed his troops to divest themselves of all baggage, which together with the horses, was left under the charge of a small guard. His troops entered the swamp in two lines. The first was composed of the volunteers, spies, and friendly Indians, under the command of Colonel Gentry. They were ordered to engage the enemy, and maintain their ground until reinforced; or, if compelled to fall back, they were directed to form immediately in rear of the second line, and await orders.

They entered the swamp in this manner at about twelve o'clock. The sun was shining pleasantly, and a quiet stillness appeared to pervade the scene around them. They passed the stream in safety, and the front line was approaching the thick hommock in front. There, too, all was silent; not an enemy to be seen; no voice was heard, nor could they discover any evidence of animal life within the dense forest before them.

There, however, lay Wild Cat and his band, and the prophet and other mighty chiefs of the nation with their followers. Wild Cat had been stimulated to desperation by what he regarded the perfidy

of General Jessup, and his imprisonment at San Augustine, from
which he had just escaped. Most of the Exiles, who remained
among the Seminoles, and were capable of bearing arms, were collected here under their respective leaders. They had retreated to
this point for the purpose of separating our troops from their horses,
and then engaging them at such superior advantage as would be
most likely to insure victory. Their spies had climbed into the
very tops of the trees, whence they had witnessed every movement
of our troops in the swamp, and given constant information to their
comrades who were on the ground, and who, acting under the
information thus received, were enabled to place themselves directly
in front of those who were pursuing them. Every warrior was
protected by a tree, and the thick foliage of the hommock shielded
every movement from the scrutiny of our spies and officers.

Soon as the first line, commanded by Colonel Gentry, came
within point-blank shot of the hommock, the allies opened a heavy
fire upon them. The saw-grass was so high as partially to protect
the bodies of our men from view; but the fire was very fatal.
Colonel Gentry, the gallant commander of the volunteers, fell at
the first fire; his son, an interesting youth, acting as sergeant-major,
was wounded almost at the same moment. Captain Childs, and
Lieutenants Rogers and Flanagan, of the same regiment, and Acting Major Sconce, and Lieutenants Hare and Gordon of the spies,
and twenty-four men, fell wounded at the very commencement of
the action.

It was hardly to be expected that militia would stand such a fire
They broke, fell back, and instead of halting in the rear of the
regulars as directed, they continued their flight across the swamp.
to the place where they left their horses; nor were the officers of
General Taylor's staff able to induce them again to join their comrades, who soon became engaged in a most deadly conflict.

But the regulars moved steadily to the charge, under Colonel
Thompson, a most gallant and estimable officer. General Taylor
says: "The weight of the enemy's fire seemed to be concentrated

N. ORR – Co.

Coacoochee, (Wild Cat.)

" upon five companies of the 6th Infantry, which not only stood
" firm, but continued to advance until their gallant commander,
" Lieut. Colonel Thompson, and his adjutant, Lieutenant Center,
" were killed; and every officer, with one exception, as well as
" most of the non-commissioned officers, including the sergeant-
" major, and four of the five orderly sergeants, were killed or
" wounded. When that portion of the regiment retired a short
" distance and re-formed, it was found that one of these companies
" had but *four men untouched.*"

Amid these difficulties, Lieut. Colonel Foster of the 4th Infantry,
with six companies, numbering about one hundred and fifty men,
gained the hommock in good order, and, after maintaining his
ground a short time, charged upon the allies and drove them from
the field, with the loss of nine Indians and one of the Exiles killed,
and eleven wounded.

The battle commenced at half-past twelve M., and continued
nearly three hours, and proved the most desperate, and to our
troops the most fatal conflict which occurred during the war. It
was past three o'clock in the afternoon when the allies gave up the
field, for which they had contended against a force more than
double their own numbers.

General Taylor and his surviving officers were now left to ascertain their loss, and contemplate the expense of subduing even a
savage people, fighting for their homes, their firesides, their *liberties.*
And we are led to think if those Northern statesmen who, for many
years subsequent to that date, were accustomed to inquire, What
has the nation to do with slavery? had been present and propounded that question to General Taylor or his officers, they would have
been silently pointed to *twenty-six dead bodies* of their deceased
comrades, then lifeless upon the ground, and to *one hundred and
twelve wounded officers and soldiers*, who were prostrated in that
swamp and hommock, suffering all the pangs which mortals are
capable of enduring; but the language of their gallant commander
better expresses his feelings than any which we can command.

12

In his official report, General Taylor says : " We suffered much,
" having twenty-six killed and one hundred and twelve wounded,
" among whom are some of our most valuable officers. * * Soon
" as the enemy were completely broken, I turned my attention to
" taking care of the wounded, to facilitate their removal to my
" baggage, where I had ordered an encampment to be formed. * *
" And here I trust I may be permitted to say, that I experienced
" one of the most trying scenes of my life ; and he who could have
" looked on it with indifference, his nerves must have been very
" differently organized from my own. Besides the killed, among
" whom were some of my personal friends, there lay one hundred
" and twelve officers and soldiers, who had accompanied me one
" hundred and forty-five miles, through an unexplored wilderness,
" without guides ; who had so gallantly beaten the enemy, under
" my orders, in his strongest positions ; and who had to be con-
" veyed back, through swamps and hommocks, from whence we set
" out, without any apparent means of doing so."

. The next day was occupied in burying the dead, making litters
for the transportation of the wounded, and preparing for their return
to Withlacoochee. One hundred and thirty-eight men had fallen
in this single conflict, victims to the policy of our Government, in
attempting to restore to a state of slavery men who abhorred and
had fled from it. The allies had also suffered severely. General
Taylor reported that ten of their dead and wounded were left on
the field.[1] But no prisoners were taken, no slaves were captured ;
and those Indians who had come from Arkansas to Florida, for the
purpose of sharing in slave-catching forays, found it a far more
dangerous employment, and one of more difficulty, than they had
expected.

On the morning of the twenty-sixth, General Taylor, with his
sick and wounded, left his encampment, and, after encountering

---

(1) Mr. Sprague says there were three hundred Indian and negro warriors engaged in
this battle, and that their loss was ten Indians and one negro killed, and eleven wounded ;
showing a great disparity between their loss and General Taylor's.

great difficulties, reached Withlacoochee on the thirty-first of De-- cember; having been absent twelve days. He made a brief official report of this expedition, and of the severe battle he had fought. This report was quietly filed away in the War Department, and but few, even of our public men, appeared to be fully conscious that he had performed meritorious service in the Florida war.[1]

But while General Taylor was thus quietly engaged in the most hazardous service, General Jessup was active in securing negroes, and employing the military power of the nation, so far as able, to seize and return fugitives to their owners. It would exceed the limits of our present work, were we to notice the efforts of various individuals claiming to have lost slaves. The Indian Bureau at Washington was engaged in this service, and applications were constantly made for slaves to the commanding officer. These applications were usually referred to some quarter-master, or pay-master, for decision; and if such inferior officer belonged to the militia, the person claimed was usually delivered over to bondage, whether the claimant had ever seen him previously or not. It is a matter of astonishment that our National Administration, guided by a Northern President (Mr. Van Buren), should have permitted a pay-master or quarter-master of militia, to sit in grave examination of the right of their fellow-men to liberty; to act as judge, jury and counselor, in cases involving the rights with which the God of Nature had endowed them.

But to the honor of our army, it was said that both officers and

(1) In 1848, General Taylor was the Whig candidate for President of the United States; and so little was the history of this war known to our statesmen or politicians, that it is believed no newspaper, or stump orator, or advocate of his election, ever related or referred to this most gallant act of his life. He had himself, during the war, exhibited no particular sympathy in the work of catching and enslaving negroes; on the contrary, he had expressed his detestation of that policy. Of course the slave power, not willing to make open war upon him, had permitted his name to rest without connecting it with the performance of any brilliant or humane acts. The casuist may say, that he ought not to have served in such a war, and that no gallantry displayed in such a cause ought to reflect credit upon any man But General Taylor, like other men, should be judged by the times, the customs, the morality of the age in which he lived.

men of the regular service, generally held the work of catching
slaves in supreme contempt. More than three hundred heavy
documentary pages were communicated to Congress on this subject,
nearly all of which are filled with extracts of letters, reports, orders,
opinions and directions concerning slaves, connected with this
Florida war.[1]

Great difficulty arose among the Indians in consequence of the
reënslavement of their friends, the Exiles. They felt the outrage
with as much apparent keenness as though it had been perpetrated
upon themselves. To prevent these difficulties, General Jessup
separated the Exiles from their Indian allies, whenever they surrendered or were taken prisoners.[2]

In pursuance of this plan, he sent Osceola and the other Indians
seized at Fort Peyton; and Micanopy, and others who had come into
his own camp for the purpose of negotiating a treaty, to Charleston,
South Carolina; while the Exiles were sent, some to Tampa Bay
and other places, to be subjected to the inspection of men who
professed to have been their previous owners.

General Jessup, in the very elaborate defense of his proceedings,
dated July, 1838, justifies this policy of separating the Indians and
Exiles by saying, that he learned the year previous, from prisoners
captured, that the Indians through the Seminole negroes had entered into arrangements with their slaves that so soon as hostilities
should commence, the latter were to join their masters, and take
up arms against the whites. This information, representing the Indians as entering into negotiation with their own slaves *through* the
"Seminole negroes" (Exiles), bears the character of fiction; yet it
is gravely set forth in an official report, and we are bound to treat
it respectfully.[3]

(1) Vide Ex. Doc., 2d Sess. XXVth Congress, No. 225.

(2) Vide General Jessup's letter to General Arbuckle, 8 Vol. Ex. Doc., 2d Sess. XXVth
Congress.

(3) Vide General Jessup's letter to Commissioner of Indian Affairs, Ex. Doc. 225, above
referred to.

Under this arrangement — separating the Indians and Exiles — all the relations of domestic life were disregarded. The Indian husband was separated from the wife he had selected among the daughters of the Exiles; and the Indian wife was separated from her more sable husband. The darker colored prisoners were hurried to Tampa Bay, and the red men and women were sent to Charleston for safe keeping.

Up to the commencement of the year 1838, General Jessup appears to have been mostly employed in efforts to obtain peace by negotiation and in directing the movements of various detachments of the army, who did not require his personal attendance, and making arrangements for the delivery of negroes to their supposed former owners; but had found very little time to mingle in the dangers of the field. Brigadier General Taylor had performed a most hazardous service; and it appeared proper that the Commanding General should also strike a blow that would distinguish his administration of the military department of the territory.

1838.] Early in January, he moved south, with about five hundred mounted men, well provided. On the twenty-fourth, at about twelve o'clock, he encountered the "allies," near the "Locka-Hatchee," and a short skirmish followed, in which the General was himself wounded somewhat severely in the arm. He lost seven men killed and thirty wounded. The enemy yielded the field to our troops, but left neither dead nor wounded upon the scene of conflict, nor is it known whether they sustained any loss whatever. General Jessup expresses the belief that there were not more than a hundred warriors engaged on the part of the enemy. On the twenty-fifth, he erected a stockade called "Fort Jupiter." Here he lay until the fifth of February, when he moved forward some twelve miles, where, it is said, some of his officers — General Easton and others — proposed that General Jessup should make terms with the Indians and their allies, and permit them to remain in the country, confining them to the southern portion of the Territory. He, however, moved forward another day's march, when, being called on by Colonel Twiggs, and learning that it was the general desire of the officers, he says he determined to send a messenger to the Indians, offering them peace.

The first messenger dispatched on this service was one of the Exiles, or, as General Jessup called him, a " Seminole negro." This man soon returned with several Indians, among whom was a sub-chief named " Hallec Hajo," who was willing to hold a conference, and expressed a desire to remain in the country; but said, if compelled, they must go West.

General Jessup insisted that " Toshkogee," the principal chief in that neighborhood, should attend, and hold a Council the next day; and that the Indians should give up their arms. Hallec Hajo at once refused to comply with such condition. He would meet in Council, but would never surrender his arms.

On the morning of the eighth of February, Toshkogee and Hallec Hajo met General Taylor agreeably to appointment. An interchange of opinions and views took place, and the General agreed to recommend the conclusion of a peace upon the *basis of allowing the allies to remain in the country*, and occupy a suitable portion of the southern part of the Territory. It was also agreed that a certain territory, near the place of negotiation, should be occupied by the Indians and their families, where they should be safe, and might remain until the views of the Executive should be ascertained.[1]

In pursuance of this arrangement of treating upon the basis of permitting the allies to remain in the country, many of the Seminoles and Exiles collected with the expectation that the agreement was to be carried out in good faith.

On the next day, General Jessup addressed a long communication to the Secretary of War, in which he gives his views upon the policy of immediate emigration somewhat at length, and advises its abandonment in the following language:

---

(1) This is the view which General Jessup gives of the transaction, Ex. Doc., 8th Vol., 2d Sess. XXVth Congress.

" In regard to the Seminoles, we have committed the error of
" attempting to remove them when their lands were not required
" for agricultural purposes ; when they were not in the way of the
" white inhabitants, and when the greater portion of their country
" was an unexplored wilderness, of the interior of which we were as
" ignorant as of the interior of China. We exhibit in our present
" contest the first instance, perhaps, since the commencement of
" authentic history, of a nation employing an army to explore a
" country, (for we can do little more than explore it,) or attempt-
" ing to remove a band of savages from one unexplored wilderness
" to another.

" As a soldier, it is my duty, I am aware, not to comment upon
" the policy of the Government, but to carry it out in accordance
" with my instructions. I have endeavored faithfully to do so ; but
" the prospect of terminating the war in any reasonable time is any
" thing but flattering. My decided opinion is, that, unless *imme-*
" *diate* emigration be abandoned, the war will continue for years to
" come, and at constantly accumulating expense. Is it not, then,
" well worthy the serious consideration of an enlightened Govern-
" ment whether, even if the wilderness we are traversing could be
" inhabited by the white man, (which is not the fact,) the object
" we are contending for would be worth the cost? I do not cer-
" tainly think it would ; indeed, I do not consider the country
" south of Chickasa-Hatchee worth the medicines we shall expend
" in driving the Indians from it."

To this communication the Secretary of War replied : " In the
" present stage of our relations with the Indians residing within
" the States and Territories east of the Mississippi, including the
" Seminoles, it is useless to recur to the principles and motives
" which induced the Government to determine their removal to the
" West. The acts of the Executive, and the laws of Congress,
" evince a determination to carry out the measure, and it is to be
" regarded as the settled policy of the country. In pursuance of
" this policy, the treaty of Payne's Landing was made with the

" Seminoles ; and the character of the officer employed on the part
" of the Government is a guarantee of the perfectly fair manner in
" which that negotiation was conducted and concluded. Whether
" the Government ought not to have waited until the Seminoles
" were pressed upon by the white population, and their lands be-
" come necessary to the agricultural wants of the community, is not
" a question for the Executive now to consider. The treaty has
" been ratified, and is the law of the land ; and the constitutional
" duty of the President requires that he should cause it to be exe-
" cuted. I cannot, therefore, authorize any arrangement with the
" Seminoles by which they will be permitted to remain, or assign
" them any portion of the Territory of Florida as their future resi-
" dence.

" The Department indulged the hope, that, with the extensive
" means placed at your disposal, the war by a vigorous effort might
" be brought to a close this campaign. If, however, you are of
" opinion that, from the nature of the country and the character
" of the enemy, such a result is impracticable, and that it is advisa-
" ble to make a temporary arrangement with the Seminoles, by
" which the safety of the settlements and posts will be secured
" throughout the summer, you are at liberty to do so."

General Jessup had previously represented the subjection of the
Seminoles as an object easily to be accomplished. He had so
represented in his letter to Mr. Blair, in 1836, which occasioned
the withdrawal of General Scott, and his own appointment to the
command of the army in Florida. He had himself been in command more than a year, and the War Department was doubtless
somewhat astonished at his recommendation now to adopt the policy
which the Indians and Exiles had from the first been ready to accept. He was probably somewhat mortified at seeing his proposition so coldly received, and the whole responsibility of carrying it
out placed upon himself, upon condition that he was *satisfied nothing better* could be accomplished. He had done all in his power
to effect the objects so much cherished by the Administration. But

the Secretary of War still urged the carrying out of the treaty of Payne's Landing, not according to its letter and spirit, but according to the unnatural and unexpected construction which General Jackson placed upon it, after complaints were made against the Seminoles by the people of Florida. It is also evident that no intention of executing it according to the supplemental treaty entered into by the Seminole Delegates while at the West, was entertained by the Administration. No measures had been taken for establishing the boundaries between the Seminoles and the Creeks; nor do we hear of any intention to fulfill that stipulation. On the contrary, it had been constantly asserted by the Secretary of War, that the Seminoles and Creeks were to be *united as one people.*

The Commanding General, in the opinion of many statesmen, had compromited the honor of the service, and violated the plighted faith of the nation by treacherously seizing Indians and Exiles who had approached the army under the white flag, which had so long been regarded as a sacred emblem of peace by all civilized nations; yet, notwithstanding these circumstances, his propositions were in spirit rejected, although in language he had been authorized to negotiate a temporary peace upon the basis he had proposed.

It is believed that the substance of this answer had become to some extent known, or suspected by the Indians, for General Jessup admits he received the decision of the Secretary of War on the seventeenth; and on the nineteenth, he directed the chiefs to meet him in Council on the twentieth, at twelve o'clock. For some cause, the Indians and their allies appear to have been indisposed to do this, and he directed Colonel Twiggs to seize them, and hold them prisoners; and he reported to the War Department that, by this movement, " five hundred and thirteen Indians, and one hundred and sixty-five negroes, were secured." [1]

Of this transaction we can only speak from the account given of it by General Jessup. From his report, certain important facts are

(1) Vide Report of General Jessup to the Secretary of War, Ex. Doc., 3d Sess. XXVth Congress.

clearly understood. For instance, he announces to the Indians and Exiles a proposition to treat with them, *upon the basis of permitting them to remain in the country.* That, for the purpose of entering into such a negotiation, they collected near Fort Jupiter; and that, without any attempt to negotiate, and while they were in his camp, they were unexpectedly seized against their will; and that Passac Micco, and fourteen others, escaped capture. Nor does General Jessup pretend that one of those six hundred and seventy-eight persons *voluntarily* surrendered. It is certain, that however honorable the intentions of General Jessup were, the Indians and the Exiles were deceived, and, as they believed, treacherously dealt with.

The official register of colored persons seized at Fort Jupiter, represents one hundred and fifty-one as properly belonging to the Seminoles, or as "*Seminole negroes,*" the term usually applied to the Exiles by General Jessup and his officers; and fourteen are represented as the slaves of citizens of Florida. These people were soon hurried off to Tampa Bay, where they were confined within the pickets, under a strong guard. Fort Brooke now presented to the eye of a stranger all the external appearances of a first class "slave factory" upon the African coast. The Exiles who had been betrayed at Fort Peyton and other places, and not delivered over to slave-hunters, were also here; and the number had so greatly increased, that many had to be sent to New Orleans for safe keeping.

When the Exiles seized at Fort Jupiter arrived at Tampa Bay, they found, among those already there, many old acquaintances, friends and relatives, who had been taken at other places. Families, in some instances long separated, were once more united; husbands, whose wives and children had been seized and long imprisoned at Tampa Bay, now rejoined their families, and were in some degree compensated for the mortification of having been made prisoners by treachery.

But fathers and husbands, whose children and wives were captured by the Creeks near Withlacoochee and other places during the previous year, now looked around for their families in vain. On making inquiry, they were informed their friends had been taken to Fort Pike, which had now become a general depot for the imprisonment of Exiles.

The Indians who had been captured by this "coup d'etat," were sent to Charleston, South Carolina, for safe keeping; and the negroes reported upon the registry as "slaves of citizens of Florida," were without ceremony delivered over to those who claimed to be their masters.

We have now reached a period of the war at which we are constrained to admit our inability to give a full or accurate history of the various captures of Exiles, or of the reënslavement of those captured.

Captain Sprague, who had the advantages of personal observation and experience during the war, says that General Hernandez of the Florida Militia, serving principally in the eastern part of the Territory, "captured some important chiefs, and restored to citizens " more than *three hundred negroes* who had been captured by the "Indians." But the means which he used for their capture is not stated.

General Jessup informs us, also, that Abraham, the negro chief, and two Indians, were sent to the Seminoles west of the Okechobee, and prevailed upon Alligator, and three hundred and sixty Indians and negroes, to surrender to Colonel Smith and General Taylor. But what proportion of this number were Exiles, we are not informed ; nor are we told of the means used, or the assurances given, to induce them to surrender. It is certain, that many of the chiefs alleged that the Cherokee Delegation assured their friends, that they would be permitted to remain in their own country, and that the President was desirous of making peace upon those terms ; and General Jessup says, that the negro chief Abraham, and another negro interpreter named Auguste, gave the same information.

Abraham had in fact dictated tho supplemental treaty, entered into by tho delegation while in the Western Country, and was made to believe, at all times, that the Government would fulfill, and abide by, the terms of this supplemental treaty. It was on this conviction that he acted, and he appears never to have doubted the good faith of the Executive until he actually arrived in the Western Country.

CHAPTER XIV.

GREAT DIFFICULTIES INTERRUPT THE PROGRESS OF THE WAR.

John Ross, the Cherokee Chief, demands the release of Wild Cat and other Chiefs — Answer of Secretary of War — Mr. Everett's resolution in Congress — Secretary's Report — General Jessup's answer — Agitation in Congress — Hon. John Quincy Adams — Hon. William Slade — Difficulty with Creek Warriors — The Exiles who had been captured by the Creeks — Arrangements for emigrating both Indians and Exiles — Indians at Charleston, and Negroes at Tampa Bay, transported to Fort Pike — Families again united — Sympathy excited — General Gaines becomes engaged in their behalf — His noble conduct — Embarrassment of Commissioner of Indian Affairs, and of the Secretary of War — Singular arrangement — Discrepancies unexplained — A Slave-dealer professes to purchase ninety of the Exiles, in order to relieve the Government — Appoints his brother-in-law an Agent to receive them — Department furnishes the necessary vouchers — Sudden change of policy — Sixty Exiles claimed by a Slave-dealer named Love — General Gaines appears on behalf of Exiles — His able defense — Court renders judgment discharging Rule — Thirty-six Exiles released by Love — Lieutenant Reynolds with the Indians, and all but these thirty-six Exiles, take passage for Fort Gibson.

WHILE General Jessup was engaged in carrying out the designs of the Administration by artifice, and by force, events of a serious character were transpiring at Washington which demanded the attention of both the Executive and himself. John Ross, principal chief of the Cherokee Nation, learning the manner in which Osceola, Wild Cat, and other Seminole chiefs and warriors, had been betrayed and seized, while visiting General Jessup under a flag of truce, by advice and at the suggestion of the Cherokee Delegation, wrote an able and very spirited letter to the Secretary of War, demanding the release of the prisoners thus captured in violation of the principles of civilized warfare.

(189)

The Secretary attempted a vindication of General Jessup, and an interesting correspondence followed, marked with great ability, in which Ross, with much force, exhibits what he seemed to regard as the perfidious treatment to which the Seminoles had been subjected, while acting under the advice of himself and his countrymen, and protected by the flag of truce, which had ever been recognized and held sacred as the inviolable emblem of peace. This was the first exposure of the manner in which this disastrous war had been conducted. Up to that time no member of Congress, or Executive officer, appears to have uttered an objection or protest against the war, or against the manner in which it was carried on. Ross was at the city of Washington, and mingled freely with members of Congress, and in private conversations called their attention to the facts stated.[1]

Mr. Everett, of Vermont,[2] a man of great experience and ability, moved a resolution (March 21) in the House of Representatives, calling on the Secretary of War for such information as he possessed touching the capture of Indians, while visiting the American army under flags of truce. The resolution was adopted, and, in reply, the Secretary of War (April 11) transmitted the answer of General Jessup, in which he rests his justification, upon the bad faith which, he alleges, the Indians had previously exhibited towards the United States. This answer occupies some fifteen documentary pages, most of which are filled with the facts already known to the reader.

---

(1) These facts may all be found in the 4th, 5th, 7th, 8th, 11th & 12th vols. of Ex. Doc., 2d Sess. XXVth Congress ; the letters of Ross and correspondence of General Jessup, and official reports, occupying several hundred pages.

(2) Horace Everett, who was many years a Representative in Congress, an ardent Whig, and constant opponent of Jackson and Van Buren. After the report of the Secretary of War in answer to his resolution had been received, Mr. Everett made a speech on the subject, exposing the manner in which the war had been conducted, and intimated that it was more immediately connected with the support of slavery than it ought to be. But while he was careful to say nothing exceptionable to the slave interest, he certainly entitled himself to the honor of being the first member who assailed the war, and the first to hold the Administration responsible for the manner in which it was prosecuted. The speech may be found at length in the Appendix to the Congressional Globe of that session.

After the report of the Secretary of War had been printed, Mr. Everett gave his views upon the facts, in a speech which attracted much attention in the country. The people were already turning their attention to the subject of slavery. Petitions were sent to Congress calling on that body to abolish the institution within the District of Columbia. The Hon. John Quincy Adams had thrown the weight of his influence in behalf of the right of petition, and was known to be opposed to the institution. Hon. William Slade, a member of the House of Representatives from Vermont, had openly avowed his deep and heart-felt sympathy with the Abolitionists, who were striving to direct the popular mind to the crimes of the "*peculiar institution*," as slavery was then called.

It was evident, that a full exposure of the causes which led to the Florida war, and of the manner in which it had been prosecuted, would tend to defeat the Democratic candidate in the next Presidential campaign. It was therefore clearly the policy of that party, and of the Administration, to maintain as great a degree of silence as possible upon all these subjects.

Among the early difficulties presented to the consideration of the War Department, was the settlement with the Creek warriors who had served under the contract made by order of General Jessup, in 1836, to give them a certain gross amount in cash, and all the *plunder they could capture*—which General Jessup and the Creeks understood to embrace negroes, as well as horses and cattle.

The General, by his order, had directed eight thousand dollars to be paid to them, and twenty dollars for each negro belonging to citizens, who had been captured by them and delivered over to the claimants.

This disposal of the public treasure by an individual, was most clearly unauthorized, either by law or by the constitution ; yet the order had been approved by the Executive, and had been made the act of the President, who thus assumed the moral and political responsibility attached to this gross violation of law, and of the Constitution.

The question how this charge upon the treasury was to be met, seems to have borne heavily upon the mind of the Commissioner of Indian Affairs, and he expressed this difficulty to General Jessup. That officer, being less familiar with matters of finance than with those of a strictly military character, replied, that the amount might with propriety be charged to the annuities due the Seminoles; but as that fund was under the supervision of Congress, it would not do to charge it over to that appropriation, lest it should create agitation.

Another difficulty was, as to the disposal of the negroes themselves. They were now said to be the "*property of the United States;*" and the question very naturally arose, what shall be done with them? This question was also propounded to General Jessup by the Commissioner of Indian Affairs. The General replied, that he thought it best to send them to Africa, for the benefit of civilization on that coast. But that could not be done except by appropriations made by Congress; and it was feared that, to ask Congress for an appropriation of that character, might lead to the disclosure of unpleasant facts.[1]

In the meantime, arrangements were made to send the prisoners, both Indians and Exiles, to the Western Country, without any particular decision in regard to the ninety negroes captured by the Creek warriors, and sent to Fort Pike as the property of the United States, and fed and clothed at the public expense for more than a year.

Agreeably to orders from the War Department, General Jessup detailed Lieutenant J. G. Reynolds to superintend the emigration, as disbursing agent, and W. G. Freeman as an assistant. These appointments were approved by the Department; and transports were engaged to take such prisoners as were at Charleston, South Carolina, around the peninsula of Florida to Tampa Bay, on the western coast, and thence to New Orleans.

---

(1) Vide Letter of Commissioner of Indian Affairs to Secretary of War, 9th May, 1838. **Ex.** Doc. 225, 2d Sess. XXVth Congress.

There were at that time many negroes at Tampa Bay, intentionally separated from the Indians, who had been sent, at the same time, to Charleston. Major Zantzinger wrote the Commissioner of Indian Affairs, to know how these negroes at Tampa Bay were to be disposed of. The Commissioner immediately answered by letter, directed to Lieutenant Reynolds, saying, " I have " to instruct you, that all of those negroes mentioned by Major " Zantzinger, which are the property of the Seminoles,[1] are to be " received with, and to constitute a portion of, the emigrating party " for all purposes of transportation and subsistence. * * * * " You will consider it your duty to call at Tampa Bay, receive this " party, and transport it to the West *with the detachment now at* " *New Orleans.*"

This direction required Lieutenant Reynolds to transport the ninety Exiles, sent to New Orleans on the second of June, 1837, to the Western Country; for they constituted a part of " the detachment at New Orleans," which he was directed to transport West. They had been captured while fleeing from our army, and of course were nearly all of them women and children, who, by the fortunes of war, had been separated from their husbands, and fathers, and brothers, that were left behind in the Indian Country. Those husbands, brothers and fathers, were among the first to capitulate in order to rejoin their families from whom they had thus been separated. Many Exiles had been betrayed and seized at Fort Peyton. Some had surrendered at Volusi; others had capitulated at Fort Jupiter; others had come in and given themselves up at different posts : and all these were assembled for transportation at " Tampa Bay," where they awaited arrangements for sending them to the Western Country.

Major General Gaines was at that time commanding the south-

---

(1) Major Zantzinger, like many other officers, appears to have thought that every negro must have a master, and he called these Exiles the property of the Seminoles, although the Agent for that Tribe had reported a few years previously, that the number of slaves owned by them did not exceed *forty.*

13

western division of the army of the United States; and Fort Pike was situated within his military district. Lieutenant Reynolds had taken the prisoners at Charleston on board the transports; had sailed around the peninsula of Florida; called at Tampa Bay; had taken on board the negroes assembled at that point, and had reached Fort Pike.

Members of familes long separated were now united. Fathers embraced their wives and children, whom they had not seen for more than a year; brothers and sons embraced their sisters and mothers; and all exhibited those deep sympathies of the human heart, which constitute the higher and holier emotions of our nature. The officers and soldiers who witnessed this scene could not but feel interested in these people, many of whose ancestors had fled from oppression generations previously, and who, for more than half a century, had been subjected to almost constant persecution. It was undoubtedly owing to these circumstances, that so many of the officers of our army became deeply interested in securing their freedom.

Major Zantzinger was in command at Fort Pike; but he could only act under the direction of his superior officers. Lieutenant Reynolds, therefore, applied to Major General Gaines for orders to Major Zantzinger to deliver the Exiles at Fort Pike to him for emigration. From the peculiar language used in this order, it is most evident that General Gaines expected some effort would be made to prevent the emigration of the Exiles, then resident at Fort Pike. The order is so unusual in its tone and language, that we insert it, as follows:

"To Major Zantzinger, or the officer commanding at Fort Pike,
" or the officer who has charge of the slaves, or other servants, be-
" longing to, or lately in possession of, Seminole Indians, now in
" charge of Lieutenant Reynolds, destined to the Arkansas: You
" will, on receipt hereof, deliver to the said Reynolds all such slaves
" or servants belonging to, or claimed by, or lately in possession of,
" the said Seminole Indians to be conducted by him in their move-

" ments to the Arkansas River, where the Indians, or their slaves
" or servants, are to be permanently located and settled : taking
" triplicate receipts for said slaves or servants, one of which will be
" forwarded to the undersigned.   " EDMUND P. GAINES,
       " *Maj. Gen. U. S. A., Commanding.*"

The above order was dated on the twenty-first of March. The
next day Lieutenant Reynolds inclosed a copy to the Commissioner
of Indian Affairs, saying, he should commence his voyage West
with the emigrants, and adding, " It is not my intention to remove
" the negroes from Fort Pike until ready for departure, as I am
" convinced that many individuals with fraudulent claims are in a
" state of readiness, and only waiting the arrival of the negroes in
" this city (New Orleans) to carry their object into effect. The
" measures I shall adopt will bar their intention."

This letter explains the reason of the precise and specific terms
in which the order of General Gaines was expressed. It is due to
the memory of General Gaines, and to the character of Lieutenant
Reynolds, that their determined efforts to preserve the liberties of
these people, so far as they were able, should find a place in history. The war had been commenced and prosecuted for the purpose of seizing and returning to bondage all those people whose
ancestors had once fled from oppression. It was the avowed policy
of the Administration to prevent these ninety Exiles, who had been
captured by the Creek Indians, from going to the Western Country,
prefering to have them consigned to slavery in Georgia or Florida,
rather than enjoy freedom in the new homes assigned to the Indians
in the West. This feeling had encouraged desperate men to make
unfounded claims to their persons : and it should be recorded to
the honor of many of our officers, that they were active and vigilant in their efforts to defeat these piratical claims, and the exertions of the President and heads of the various Executive Departments, to consign these people to interminable bondage. In order
to do justice on this subject, it is necessary to permit all concerned

to speak for themselves, so far as convenience will allow. To carry out this object, the reader will excuse our frequent quotations from official documents.

On the twenty-sixth of March, Lieutenant Reynolds wrote the Commissioner of Indian Affairs, dating his letter at "New Barracks," below New Orleans, saying, "The Indian negroes will be "received at Fort Pike, and brought to this place, via the Missis- "sippi River. This course was adopted with the concurrence of "General Gaines. Everything will be in readiness to embark soon "as the boat arrives. General Gaines has directed that the guard "under the direction of Lieutenant Wheaton shall proceed with "me."

Major Zantzinger, who commanded at Fort Pike, appears to have felt some delicacy at delivering up the negroes on the order of General Gaines, and, with those impressions, wrote General Jessup, inquiring as to that point. He received an answer, dated seventh of April, approving his course, and saying, "the removal of the "negroes was *proper;* they were either *free,* or the property of the "Indians."

All these proceedings were reported to the proper Department at Washington. About the time, or soon after, they would naturally reach that city, William Armstrong, Acting Superintendent of the Indians in the Western Territory, evidently in the joint service of our Government and of the Creek Indians, addressed a note to the Commissioner of Indian Affairs, dated at Washington City, April twenty-third, 1838, saying, "When General Jessup called upon "volunteers to go to Florida, he promised them all the *property* "they could capture. Accordingly, the Creeks captured near *one* "*hundred negroes,* which they left in possession of the officers of "the United States. *What has become of these negroes?* Will "they receive them, or their value, as promised?"

The difficulty attending the transformation of men into chattels now increased so much, that the Commissioner of Indian Affairs addressed a letter to the Hon. Secretary of War, which is so characteristic of the manner in which the administration of our Government was then conducted, that we give the letter in full:

"WAR DEPARTMENT,
" *Office of Indian Affairs*, May 1, 1838.

"SIR : I have the honor to submit for the consideration and de-
" cision of the Department a question that has been presented by
" the Superintendent of the Western Territory, (Captain Arm-
" strong.)

"In September last, General Jessup advised the Department
" that he had purchased from the Creek warriors all the negroes
" (about eighty in number), captured by them, for $8,000, and
" this purchase was approved on the seventh of October. At a
" subsequent date, he wrote that he had supplied Lieutenant Searle
" with funds, and directed him to make the payment. It is believed,
" however, that the warriors refused to take the sum named, Lieu-
" tenant Searle having made no such payment, and the delegation
" here asserting that they never received it. It is now asked,
" whether they will be permitted to take the negroes, or be paid
" their value? It was suggested by General Jessup, that the con-
" sideration for the captives would be a proper charge on the Semi-
" nole annuity. But this would deprive the friendly portion, who
" have emigrated, of what they are justly, and by law, entitled to,
" and to a certain extent would be paying the Creeks with their
" own money; for the fourth Article of the Treaty with the Semi-
" noles, of May ninth, 1832, provides, that 'the annuities then
" granted shall be added to the Creek annuities, and the whole
" amount be so divided that the chiefs and warriors of the Semi-
" nole Indians may receive their equitable proportion of the same
" as members of the Creek confederation.' Independently of this
" difficulty, I would respectfully suggest, whether there are not
" *other objections to the purchase of these negroes by the United*
" *States?* It seems to me, that a proposition to Congress *to ap-*
" *propriate money to pay for them, and for their transportation*

" *to Africa, could its authority for that course be obtained, or for*
" *any other disposition of them,* WOULD OCCASION GREAT AND EX-
" TENSIVE EXCITEMENT. Such a relation assumed by the United
" States, for however laudable an object, would, it appears proba-
" ble, place the country in no enviable attitude, especially at this
" juncture, when the *public mind here and elsewhere is so sensi-*
" *tive upon the subject of slavery.* The alternative would seem to
" be, to deliver the negroes to the Creeks, as originally agreed on.
" The subject involves so many delicate considerations, that I re-
" spectfully invite your attention to it, and your direction as to the
" answer to be given to the delegation now in the city. As early
" a decision of this question as practicable, is very desirable : the
" Indians intending to leave this place in four or five days, and
" being anxious that this matter should be disposed of before they
" go.

" Very respectfully,

" Your most obedient servant,

" C. A. HARRIS, *Commissioner.*

" Captain S. COOPER, Acting Sec'y of War."

" P. S.—If it should be determined to deliver them to the
" Creeks, I would suggest, as the opinion of this office, that it
" would be *impolitic for them to be taken to the country West,* and
" that so far as the Department may of right interfere in regard to
" the ultimate disposition, *it should endeavor to have it effected* IN
" SOME OTHER MODE. C. A. H."

It is no part of our duty to comment on these proceedings;
yet we are constrained to say, that no historian has, or can
explain the reason of delay on the part of the Creek Indians,
in regard to their claim to these people, for more than an entire
year, upon any principles of consistent action. General Jessup
said, in his official communications, they *had received their pay,*
and that " the negroes *were the property of the Government;*"
and the Department had approved his whole course on this subject.
The Creeks, so far as we can learn, left the country and went West,

perfectly satisfied. This Delegation had been some months in Washington, and, as the Commissioner of Indian Affairs says, were to leave in four or five days; when, for the first time, they mentioned the subject, although the negroes had been detained from them, as they allege, in direct violation of their contract. They appear to have rested satisfied until difficulties from other quarters were presented to the Administration. And these letters may all easily be explained, as the carrying out of a previous understanding between these officers and the Creek Indians. However that may be, the Commissioner of Indian Affairs wrote Captain Armstrong, Superintendent of the Western Territory, as follows:

"WAR DEPARTMENT,
"*Office of Indian Affairs*, May 5, 1838.

"SIR: The Secretary of War has directed that the negroes be-
"longing to the Seminoles, and captured by the warriors in Florida,
"shall be placed at the disposal of the Delegation now in this city.
"But before this can be carried into effect, it will be necessary to
"be satisfied that the warriors have not received the $8,000 prom-
"ised in the agreement with General Jessup; to ascertain accu-
"rately their number and identity, and the claims of citizens upon
"any of them. For all to which such claims can be established,
"$20 each will be allowed. From the information now here, the
"number is supposed to be between sixty and seventy, the original
"number having been reduced by sickness. All the facts herein
"indicated will be required as early as practicable; but some time
"must necessarily elapse. It is the opinion of the Department,
"that it will be impolitic to take these negroes West, and that they
"should be otherwise disposed of. Any arrangement the Delega-
"tion may make respecting them, and submit to this office, will be
"sanctioned, and instructions given for such action as may be
"proper on the part of the Government.
                              "Very, &c.,   C. A. HARRIS.
"Capt. WM. ARMSTRONG,
        "Washington."

One feature in these communications stands out prominently to the view of the reader : the number of these victims appears to have undergone constant diminution. General Jessup reported the number sent to Fort Pike at *ninety*. In his previous letter, addressed to the Secretary of War, Commissioner Harris states the number at eighty; and in this communication, written four days subsequently, he states the number to be between sixty and seventy; while the official registry shows there was one hundred and three — of whom some, however, undoubtedly died.

If the honorable Secretary of War intended these people should be delivered over to the Creek Indians as their *property*, it would be difficult to understand by what law he should himself attempt to control them, in the subsequent disposition of their legalized chattels, or by what authority he should object to their going West.

It will however be seen that one point yet remained undecided. The negroes were not to be delivered until it was ascertained that the Creeks had *not* received the eight thousand dollars, agreeably to the order of General Jessup in September, 1837.

Fortunately, a Lieutenant Sloan, who had acted as a disbursing agent of the United States, was at that precise time in Washington City. He stated to the Commissioner of Indian Affairs, in a letter dated May sixth, being the day after this decision of the Secretary of War, assuring him that he had learned *from Lieutenant Searle himself that the Indians refused* to accept the eight thousand dollars for their interest in the negroes. These statements constituted a series of supposed facts, which appears to have been regarded as necessary to authorize the subsequent proceedings.

This evidence was, accordingly, deemed satisfactory; and the Creek Indians were now declared to be the owners of these ninety Exiles, under the original contract made between them and General Jessup, in 1836 : thus abrogating the order of General Jessup, No. 175, and setting aside the approval of that order by the Department of War itself — which was dated the seventh of October, 1837—leaving the United States to sustain the loss incurred by feeding and clothing the prisoners, and guarding them for thirteen months.

At this time a slave-dealer by the name of James C. Watson, said to reside in Georgia, happened to be also at the seat of Government, as was common for Southern gentlemen during the sessions of Congress. To this man the officers of Government now applied for aid, in extricating themselves from the difficulty into which they had been brought by this slave-dealing transaction. Even the Secretary of War is said to have encouraged Watson to purchase those negroes of the Creek Indians.[1] By request of these public functionaries, and at their instance, Mr. Watson declares he was induced to purchase the negroes, and to give between fourteen and fifteen thousand dollars for them.[2] It was perhaps the heaviest purchase of slaves made in the city of Washington during that year, and certainly the most dignified transaction in human flesh that ever took place at the capital of our nation, or of any other civilized people; inasmuch as the high officers of this enlightened and Christian confederation of States constituted a negotiating party to this important sale of human beings.

The purchase appears to have taken place on the seventh of May; and Watson, being unable to go immediately to New Orleans, authorized his brother-in-law, Nathaniel F. Collins of Alabama, as his agent and attorney, to repair to that city and take possession of the prisoners. Yet the whole business appears to have been carried on in the name of the Creek Indians.

On the eighth of May, five persons, styling themselves " chiefs, head-men and delegates of the Creek Tribe of Indians," filed with the Commissioner of Indian Affairs a request, stating that they had appointed Nathaniel F. Collins, Esq., of Alabama, their agent and attorney, to demand and receive from General Jessup the negro slaves which the Creek warriors had captured in Florida, under

(1) Vide Watson's Petition and proofs, in support of his claim, presented to Congress — 1st Sess. XXVIth Cong.— now on file in the office of the Clerk of the House of Representatives.

(2) Vide Watson's Statement of facts in this case, on file with the above papers.

their agreement with that officer, made in September, 1836, and requesting the Department to furnish the proper order for obtaining possession of the slaves from the officer having them in charge. This request was communicated to the Secretary of War the next day, by the Commissioner of Indian Affairs, and constitutes a part of the record; and, coming from that department of government most implicated in this slave-dealing transaction, we place it before the reader :

" WAR DEPARTMENT,
" <i>Office of Indian Affairs</i>, May 9, 1838.

" SIR : The decision made a few days since, requesting that the " negroes captured by the Creek warriors in Florida, should, in " compliance with the engagement of General Jessup, be delivered " to the Delegation now here, has been communicated to them with " the intimation that, when they had determined what disposition " would be made of them, and communicated information of the " same to this Department, the necessary orders would be issued. " In a communication just received from the Delegation, they state " they have appointed Nathaniel F. Collins, of Alabama, their " attorney in fact to receive the negroes. I have the honor to " request that an order be issued to the commanding officer at Fort " Pike ; to Major Isaac Clark, at New Orleans ; to the command- " ing officer in Florida, and to any other officer who may have " charge of them, to deliver to Mr. Collins all the negroes in ques- " tion. He will, of course, hold them subject to the lawful claims " of all white persons. Abraham and his family should be except- " ed, in consequence of a promise made by General Jessup. The " officers should be instructed to use due caution, so as to deliver " only those captured by the Creeks. It is proper to remark, that " it appears from a letter received from Lieutenant Sloan, that " these Indians refused to receive the $8,000, offered them under " the direction of General Jessup, for their interest in these negroes.

" Very respectfully,
" Your most obedient servant,

"Capt. S. Cooper, Acting Sec. of War."   " C. A. HARRIS.

On the same day, Mr. Collins was furnished with written instructions, which, being also important, are presented to the reader:

"WAR DEPARTMENT,
" *Office of Indian Affairs*, May 9, 1838.

"SIR: Having been notified by the Creek Delegation that they " have appointed you their agent and attorney in fact, to receive " the negroes captured by their warriors in Florida, which, by the " decision of the Secretary of War, are to be delivered up to them, " in conformity to the agreement made with them by General Jes- " sup, I have the honor to transmit herewith the copy of a commu- " nication to the Secretary of War on the subject, which has " received his approval. Orders will be given to the officers " therein named to carry the measure into effect, in conformity " to the recommendation. Captain Morrison, Superintendent of " Seminole Emigration at Tampa Bay, and Lieutenant Reynolds, " engaged in removing a party of the same, at New Orleans, have " been instructed to assist and coöperate in the matter. Here- " with you will receive the copy of a list of negroes captured by " General Jessup, which, it is believed, embraces the negroes to " which the Creeks are entitled; but as this is not certain, much " caution should be used in identifying them. It is supposed that " all these negroes now alive are at Fort Pike; but some of them " may be at Tampa Bay, or other places: it will be for you to find " them. No expense of any nature whatever, growing out of this " matter, will be paid by the United States.

"C. A. HARRIS, *Comm'r.*
"N. F. COLLINS,
"Washington, D. C."

Preparations being now perfected, and the whole matter being fully understood, Mr. Collins left Washington on the following morning, prepared to bring those fathers, and mothers, and children, back to servitude in Georgia, from which their ancestors had fled nearly a hundred years previously; and this nefarious work was thus encouraged and sanctioned by our Government.

Of these movements the Exiles were ignorant. Many hearts were moved in sympathy for them, and many of our military officers were active in their endeavors to defeat the machinations of the President and the War Department.

Lieutenant Reynolds found it necessary to return to Florida before leaving New Orleans with his party of Emigrants. While he was absent, the efforts of slaveholders to reënslave these people appeared to increase, and they became more bold, although Collins had not yet appeared, clothed with the authority of Government, to effect their enslavement.

General Gaines, commanding the Western Military District of the United States, and residing at New Orleans, as if premonished of the arrival of this national slave catcher, issued his peremptory order (April 29), directing Major Clark, Acting Quarter-Master at New Orleans, to make arrangements for the *immediate* embarkation and emigration of the Seminole Indians and *black prisoners of war*, at that time in Louisiana, to the place of their destination on the Arkansas River, near Fort Gibson.

Major Clark being thus placed in charge of the prisoners for the purpose of emigrating them, at once informed the Commissioner of Indian Affairs, that claims were " made for about seventy of the " Seminole negroes, and the courts here have issued their warrants " to take them. The United States District Attorney has been " consulted. He gives it as his opinion, that the Sheriff must be " allowed to serve the process. It appears they are claims from " Georgia, purchased from *Creek Indians*. No movement of the " Indians or negroes can be made at present. The Indians are " almost in a state of mutiny."

This state of feeling arose from these attempts again to separate the Indians and negroes. Many of them were intermarried : they had been separated ; their families broken up, but were now reünited, and they determined to die rather than be again separated. The Exiles had also fought boldly beside the Indians ; they had encountered dangers together, and had become attached to each other; and soon as the subject of surrendering the Exiles to bondage was named, the Indians became enraged, threatening violence and death to those who should attempt again to separate them from the Exiles.

The claimants mentioned by Major Clark, were from *Georgia.* The pirates who robbed E-con-chattimico and Walker of their slaves and seized the Exiles resident with those chiefs, as stated in a former chapter, were from Georgia. Watson, the more dignified dealer in human flesh, and acting in accordance with the advice of the Secretary of War, was also from Georgia; and all these claims were said to be derived from Creek Indians, who, as we have seen, professed to own all the Exiles who fled from Georgia after the close of the Revolution, and prior to 1802, together with their descendants.

Information, respecting these difficulties of reënslaving the Exiles, reached the authorities at Washington, and created great embarrassment. The War Department appears never to have anticipated that negroes, who were already prisoners of war, would find friends or means to awaken the sympathy of others. But it was clear that any litigation would make the public acquainted with the facts.

It will be recollected that on the tenth of May, the Commissioner of Indian Affairs wrote an order, directed to General Jessup, to deliver up near one hundred of these Exiles to Collins, the Agent of Watson, and two days later — that is, on the twelfth of May — he wrote Thomas Slidell, District Attorney of the United States at New Orleans, saying, " It is represented to this Department, that " the emigration of the Seminoles, now near New Orleans, has " been impeded by claims set up to some of their negroes. I am " directed by the Secretary of War to request that you will give " the Indians your advice and assistance, and by all proper and " legal means protect them from injustice and from harrassing and " improper interferences with their property and persons. It is of " the highest importance that, if possible, no impediments should

" be suffered to be thrown in the way of their speedy conveyance
" to their country, west of Arkansas."

It is a historical curiosity, that the Secretary of War should so
often change his policy. He had, as the reader is aware, exerted
his influence to prevent those Exiles, who had been captured by the
Creeks, from going West.

On the fifth of May, Commissioner Harris declared — " *it is the*
" *opinion of the Department that it will be impolitic to take these*
" *negroes West;"* and on the ninth, acting under the direction of
the Secretary of War, he furnished Mr. Collins with authority to
demand and receive these people, and instructions were also issued
" to the officer commanding at Fort Pike ; to Major Isaac Clark at
" New Orleans; to the commanding officer at Florida, and to any
" other officer who may have the negroes in charge," to deliver
them to Mr. Collins ; while three days afterwards he assures Mr.
Slidell, as before stated, " It is of the *highest importance that, if*
" *possible, no impediments should be suffered to be thrown in the*
" *way of their speedy conveyance to their country, west of Ar-*
" *kansas."* This letter to Mr. Slidell was inclosed in another of
the same date, addressed to Major Clark, as follows :

" SIR : I have the honor to acknowledge the receipt to-day of
" your letter of the third instant.

" The enclosed copy of a letter of this date to the United States
" District Attorney will show you what measures have been adopted
" in relation to the claims set up to the Seminole negroes. This is
" all that this Department can do in this matter.

" *It is very much to be regretted, that anything has occurred to*
" *prevent the speedy emigration of these Indians.* I will be greatly
" obliged to you, should no emigrating agent be at New Orleans,
" to give all the aid in your power in removing the difficulties which
" are thrown in their way."

While the Executive officers at Washington, the Creek Indians,
and the slave-dealer Watson, were arranging their contracts and per-

fecting their plans for enslaving those Exiles, who had been captured with the assistance of the Creek warriors, an important and most spirited contest was progressing in New Orleans.

Before one of the courts of the State of Louisiana, a slave-dealer by the name of Love, claimed title to the bodies, the bones and muscles, the blood and sinews, of some sixty of these persons, held by the United States as *prisoners of war*. They had been captured by our troops as hostiles; had been held for thirteen months as prisoners of war; had been fed, and clothed, and guarded, at the expense of the people of the United States: but they were now claimed as the *property* of Love. This absurdity was presented before an enlightened court as a grave question of international law; and a determined effort was put forth before that State tribunal to change the law of nations; to modify the law of Nature and of Nature's God, so far as to transform men into chattels, and declare these prisoners of war to be the property of their fellow men.

Love demanded the Exiles of General Gaines, who was in actual command of the Western Military District of the United States, and by virtue of his office held control of the Exiles while in his district. Bred to the profession of arms, he had made himself familiar with those principles of natural, of international, law which point out the rights of belligerents, whether they belong to the victorious or the vanquished nation. Being advised that efforts were making to get possession of these Exiles for the purpose of reënslaving them, he indicated to the officer in command at the barracks the propriety of retaining possession of them as he would of other *prisoners of war*.

On the second of May, the Sheriff of New Orleans appeared at the barracks, and desired to pass the line of sentinels for the purpose of serving his process; but the sentinel, punctilious to his duty, refused to let him enter. The Sheriff then returned his writ with the following indorsement thereon :

" Received May second, 1838, and demanded the within slaves
" of General Gaines, the defendant, who answered me, that he never

" had the within described *slaves* in his possession, or under his
" control. I found the slaves at the barracks of the United States,
" but the officers in charge of the same refused to deliver them to
" me.   Returned May eighth, 1838.

" FREDERICK BUISSON, *Sheriff*."

The Exiles still remained in the barracks under the officers in
charge of them ; and on the ninth of May, General Gaines sued
out a rule to set aside the order of sequestration upon the grounds,
" that the negroes were '*prisoners of war*' of the United States,
" taken in combat with the Seminole Indians ; that the control of
" the United States over said negroes, and their right to the control
" of such negroes as *prisoners of war*, could not be taken away by
" the sequestration issued."

Thus was the manhood of these colored people asserted by this
military officer of the United States at that day, when few members of Congress would have hazarded their reputation by the
avowal of similar doctrines. Twenty-three years previously, as
the reader has already been informed, General Gaines gave to
the War Department notice that " fugitives and outlaws had taken
" possession of a fort on the Appalachicola River."   Twenty-two
years previously, he had detailed General Clinch, with his regiment
and five hundred Creek warriors, to destroy " Blount's Fort," and
take the fugitive slaves and return them to their owners.   He had
only two years previously gone to Florida, marched into the Indian
Territory, and fought them bravely for several days.   He now saw
these Exiles and Indians in a different situation.   He witnessed
their attachment to each other as parents and children, as husbands
and wives, as members of the human family, and his sympathy
was aroused — his humanity was awakened.   His finer feelings being called forth, he possessed the firmness, the independence, to
act according to the dictates of his conscience and judgment.[1]

(1) Several years after this transaction, the Author happened to meet this war-worn veteran, and as the old hero recounted this incident of his life with warm and glowing eloquence, his eye kindled, his countenance lighted up with pleasure, and he spoke of it with
more apparent satisfaction than he ever referred to his most brilliant military achievement.

He assumed the responsibility of paying costs and damages, caused himself to be made defendant in the case, and, having obtained a rule on the sheriff to show cause why the negroes should not be delivered as prisoners of war to him, as commander of that Military District, he appeared in person at the bar of the court, and ably vindicated the rights of Government, of himself, and of the prisoners.

"The laws (said he) of the United States authorize the late and " existing war against the Seminole nation of Indians, and against " all persons in their service. The negroes claimed by the plaintiff " were found in the service of the Indians, speaking the same " language, and, like the inhabitants of all savage nations, aiding " and assisting in the war. They were captured and taken by the " United States forces *as prisoners of war*, and they are now in " charge of a United States officer, Lieutenant Reynolds, acting " pursuant to the orders of the President of the United States, " directing him to superintend their transportation from the theatre " of war in Florida, to a place set apart for their location, west of " the State of Arkansas, *as prisoners of war*, as well as servants " of the Seminole Indians, who are also *prisoners of war*.

"The laws of war, as embraced in the works of Brynkershoeck, " Vattel and Wheaton, clearly sanction the principle, that all per- " sons taken in battle, or who may be forced to surrender, whether " officers, soldiers, or followers of the enemy's army, *are prisoners* " *of war*. * * *

"Among savage nations, it is universally known and admitted, " that in war they have no *non-combatants*, excepting only such as " are physically incapable of wielding arms. Every man, without " regard to age or color; every boy able to fire a gun, or wield a " hatchet, or an arrow, is a *warrior*. And every woman is a " laborer, in the collection and preparation of subsistence and " clothing for the warriors: all are therefore liable, when captured " in a state of hostility, to be treated *as prisoners of war*."

He declared himself "lawlessly taxed with this investigation,

14

" and lawlessly threatened with heavy damages and costs, and
" forced to be defendant, without any legal or rational grounds of
" action against him. I am (said he) authorized, in virtue of my
" official station as Major General, commanding the Western Divis-
" ion of the Army of the United States of America, to serve them
" honestly and faithfully against their enemies and opposers, whom-
" soever, and to obey the orders of the President of the United
" States, etc. Under this official pledge, I deem it my duty to
" afford every officer of the army whatever facilities may be neces-
" sary and proper, to enable them to perform whatever duty is
" confided to them by the President of the United States. In pur-
" suance of this authority, I ordered Major Clark to furnish trans-
" portation, for enabling Lieutenant Reynolds, and the officers on
" duty with him, to convey the prisoners of war to the place of their
" destination in the Western Country.

" But it seems that the counsel for the claimant has flattered
" himself that I should make the most convenient and accommo-
" dating defendant imaginable. I was expected to take *the respon-*
" *sibility* of doing whatever the voracious claimant might desire,
" without coming into this honorable court. I take leave to apprise
" the court, for the benefit of all concerned, that I have never
" hesitated to assume the responsibility of *doing my duty*, or of
" doing *justice;* but I have not yet learned, while acting in my
" official capacity on oath, to take the responsibility of doing that
" which is *repugnant to law, unjust* and *iniquitous,* as I verily
" believe any favor shown to this claim would be.

" The court appears to labor under the impression, that the
" negroes in question were captured by the Seminole Indians, in
" the course of their hostile incursions upon our frontier inhabitants.
" *Is this the fact?* I will assume, for the learned counsel of the
" claimant, that he *will never have the temerity to assert that they*
" *are among the number taken from our frontier inhabitants in*
" *the present, or in any former war.*"

The gallant General, as well as some other well informed officers, appears to have been conscious of the real character of these Exiles, as will have been noticed in his last remark, assuring the court, that they were *never captured from the white people* "in the pres ent, or in *any former war.*"

The ground which he assumed, that the captives were prisoners of war, subject to the orders of the Executive, was so self-evidently true that it could not be met or overthrown, by reason or by argu ment.

His honor the Judge, in delivering his opinion discharging the rule, disregarded all claims to right on the part of the Exiles. They being black, under the laws of Louisiana, were presumed to be slaves to some person ; and he spoke with exultation of the fact, that neither General Gaines nor the United States had claimed them as *slaves ;* and he declared it would be infinitely more wise and natural for the United States to hold them as lawful *prize* to the captors, than it would be to send them with the Indians to cul tivate their lands in time of peace, and swell the number of our enemies in times of war ; but, on this motion, he thought the court bound to regard the facts set forth in the plaintiff's claim as true, and he therefore discharged the rule, and made the order of seques tration absolute.

There now appeared no hope of escape for these people ; they seemed to be the sport of fortune. For more than a century they and their ancestors had set at defiance the efforts of slaveholders, assisted by Government, to reënslave them ; but they now appeared to be within the power of those who were anxious to consign them to bondage.

On the fifteenth of May, Lieutenant Reynolds, having returned to New Orleans, wrote the Commissioner of Indian Affairs, saying, " I arrived at this place from Tampa Bay yesterday ; was detained " longer than I expected to be, in consequence of the absence of " General Jessup from Fort Brooke. Arrangements are made for " the embarkation of the party for ' Fort Gibson,' with the excep· " tion of sixty-seven of the negroes, who are claimed by persons

" from Georgia. The civil authorities, I understand, require that
" these negroes be not removed. It appears that General Gaines
" presented himself as defendant, and contended, that as the negroes
" were *prisoners of war*, the civil authority had no right to wrest
" them from the Government's hands. The court however decided
" contrary, acknowledging the Indians alone as *prisoners*, and the
" negroes as the *property* of the Indians. The case will not come
" on for some time, and, deeming (from all that I can learn) that
" the claim is fraudulent, it will be necessary that they remain."

Lieutenant Reynolds was delayed until the twenty-first of May
before he was able to embark the other prisoners. One steamer left
on the nineteenth ; and on the twenty-first, he wrote the Commissioner of Indian Affairs, saying, " Thirty-one of the negroes, out
" of the sixty-seven, have been selected by the claimants. These
" negroes, I am informed, do not belong to the Indians on whom
" the claims have been made."

This opened up new hopes for those to whom the claimants admitted they had no title. There is, however, something about this
surrender which we are not able to explain. It is certain that
Lieutenant Reynolds left New Orleans on the twenty-first of May
with all the prisoners, both Indians and negroes then at that city,
except thirty-one left in charge of the sheriff, and seven Spanish
maroons, whom he discharged. The remaining thirty-one were left
in the charge of the sheriff, with the slave-catching vultures watching, and eager to fasten their talons upon them so soon as opportunity should permit. The separation was painful. Families were
again severed : parents were torn from their children, and brothers
and sisters compelled to bid adieu to each other ; and as they could
see no escape for those left at New Orleans, they regarded the separation as final.

But the other prisoners were on board. Lieutenant Reynolds
and other officers had done what they could, and they desired soon
as possible to get the hapless Exiles, who yet remained in their possession, beyond the reach of slave-hunters and slave-catchers. That

mysterious power, steam, was now applied; and rapidly the vessel was driven against the strong current of the Mississippi, as the sable passengers cast their last, lingering look toward their friends who remained behind, the victims of a tyranny—an oppression—which yet disgraces the civilization of the age in which we live. The Indians were also thoughtful and sad, as they cast their eyes back towards their beloved Florida, the scenes amidst which they had been born and reared; where they had fought; where their brethren had been slain; where their fathers rested peacefully in their graves. Many bitter sighs were heard, and many tears fell from the eyes of those prisoners as they resumed their voyage, for unknown homes in the Western Country.

CHAPTER XV.

DIFFICULTIES IN ENSLAVING EXILES CONTINUED.

Collins, Agent for the Slave-dealer, reaches Fort Pike — Prisoners gone — He repairs to New Orleans — reaches that City one day after the Exiles and Indians had left — He follows them up the River — Whole number of Prisoners on the two boats — They stop a few hours at Vicksburg — Collins overtakes them — Hands his Order to Reynolds — They consult together — Difficulty in separating Indians from Negroes — They all proceed together — Reynolds and Collins endeavor to persuade Indians to deliver over Negroes — They refuse — They reach Little Rock — Call on Governor Roane for military aid — His emphatic Answer — They proceed to Fort Gibson — Call on General Arbuckle to separate them — He refuses — Collins gives up all as lost — His Letter to Commissioner of Indian Affairs

Collins, the agent of Watson, left the City of Washington on the tenth of May with full powers to act for the Creek chiefs as well as for his principal; fully provided, also, with orders from the Commissioner of Indian Affairs, directing all officers of the United States, in whose custody the Exiles might be, to deliver them to this agent of the slave-dealer. Expecting to find his victims at Fort Pike, he repaired to that place; but on his arrival found they had left for New Orleans some days previously. He forthwith followed them, and reached that city on the twenty-second of June, being one day after Reynolds and his prisoners had left that city for Fort Gibson.

Thus it will be seen, that the efforts of General Gaines, and the active vigilance of Major Clarke and Lieutenant Reynolds, had barely succeeded in getting these people under way for their western homes, when the authority for their reënslavement arrived.

Vexed and mortified at this disappointment, Collins took passage on the first packet bound up the river, determined to secure the victims of Watson's cupidity wherever he should find them.

While Collins was thus speeding his way up the river, Reynolds and his charge, unconscious that the slave-hunter was on their track, stopped at Vicksburg for a few hours to obtain supplies for their journey. While passing up the river, Reynolds wrote a report to the Commissioner of Indian Affairs, stating that on the boat which left New Orleans on the nineteenth, six hundred and seventy-four prisoners had been placed for emigration ; that on the boat which left the twenty-first, on which he had taken passage, there were four hundred and fifty-three—making in all twelve hundred and twenty-one Indians and negroes, who were now emigrating to the Western Country. While they were lying at Vicksburg, Collins arrived, and, as he states, " succeeded in getting the order of the Commissioner of Indian Affairs handed to Reynolds." This was undoubtedly correct, for Reynolds wrote the Department the same day, saying, " Since my letter this morning, enclosing an abstract of my " muster-roll, Mr. Collins, the attorney, recognized by you, has " sent off various papers, in relation to certain claims for negroes " taken by the Creek Volunteers, and *your order has been received.* " I have therefore made arrangements with Mr. Collins to accom- " pany me to Little Rock on board of my boat, that no time may " be lost in the emigration on the passage from here thither. Due " care will be had in selecting such only as come within your order, " as also to apprise the chiefs and other Indians with regard to the " claim. The excitement evinced at New Orleans on the part of " the Indians, convinced me of the necessity of this measure. I " think that, between this and Little Rock, I will be enabled to " persuade them to consent without any resistance on their part."

As stated in this letter, Mr. Collins took passage at Vicksburg with Lieutenant Reynolds, and agreed to go on with him and his prisoners, until they could persuade the Indians to separate from their friends and companions, their wives and children, or until they could obtain a military force sufficient to compel the separation. Mr. Reynolds says that the excitement on the part of the Indians at New Orleans, had convinced him of the necessity of this measure ; and the only doubt of his perfect sincerity rests on the assertion, that he thought he could, while on the voyage, induce the Indians to *consent to such separation.*

On the twenty-seventh, they left Vicksburg for Fort Gibson. While on their passage, they had full opportunity to deliberate and consult together as to the best mode of carrying out the plan of transforming this small portion of mankind into property; but the universal laws of Nature and of Nature's God appeared to conflict with this slave-dealing theory. While on the passage up the river, Mr. Reynolds assembled the Indian chiefs and warriors, and laid before them the facts concerning the claim of Watson, and, as he says, "explained every thing calculated to appease them." But the result we give in his own words, expressed in a letter dated at Little Rock, Arkansas, June second, being one week after they left Vicksburg, in which he says : "They (the Indians) at once demurred : Micanopy " taking the lead, saying, it was contrary to the express words of " General Jessup, and would listen to nothing calculated to dis- " possess them of their negroes. Finding them thus determined, I " prevented any communication with them on the subject until " reaching this place, when they were again called together, and I " repeated all that had been mentioned to them before. I told them " it was needless to object ; my orders were positive, and must be " obeyed. All was of no use ; they became, if anything, more " vexed than before, and left me much exasperated. Mr. Collins " witnessed my exertions to carry out your instructions ; indeed, " sir, I have been excessively perplexed with these Indians and " negroes. I see no method in the absence of force by which pos- " session of the negroes can be had. The authorities here show a " decided inclination to protect the Indians, and there is no doubt " every attempt will fail on our part. I have in no instance acted " with duplicity. The statements made, have been as they actually

" exist. Thirty-one of the number left at New Orleans are on the " official list handed me by Mr. Collins."

The whole party were detained several days at Little Rock in consequence of the low stage of water. While waiting here, Collins appears to have become impatient, and anxious to get possession of the negroes. Indeed, from the closing remark of Mr. Reynolds's letter, last quoted, we are led to suspect that little sympathy existed between Reynolds and this agent of the slave-dealer; nor is it unlikely that an officer, bred up in the cultivation of a high and chivalrous sense of honor, would feel some repugnance at being constrained to associate with any man employed in the business which brought Collins to the Western Country. Knowing, however, that the Executive of the United States had become in fact a party in this disreputable transaction, he endeavored to manifest at least a respect for those officers of Government who had become participants in it.

On the third of June, Lieutenant Reynolds addressed an official letter to Samuel C. Roane, Governor of Arkansas, stating the circumstances in which he was placed. He set forth the claim of the Creeks, and their sale to Watson, together with the fact that Collins was then at Little Rock, anxious to obtain possession of the negroes; that he (Reynolds) could not deliver them to Collins without assistance, and on that account demanded of his Excellency assistance of the civil authority to aid him in carrying out the policy of the Federal Government.

Here again the workings of the human heart, and the laws of human nature, cast insurmountable obstacles in the way of carrying out the Executive designs. True, Arkansas was a slave State, and her Governor was a slaveholder, characterized by that bold and generous nature which usually distinguishes the pioneers of the West; but his letter breathes such a spirit of independence, such a bold and unhesitating regard for justice and propriety, that we prefer to let his Excellency speak for himself. The letter is couched in the following language :

"Executive Office,
"*Little Rock*, June 4th, 1838.

"Sir: Your note of this day has been duly received, in which
"you call on me as the Executive of the State of Arkansas to fur-
"nish you military force, sufficient to coerce obedience to your in-
"structions to surrender a number of negroes, now with the Semi-
"nole Indians under your command ; and stating that the Indians
"manifest a hostile determination not to permit the negroes in ques-
"tion to be surrendered to the agent or attorney of the Creek In-
"dians.   I have also examined the copies of the order from the
"War Department, directed to you on this subject, as well as the
"schedule of the negroes and letter of attorney, in the possession of
"Mr. N. F. Collins, the Creek agent or attorney, to receive the
"negroes in controversy.   After due reflection on the subject, I
"have determined not to afford you any assistance to carry these
"instructions into effect, and respectfully request of you not to
"attempt to turn over those negroes to the claimants within the
"State of Arkansas, and more especially in the neighborhood of
"Little Rock.   And *I require of you to proceed* with your com-
"mand of Indians and *negroes* to their place of destination with
"the least practicable delay, that the citizens of Little Rock and its
"vicinity may be relieved from the annoyance of a hostile band of
"Indians and *savage negroes.*

" Without prejudging the claim of the Creek Indians to the
"negroes, from the nature of things it is wholly impracticable for
"the claimants to make a proper designation of the negroes claimed.
" *There are no witnesses here that can identify the negroes* — not
"even the person setting up the claim.   And had the Government
"intended to dispose of those negroes to the Creek Indians, it
"should have been done in Florida, and not bring Indians and
"negroes into Arkansas, the vicinity of their future residence, and
"then *irritate* the Indians to madness, and turn them loose on our
"frontier, where we have no adequate protection — the massacre of
"our citizens would be the inevitable consequence.

"I have just visited the chiefs of your command, and assured
"them that their negroes should not be taken from them, and they
"have pledged themselves that their people should go on to their
"country peaceably. Your immediate departure will insure peace
"and avert the outrages you had such good cause to expect.

"You will transmit this note to the proper Department at Wash
"ington as a justification of the course you may pursue in accord-
"ance with it.

"I am, respectfully,
"Your obedient servant,
"JNO. G. REYNOLDS,   SAM. C. ROANE.
"1st Lieut. U. S. M. C., and Disb'g Agent, Ind. Dep't."

This letter of Governor Roane certainly indicated to Mr. Collins
a strong repugnance to the policy adopted by the War Department,
and must have convinced him that his mission was, at least, un-
popular among men removed from the moral atmosphere in which
the Executive appeared to live. We are not informed of its effects
upon Mr. Reynolds; but that gentleman could not have been very
greatly disappointed, as he had clearly predicted the failure of all
attempts to separate the Indians and negroes.

A rise in the Arkansas River enabled them to resume their journey. They reached Fort Gibson on the twelfth of June, and both
Indians and negroes were turned over to the care of Captain Ste-
phenson, the agent appointed to reside with the Western Seminoles.
Here Mr. Reynolds and Mr. Collins expected to make a final effort
to separate the Indians and negroes, in order that the latter might
be transported back to that interminable slavery which all knew
awaited their return to Georgia. For this purpose, Lieutenant
Reynolds addressed Brigadier General Arbuckle, in command at
Fort Gibson; but, as the correspondence between these officers
brought the important mission of Mr. Collins in that Western
Country to a close, we will present these letters to the reader.

On the twelfth of June, the day of his arrival, Lieutenant Reynolds addressed General Arbuckle the following note:

" GENERAL : I herewith enclose orders, received from the Com-
" missioner of Indian Affairs, for the surrender of a certain number
" of negroes, belonging to the Seminole Indians, to Mr. N. F.
" Collins, the attorney appointed by the Creek Delegation which
" recently visited Washington, which appointment has been ratified
" by the Department ; and feeling myself bound to turn over all in
" my possession, in obedience to such orders, and the Seminole
" chiefs and Indians refusing *positively* to give them up, I have to
" request the employment of such a force, General, as you may
" deem *adequate* for carrying into effect my instructions.

"I am, General, very respectfully,

" Your obedient servant,

"JNO. G. REYNOLDS,

"*1st Lieut. U. S. M. C., and Disb'g Agent, Ind. Dept.*

" General M. ARBUCKLE,

" Commanding, etc., Fort Gibson."

General Arbuckle was in command of the military forces of the
United States in that Western Country, and of course felt great
responsibility in regard to maintaining peaceful relations with the
Indians of that region. Having maturely reflected upon the communication of Mr. Reynolds, he returned the following answer :

"HEAD QUARTERS WESTERN DEPARTMENT, THIRD DIVISION, }
Fort Gibson, June 13th, 1838. }

" SIR : I have received your letter of the 12th instant, with the
" papers accompanying it, in which you request me to furnish such
" a force as I deem adequate, to enable you to turn over a number
" of negroes that were captured by the Creek warriors in Florida,
" to Nathaniel F. Collins, their attorney.

" I have given your application much reflection, and have deter-
" mined to decline a compliance therewith for the following reasons:

" First. The difficulty and uncertainty of identifying the negroes
" actually captured by the Creek warriors, who are now with their
" former owners, and in company with a large number of other
" Indian negroes, and there being no individual of character present
" (as far as I am informed) who could with certainty designate

" them. Secondly. The Seminole chiefs positively declare that
" General Jessup promised that the negroes taken from them by
" the Creek warriors should be returned; and there is reason to
" believe that such a promise was made, other than the declaration
" of the chiefs.

"In addition to the above, it is proper that I should state, that
" the Seminole chiefs, at the council I held with them yesterday,
" voluntarily pledged themselves to give up the negroes in question,
" provided the President of the United States should, after being
" informed of the facts in the case, so decide; yet they state that
" many of the negroes have died, and that several are claimed to
" have been captured that were brought in by their owners when
" they surrendered.

"I am, Sir, very respectfully,

"Your obedient servant,

"M. ARBUCKLE,

Brevet Brigadier General, Commanding.

"J. G. REYNOLDS,

"1st Lieut. U. S. M. C., and Disb'g Agent, Ind. Dept."

Collins now gave up all as lost. He appears to have realized,
that almost every officer of the army west of Florida, had conspired
against this policy of enslaving the Exiles, while he himself seemed
to entertain no doubt of the honor and rectitude of his own position;
and in order to do him justice, and render our narrative brief as
consistent, we here insert so much of his report to the Commissioner
of Indian Affairs, drawn up after his return to Alabama, as relates
to his mission up to the time of leaving Fort Gibson, on his return.
It is as follows:

"TUSKOGEE, ALABAMA, July 29, 1838.

"SIR: Immediately after my arrival (about the first of this
" month), I was taken sick with the fever, from which I am just
" recovering, which will account for the delay in communicating
" the result of my mission to procure the Seminole negroes that
" were to have been turned over to me, as agent of the Creek
" Indians.

"I left Washington on the 10th of May, and arrived in New
"Orleans on the 22d, the day after Lieutenant Reynolds had left
"there with the Indians and all the negroes, except thirty-two that
"were detained by the civil authority, at the instance of Love. I
"did not overtake Reynolds until he arrived at Vicksburg, when,
"after some exertion, I succeeded in having his order handed to
"him; and he came ashore, and suggested the probability of his
"being able to induce the Indians to consent to deliver the negroes
"willingly (between thirty-five and forty of which, by a comparison
"of our lists, we found he had in his possession), if I would go on
"board and proceed up the river with him. This I acceded to, as
"I was anxious to pursue such a course as would tend, ever so
"remotely, to conciliate the Indians, and harmonize with the views
"of the officer in charge. The experience of a day or two however
"proved that these calculations were erroneous, and I went on to
"Little Rock, to get a force to coerce their delivery. On our
"arrival there, Lieutenant R. called upon the acting Governor of
"Arkansas for assistance ; *but from some cause or other* he refused
"it, as will be seen by the correspondence forwarded you by Lieu-
"tenant R. I then proceeded with the party to Fort Gibson,
"calculating certainly on being able to obtain the necessary assist-
"ance at that place. Lieutenant R., on arriving within three
"miles of the fort, landed one of the boats, and proceeded with the
"other (having all the negroes and some Indians) directly to the
"fort, and made known to General Arbuckle the situation of the
"affair, and presented him with all the papers. He held a lengthy
"interview with the Seminole chiefs, in which the various talks
"and promises of General Jessup were detailed, the number and
"identity of the negroes denied, and the validity of the whole trans-
"action questioned, etc. ; and hence the conclusion, as he had
"received no order in relation to the negroes, he should not inter-
"fere ; and directed Lieutenant R. to land them with the In-
"dians. First, however, to conclude the farce, he exacted from
"each chief separately the promise, *if the President should decide*

" *that the negroes should be given up*, that they would deliver them
" to him., This of course they promised ; any explanation or re-
" monstrance urged by me was unavailing."

CHAPTER XVI.

FURTHER DIFFICULTIES IN THE WORK OF ENSLAVING THE EXILES.

General Gaines in person defends those left at New Orleans — He appeals from the judgment — Effect of appeal — Authorities at Washington informed of difficulties — General Jessup retires from the command — General Taylor succeeds him — He refuses to follow policy of General Jessup — Recognizes no prisoners as slaves — Letter from Adjutant General — He promptly refuses to have any thing to do in Watson's slave-dealing transaction — This indignant answer is received without reply by Department — Other persons claim the Exiles detained at New Orleans — Commissioner driven to the necessity of declaring correct law on the subject — Same as that avowed by General Gaines, by General Taylor, and by Hon. J. Q. Adams — Claim of Colonel Humphreys for slaves — Jessup's answer — Reynolds returns from Fort Gibson to New Orleans — Collins reaches the city same day — Inquires as to the situation of the thirty-one Exiles left there — Is referred to Major Clark — Clark's answer — Collins leaves city in disgust — His Letter to Secretary of War charging Reynolds with misconduct — Exiles remaining at New Orleans are delivered to Reynolds — Are sent to Fort Gibson — Join their friends — All are left however without permanent homes or lands — Intention of the Administration to compel them to unite with the Creeks — They refuse — Cherokees tender them lands — They settle upon Cherokee territory.

AFTER the emigrating company of Indians and Exiles had left
1838.] New Orleans, under charge of Lieutenant Reynolds, Gen'l
Gaines assumed upon himself the whole responsibility of
defending the thirty-one who remained in that city; for as yet there
had been no trial upon the merits of the case, although it was pretty
evident that the judge was strongly impressed in favor of reënslaving
them. The cause was duly brought to a hearing, and, after argument
and consideration, the court gave judgment in favor of the claimants.

This was no more than had been expected   General Gaines,
faithful to his own convictions of justice, took an appeal to a higher

(224)

tribunal; and this appeal rendered it necessary for the court to fix a time within which the claimants should enter bail for costs and damages, or the negroes would be delivered up to General Gaines by the sheriff.

In the meantime, the Executive officers at Washington had become informed of the difficulties which had lain across the path of Mr. Collins, and felt it to be desirable that the whole matter should be arranged with as little discussion as possible.

General Jessup retired from the command of the army in Florida on the fifteenth of May, and returned to Washington, leaving General Zachary Taylor as commander-in-chief of our military forces in that Territory. He had shown himself prompt in the execution of all orders; cool, deliberate, and firm in battle; faithful to his men, to himself and his country; but, up to this time, he had manifested no particular zeal in the capture of negroes. Indeed, although he had penetrated farther into the Indian Country than any other officer — had fought the bloodiest battles of any commander in Florida, yet he refused to draw any distinctions among his prisoners. With him Indians and negroes were equally *prisoners of war*, and entitled to the same treatment. Nor would he listen to men who professed to own the persons whom he captured, or who had surrendered themselves as prisoners.

The Administration having been a party in the sale to Watson, determined to carry out the slave-dealing arrangement with him; at least so far as regarded the thirty-one negroes who yet remained in New Orleans. In order to effect this object, it was deemed necessary to have the coöperation and aid of General Taylor. The Adjutant General, therefore, addressed him on the subject, enclosing to him the letter of the Commissioner of Indian Affairs, dated the ninth of May, addressed to the Secretary of War, and heretofore referred to. General Taylor evidently thought the honor of the service would be compromited by this slave-dealing transaction. He subsequently became President of the United States; and as the reader will feel anxious to understand precisely the views which he

15

entertained, we give that portion of his letter to the Adjutant General which relates to this subject. It is in the following words:

"I have the honor to acknowledge your communication of the
"tenth of May, 1838, accompanied by one of the ninth from the
"Commissioner of Indian Affairs, addressed to Captain Cooper,
"Acting Secretary of War, on the subject of turning over certain
"negroes, captured by the Creek warriors in Florida, to a Mr. Col-
"lins, their agent, in compliance with an engagement of General
"Jessup.

"I know nothing of the negroes in question, nor of the subject,
"further than what is contained in the communication above re-
"ferred to ; *but I must state distinctly for the information of all
"concerned, that, while I shall hold myself ever ready to do the
"utmost in my power to get the Indians and their negroes out of
"Florida, as well as to remove them to their new homes west of
"the Mississippi*, I CANNOT FOR A MOMENT CONSENT TO MEDDLE
"WITH THIS TRANSACTION, *or to be concerned for the benefit of Col-
"lins, the Creek Indians, or any one else.*"

This language was received at the War Department without
reproof, although the Secretary was from South Carolina, bred
up in the chivalrous doctrines of the Palmetto State. He quietly
suffered a Brigadier General thus plainly to express his contempt
for this slave-dealing transaction, in which not only the War Department, but the President of the United States, was involved.
He appears to have been willing to encounter almost any kind of
disrespect, rather than call public attention to the subject.

In the meantime other claims were presented to the Department
for those Exiles, or portions of those, who had been captured by
the Creeks.[1] Gad Humphreys filed with the Secretary of War a
list of forty-seven slaves who had fled from him in 1830, stating

---

(1) Vide Letter of Major Isaac Clark to Commissioner of Indian Affairs, Sept. 18, 1838.
Ex. Doc. 225, 3d Sess. XXVth Congress.

that they had gone to the Seminoles, and that a part of them had been sent to Fort Pike.

Colonel Humphreys appeared to regard himself as entitled to the possession of those people; although by the treaty of Payne's Landing the Seminoles had paid for all slaves residing with them prior to 1832; and had been released from all further demands on account of such slaves.

Colonel Humphreys stated that his claim had been examined by the late agent, General Wiley Thompson, and decided *against* him; but insisted that the decision was wrong, and avowed his ability to show it erroneous by proper proof whenever he should have an opportunity, and again demanded that the slaves should be brought back to Florida, where he could present his proof without trouble. This letter was inclosed in one directed to Mr. Downing, Delegate in Congress from Florida, and by him transmitted to the Secretary of War, and by that officer referred to the Commissioner of Indian Affairs. Thus driven to the wall, the Commissioner of Indian Affairs came out in plain and unmistakable language, asserting the doctrine, that the Government held the power and constitutional right to dispose of prisoners taken in war, whatever their character may be. This doctrine had been eloquently sustained by General Gaines, on the trial in New Orleans. It was the doctrine avowed by Hon. John Quincy Adams in the House of Representatives, during the next session of Congress; but it called down upon him much abuse in that body, and in the Democratic papers of the country. The Commissioner's report to the Secretary of War set forth in distinct language, that the claims of individuals to slaves were precluded by the action of the Government in sending these people West; that they had been captured by the army and disposed of by the Executive, and the action of the Department could not be changed in consequence of individuals claiming them as slaves. In short, he repeated the doctrine advanced by General Gaines at New Orleans. The report also confirmed the policy of General Taylor in disregarding the claims of individuals to persons captured by the army, and was a tacit condemnation of that pursued by General Jessup, and previously sanctioned by the Secretary of War. This report was passed over to the Secretary.

That officer (Mr. Poinsett) having received this report, transmitted it to Colonel Humphreys. This drew from that gentleman a still more elaborate argument in favor of his claim, which occupies nearly four heavy pages in documentary form. This was also transmitted to Mr. Downing, and by him passed over to the Secretary of War; but we are not informed whether the Secretary of War replied to this second argument or not.

It is, however, important to the truth of history to notice this recognition of the doctrine by a slave-holding Secretary of War, that the Executive in time of war may separate slaves from their masters, and send them out of the country, without regard to the relation previously subsisting between them and their owners. The principle was thus recognized by Mr. Poinsett, although a citizen of South Carolina, acting under the advice and direction of Mr. Van Buren, a Democratic President of the United States.

General Jessup also, in a report to the War Department, declared, that, in his opinion, the treaty of Payne's Landing exonerated the Indians from all claims for slaves which accrued prior to that date, and that Colonel Humphreys and other claimants could only demand a proportion of the seven thousand dollars allowed by the Indians for slaves then residing among them. This suggestion was obviously just, and was approved by the Secretary of War; and we are naturally led to inquire, why the same obviously just rule was not applied to some hundreds of other cases precisely like that of Colonel Humphreys?

In the meantime, Lieutenant Reynolds having accomplished his mission, so far as the emigration of the captives shipped on board the two boats which left New Orleans on the nineteenth and twenty-first of May were concerned, returned to that city in order to complete the duties assigned him in regard to the thirty-one prisoners who had been detained there by legal sequestration. Collins, faithful to the trust reposed in him, also returned to New Orleans with the full purpose of securing those people as slaves to Watson. They reached the city on the twenty-third, and found the slaves still in the possession of the Sheriff; as the time assigned by the court within which the plaintiff was to enter bail had not expired.

On the twenty-fifth of June, Mr. Collins addressed a note to Mr. Reynolds, inquiring whether there had been any decision of the court upon the claim of Love to the Seminole negroes left at that place; and what number he (Reynolds) was satisfied belonged to the Creek Indians; and demanding that such as belonged to them should be delivered to him, under the order of the Commissioner of "Indian Affairs."

Mr. Reynolds replied that he understood the case had been dismissed; but as he (Reynolds) was then acting under a superior officer (Major Clark), he would refer Mr. Collins to him.

On the following day, Collins addressed Major Clark on the subject; but receiving no answer, and becoming vexed and disgusted with the business, he left the city on the twenty-seventh for his home in Alabama. In justice to Mr. Collins, we let him speak for himself, and quote the remainder of his report to the Commissioner of Indian Affairs, being that portion which relates to his efforts to get possession of these thirty-one Exiles. It reads as follows:

"On arriving at New Orleans on my return, I found the repre-
"sentatives of Love had withdrawn their claim against those thirty-
"two negroes that were left there, thirty-one of which Lieutenant R.
"expressed himself satisfied belonged to the claim. I addressed a
"note to Lieutenant R. requesting that such of the negroes as he
"was satisfied of the identity might be turned over to me; he in
"turn referred me to Major Clark who was his senior officer, and
"who had received similar instructions to his own. I had, in com-
"pany with Lieutenant R. the day before, called upon Major Clark,
"and learned his determination in relation to the negroes. He did
"not recognize the validity of his order, inasmuch as 'By order

" of the Secretary of War' did not precede your signature, and
" had even the hardihood to state, that, by an examination of the
" lists, none of those negroes in New Orleans were embraced in
" the claim I presented, and subsequently ordered Lieutenant Rey-
" nolds to send the negroes forthwith to Arkansas.   After I saw a
" settled and determined purpose to thwart me there as well as
" elsewhere, I left New Orleans on the next day for this place, and
" since my arrival here, I have learned by a letter from Lieutenant
" Reynolds, that the negroes were sent off the next day after I left.

    " Captain Morrison I did not see.   Not perhaps being as fruitful
" in expedients as some others of them, he stopped at Fort Jack-
" son, and sent to New Orleans for transportation outfit, etc., and
" passed the city on his way up, without but few knowing who he
" was, or anything else in relation to him.   I learned indirectly
" from Major Clark, (who probably did not intend this admission
" for me,) that he had between twenty and thirty of the negroes on
" board belonging to this claim.

" I am, sir, with the highest respect,

" Yours, etc.,

" C. A. Harris, Esq.,   N. F. COLLINS.
    " Comm'r Indian Affairs, Washington, D. C."

It is most obvious that Collins believed that the military officers
of Government, who were serving at a distance from Washington,
viewed his mission with no particular favor, and he evidently retired
from New Orleans with some degree of indignation.

In the meantime, the claimant Love, despairing of obtaining the
negroes, refused to enter bail for costs and damages, in case the
suit should be determined against him in the higher court, and the
sheriff delivered them over to Mr. Reynolds on the same day that
Collins left the city.   On the next day, Mr. Reynolds wrote the
Commissioner of Indian Affairs, saying, " The thirty-one negroes
" who were arrested, seized from me and lodged in the jail of this
" city, were last evening surrendered to me.   The Creek attorney
" (N. F. Collins, Esq.) nor any authorized agent being present,

" and not wishing to detain them at the expense of the Government,
" they were immediately embarked and dispatched West, with
" twenty-five days' provisions, under the charge of Assistant Con-
" ductor Benjamin, who, to satisfy the Indians, had been left with
" the negroes at the period of the service of the process; of which
" fact I informed the Department at the time."

These thirty-one prisoners who had been thus detained, were now
once more under way for their western home. Their hearts appeared to beat more freely as the noble steamer, which bore them
on their way to their friends and future homes, cut loose from her
moorings and sped her way toward her destined port. On board
that happy craft, also, were many smiles and hearty congratulations
exchanged among those children of the forest, who had been borne
along on the tide of ever-varying circumstances. Although helpless and penniless, and apparently friendless, they had almost
miraculously escaped the meshes which our Government and the
slave-dealers had spread for their destruction. In due time they
reached Fort Gibson, and were delivered over to the care of the
proper agent, who conducted them to their friends. And now
some nine hundred Seminoles, and some three to four hundred
Exiles, had reached the Indian Country; they constituted the first
party of that nation who, driven from their homes — their native
wilds — had consented to be taken to a strange land.

They had been assured by General Jessup and all officers who
spoke for the Government, that the treaty of Payne's Landing was
to be complied with. To enforce that treaty had been the order of
General Jackson. General Cass had declared that the *Indians
must comply with that treaty;* while, to our Indian agents, he
asserted it to be the policy of the Government to *unite the Creeks
and Seminoles as one people.*

But the Indians and Exiles were constantly assured, that they
were to have a tract of country set off to their separate use; and
when they entered into the articles of capitulation with General
Jessup, on the eighteenth of March, 1837, that officer, on behalf

of the United States, had stipulated to protect the Indians and "their allies" in the enjoyment of their lives and property.

But now the turpitude and guilt of the Executive were revealed. The orders of the agent directed him to take them on to the territory assigned to the Creeks. This would subject them to Creek jurisdiction and Creek laws; and they were perfectly conscious that every Exile would be immediately enslaved. Yet there was no country which they could call their own. The perfidious pretense of enforcing the treaty of Payne's Landing, without giving them a separate territory according to the supplemental treaty, now stood exposed in its proper light. Abraham was a man of influence with his brethren. He had used his utmost efforts to induce them to emigrate. He had been honest. He believed in the integrity of our nation, of its people, its government; but his error had been fatal. The Exiles were in the Western Country, without a home, and with no means of support, except the stipulation of Government to furnish them provisions for one year.

It was at this time, when a Christian government had violated its faith, most solemnly pledged, in order to enslave a people who for ages had been free, that a Pagan government performed towards the Exiles and Seminoles the Christian duty, the hospitality, of furnishing them temporary homes. The Cherokees had volunteered to exert their influence with the Indians and Exiles in favor of peace. They had induced many of them to come into the American camp under flags of truce which had been violated, and their persons seized, held prisoners, and sent West. They had themselves, apparently, been involved in this treachery practiced by our Government, and, under these circumstances, they consented to share their own possessions with the Seminoles and Exiles until further arrangements were made; they consented to have the Seminoles and Exiles settle on their land for the present, until the Government could be induced to fulfill its most sacred compacts with these victims of slaveholding persecutions.

CHAPTER XVII.

THE Indians and Exiles who had emigrated, now found themselves separated at the distance of more than a thousand
1838.] miles from their brethren in Florida, with whom they
could hold no intercourse. They were without a country—without
permanent homes—residing upon the lands of the Cherokees, at
the mere sufferance of that Tribe, whose humanity had been awakened, and whose sympathy had been extended to them. Their
situation and discontent were duly communicated to the Executive;
but it appears to have been regarded as of too little importance to
receive attention.

But while the President and the War Department disregarded
all complaints coming from the Seminoles and Exiles, they relaxed
no effort to secure Watson in the possession of the ninety human
beings whom he had purchased of the Creek Indians, at the request
of the Executive.

As the last resort, instructions were sent to General Arbuckle,
commanding in the West, to make investigations, and ascertain

what more could be done for the reënslavement of those people.
That officer replied to this communication as follows:

"HEAD QUARTERS 2D DEPARTMENT, WESTERN DIVISION,}
Fort Gibson, Aug. 27th, 1838.   }

"SIR: I had the honor, on the 22d instant, to receive your in-
"structions of the 21st ultimo, together with the papers to which
"they refer. I extremely regret that the United States is liable to
"suffer loss in consequence of the Creek warriors having sold, and
"received pay, for the negroes they captured from the Seminole
"Indians in Florida; and these negroes having been imprudently
"returned to the possession of their former owners at New Orleans,
"and brought to this place, with two hundred or more other ne-
"groes belonging to the Seminoles. Owing to these transactions, it
"would be extremely difficult, if not impossible, to identify at most
"but few of them; and from the present position of this case, it is
"not probable *that one of the negroes will be obtained except by
"force.* For further information in relation to this subject, I beg
"leave to refer you to my letter to Captain Armstrong, Acting
"Superintendent of the Western Territory, of this date, a copy of
"which is herewith enclosed. I shall do all in my power to pre-
"vent loss to the Government, and will at an early period have
"the honor to advise you of the measures taken in the case.

"I have the honor to be, Sir, with great respect,
"Your obedient servant,
"M. ARBUCKLE,
"Hon. J. R. POINSETT,   *Brevet Brig. Gen'l, U. S. A.*
"Secretary of War."

The letter to Captain Armstrong, Superintendent of the Western
Territory, was as follows:

"HEAD QUARTERS 2D DEPARTMENT, WESTERN DIVISION,}
Fort Gibson, Aug. 27, 1838.   }

"SIR: I received by the last mail, from the honorable the Sec-
"retary of War, a communication under date of the 21st ultimo,
"on the subject of the negroes captured by the Creek warriors,
"together with a letter from the Commissioner of Indian Affairs to

" the Secretary of War, under date of the 19th ultimo, relating to
" this subject, copies of which are herewith enclosed. All other
" papers or transactions in relation to this matter, it is presumed,
" you are apprized of. It will be seen by the communication first
" referred to, that it was not known at Washington, at the date of
" that letter, that the Creek warriors had been paid for the negroes.
" That circumstance, however just to the warriors and proper, so
" far as you have had an agency in the affair, will increase the
" difficulty of obtaining the negroes, as it is believed the Creek
" warriors will not now give themselves any trouble to have the
" negroes delivered to the individuals to whom they sold them.
" And notwithstanding the pledge of the Seminole chiefs to me, to
" surrender the negroes in the event the Government should so
" require (after reconsidering their claim to them), I do not be-
" lieve they will comply with their promise, with the knowledge
" that the negroes are to be taken from this country as the servants
" of a white man. Finally, as the Seminoles are greatly under the
" influence of their negroes, there is scarcely a hope that the cap-
" tured negroes will be surrendered without the application of force
" (which is not required) ; and, in that event, it is not probable
" they could be had, as they would no doubt run away the moment
" they are informed a military force is to be employed to take them.
" And in such case, it is believed, they would be assisted, when
" necessary, by most of the Seminoles, and by all the Seminole and
" Creek negroes ; and if the captured negroes could be placed in
" the possession of the Creek agent, he would not detain them a
" moment without he had a suitable guard for that purpose. I
" am therefore of the opinion, that the best means that can now be
" resorted to, to prevent loss to the United States, is, if possible,
" to induce the Seminoles to refund, from their annuity, the sum
" paid to the Creek warriors for the negroes, and the interest on
" the same until paid. I will be much gratified if you can visit
" this post in six or eight days, when the Seminole chiefs can be
" assembled here, with the object of inducing them to agree to the

" measure proposed, or such other as may be deemed advisable.
" In the event that it may not be convenient for you to be at this
" post at an early period, I request that you will favor me with
" your views on the subject of this communication by the return of
" mail.

" I am, Sir, with much respect,
" Your obedient servant,
" M. ARBUCKLE,

" Capt. W. ARMSTRONG,   *Brevet Brig. Gen'l, U. S. A.*
" Acting Sup't W. Ter., Choctaw Agency."

This correspondence might well have concluded the efforts of the
Executive to deliver these ninety Exiles to the slave-dealer. It
were unnecessary to say, that General Arbuckle's labors in this behalf proved useless. He had foretold such failure in his letter to
the War Department. In January, 1837, the Creek warriors captured these people, and for almost two years the influence of the
Executive had been exerted to enslave them; but a series of incidents, unequaled in real life, had constantly succeeded each other,
preventing the consummation of this intended crime; yet the slave
power was inexorable in its demands.

These circumstances failed to convince the President that it was
useless for the Executive of a great nation to contend against the
plainest dictates of justice; against those convictions of right which
dwell in the breast of every human being who has not extinguished
the moral feelings of his nature.

Collins having returned to his plantation in Alabama, deliberately
drew up and transmitted his report to the Commissioner of Indian
Affairs, which we have heretofore quoted. But when he was subsequently informed that the thirty-two Exiles who were in the hands
of the Sheriff at New Orleans had, on the day of his leaving that
city, been delivered over to Reynolds, and sent West, his indignation was further excited, and he immediately wrote the Commissioner of Indian Affairs again more distinctly charging the officers
engaged in the emigration of these people with bad faith. He
wrote as follows:

"MONTGOMERY, ALABAMA, Aug. 8, 1838.

" SIR : Since writing you a week since, I have understood that
" Lieutenant Reynolds has informed you that on his arrival in New
" Orleans the negroes that were detained there had been surren-
" dered to him, and that, in consequence of my not being there,
" they were sent off to, etc. After seeing so much duplicity and
" management as has been manifested by the officers with whom
" I have recently had intercourse, particularly Lieutenant R., I am
" not surprised at the above statement. Lieutenant R. is well
" apprised that the negroes had been turned over to him while I
" was in New Orleans; and it is also susceptible of proof that
" during my stay there arrrangements were privately making to
" charter a boat to transport them. After I learned this, I pur-
" posely threw myself in his way ; but he said not a word to me in
" relation to the negroes, until I addressed him the note which is
" herewith enclosed. After receiving his answer, I, in his presence,
" addressed the enclosed copy to Major Clark ; but before I had
" procured a messenger to carry it to Major C., Lieutenant R.,
" after being a short time absent from the room, returned, and in-
" formed me he had seen the Sheriff, and he had refused to turn
" over the negroes to him, which rendered it, as I conceived, un-
" necessary to send the note to Major C. After my return home,
" he wrote that (the next day after I left it seems) the Sheriff re-
" viewed his decision, and a *second time* turned them over to Lieu-
" tenant R. ; and as he states in his letter to me, that Major Clark
" *ordered them to proceed forthwith to Arkansas.* Why was it
" necessary, then, for me to have been there, since he had yielded
" everything to his senior officer, and that officer he knew had de-
" termined not to respect the order he had received, and had de-
" termined (as his previous statement and subsequent conduct
" prove) to send them forthwith to Arkansas ? It is about such a
" subterfuge as the Sheriff turning the negroes and withholding
" them after my letter to Major C. was seen, and then turning
" them over again after it was known I had left. It is due Lieu-

" tenant R. to observe, that he stated to me the Sheriff had told
" him a lie. I know not what object he could have had in view in
" doing so.

" I remained in New Orleans four days, in which time I became
" convinced from the maneuvering that was evinced that nothing
" would be gained by a longer stay, and as the sickly season was
" approaching, I left with the conviction that the Sheriff would alter
" his decision as soon as I left there.

" I am, with the highest respect, sir,

" Yours, etc.,

" C. A. HARRIS, Esq.,   N. F. COLLINS,
" Commissioner Indian Affairs.   *Agent Creek Warriors.*"

It is worthy of notice that this agent of a slave-dealer should thus
address, to one of the Executive Departments of this august
nation, complaints against the sworn officers of our Government;
but it is still more worthy of note that the War Department should
call on its authorized and sworn agents to respond to complaints
coming from such a source. Copies of Collins's two letters were
immediately enclosed to Lieutenant Reynolds, accompanied by a
letter from Commissioner Harris, of which we give a copy:

" WAR DEPARTMENT,
Office of Commissioner of Indian Affairs,
August 27, 1837. }

" SIR : I enclose copies of two letters from N. F. Collins, Esq.,
" (one of the twenty-ninth ultimo and the other of the eighteenth
" instant,) in relation to the negroes which you were directed to
" turn over to him as the agent of the Creeks. From these papers,
" and from other information received here, it would seem there has
" been great disregard, if not a violation, of the orders of the War
" Department in this matter. I trust you will be able to make
" such explanations of your conduct as will relieve you from cen-
" sure — *a prompt answer is desired.*

" It may not be amiss to inform you that, when on duty in the
" Indian Department, you are bound to obey the orders of no mili-
" tary officer, unless you have been placed under his direction.

" Captain Morrison is the only army officer authorized to control
" your movements.

" Very, etc.,

"Lieut. J. G. REYNOLDS. C. A. HARRIS, *Commissioner.*"

These intimations to Lieutenant Reynolds of *censure*, and the
distinct call for *explanations*, could be neither misinterpreted nor
misunderstood ; and, although the complaints and charges had been
preferred not merely by a man in private life, but by an individual
whose very employment as an assistant slave-dealer had rendered
him odious and infamous among honorable men, yet this officer who
had fought under the flag of his country, and was ready at any
moment to peril his life in the support of his country's honor, was
now constrained to meet charges coming from an infamous source.
The surprise of Lieutenant Reynolds at this procedure was expressed in the following letter :

" NEW ORLEANS, Sept. 20, 1838.

" SIR : Your letter, dated twenty-seventh ultimo, enclosing
" copies of two communications received at your office from Mr. N.
" F. Collins, the Creek attorney, came to hand on the tenth in-
" stant. I was surprised at being called upon to answer for ' my
" conduct ' toward Mr. Collins, as also the Department for disre-
" garding its orders. Indeed, sir, I have been, in my own estima-
" tion, too faithful a servant in the special department in which it
" was the pleasure of General Jessup to assign, and you to con-
" tinue, me, to make a defense to the allegations advanced by Col-
" lins. At the time of Mr. Collins's departure from this city, he
" did not evince that virulence of feeling that he has thought proper
" to express in his letter ; on the contrary, he was then apparently
" under the full conviction that I had done all that was possible to
" aid him, and carry out the orders received in relation to the
" negroes in question. What object could I possibly have in wish-
" ing clandestinely, and in the very face of orders, to send those
" negroes to Arkansas ? Had Mr. Collins been here, sir, so far as

"I was concerned, he should have had the negroes upon *identity*.
"I enclose papers, sir, from various gentlemen to disprove the asser-
"tion of Mr. Collins, 'that the negroes were in my possession du-
"ring the time he was here ;' on the contrary, they did not come
"into my hands until some time after his departure.   It is true, I
"have frequently referred to Major Clark for advice in matters
"relative to my official situation.   It was on account of the high
"regard I have of his character as a gentleman, and an officer of
"long standing and experience, and whose integrity stands pre-
"eminently and deservedly high.

"I have the honor to be, sir, very respectfully,

"Your obd't servant,

"JNO. G. REYNOLDS,

U. S. M. C. Dib. Agent, Ind. Dep't.

"C. A. Harris,
"Com. Ind. Affairs, Washington City, D. C.

We have too little space in this work to copy official papers to
any considerable extent.   Those which accompanied Lieutenant
Reynolds's reply were —

First. A full statement of facts from Sheriff Buisson, showing
that the thirty-one prisoners, who had been in his charge, were
not turned over to Major Clark until the twenty-eighth of June,
1838.

Second. A full statement of facts by George Whitman, owner of
the steamboat, who contracted to carry the prisoners West.

Third. A similar statement by Major Clark of the facts that
came within his knowledge, accompanied by a copy of a communication from Jno. C. Casey, Acting Seminole Agent.

All these statements showed that Lieutenant Reynolds had
strictly obeyed his orders ; and whether they proved satisfactory to
the War Department or not, we are unable to state.   It is, however,
believed, that no further proceedings were had in relation to the
conduct of that officer.

Mr. Collins, finding that he possessed some influence with the
War Department, on the eighteenth of October, wrote the Commissioner of Indian Affairs, saying, "I have now to request that,

" should General Arbuckle be unable to comply with the instruc-
" tions I understand he has received, (which from my knowledge
" of the Indian character I have no doubt he will,) this claim may
" be laid before the agent who may be appointed to investigate the
" claims of the Creeks with the necessary documents; that it may
" be examined and reported on by him."

In answer to this letter, Mr. Crawford, Acting Commmissioner
of Indian Affairs, replied, stating that General Arbuckle had, on
the twenty-eighth of September, informed the Department that the
negroes could only be obtained by military force. Mr. Crawford
also assured Mr. Collins that General Arbuckle had been instructed
to act in concert with Captain Armstrong for the purpose of obtaining a treaty with the Indians by which provisions for this claim
would be made ; and that the necessary papers had been transmitted to those gentleman to enable them to act with a correct understanding of the subject.

But the Creek Indians appear to have become impressed with
the opinion, that the whole proceeding was either unjust or dishonorable, and they wholly refused to participate any further in the
transaction.

The Exiles and Indians were now living on the Cherokee lands.
The Creeks would have nothing further to do with Watson, nor with
the United States, in regard to the *captured* negroes. The Seminole
Indians showed no disposition to surrender them to slavery, and the
Exiles themselves exhibited no intention of going voluntarily into
bondage. General Arbuckle advised against the employment of a
military force to effect that object; and to all present appearances
these ninety Exiles had, through a train of mysterious incidents,
been preserved from bondage. The Florida War had become un-
popular ; and Watson, the purchaser of the supposed slaves, had
warm personal friends among the Whigs of Georgia. They were
quite willing to subject Mr. Van Buren to any degree of odium in
their power. Watson, therefore, sent his petition to Congress, asking indemnity for the loss of slaves whom he had purchased of the

16

Creeks at the instance, and by the recommendation, of the Executive officers of Government.

In order to sustain the claim of Watson, it was necessary to place the facts attending this transaction before the House of Representatives. For this purpose a resolution was adopted, on the twenty-eighth of January, 1839, calling on the Secretary of War for "such information as was to be found in his office touching the " capture of negroes and other property from the hostile Indians, " during the present war in Florida."

In answer to this resolution, the Secretary of War, on the twenty-seventh of February, made report, embracing one hundred and twenty-six pages of printed matter. It was numbered H. Doc. 225, and ordered to be printed. From that document much information has been obtained in regard to the capture and emigration of this first party of Indians and Exiles to the Western Country.

The result of this speculation in human flesh is so essential to a correct appreciation of the whole transaction, that we deem it proper to give, in this connection, the proceedings of Congress upon that subject; although it may appear to be rather a digression from the chronological narration of events which constitute the subject of our history.

It will be recollected that the Commissioner of Indian Affairs, in his letter to the Secretary of War, dated the first of May, 1838, suggests that it might create agitation, were the Department to ask Congress for an appropriation of money to carry these Exiles to Africa, or for any other disposition of them; that, to suppress all discussion in Congress upon the subject of slavery, gag-resolutions and gag-rules had been adopted at each session since 1835. It was under the operation of these rules that the advocates of slavery expected to pass a bill to indemnify Watson for his loss in failing to enslave these Exiles.

1839.] During the summer of 1839, the document, No. 225, above referred to, was printed. According to the practice of that day, few, even of the members of Congress, examined these documents. A copy of this, however, was placed on file, with Watson's petition and other papers, as evidence on which his claim rested.

At the commencement of the next session, the Author of this work, being a member of the House of Representatives, was placed upon the committee of Claims; at the head of which was Hon. David Russel, of Washington County, New York, a man of great industry, integrity and ability; always independent, according to the general views of that day, and upright in the discharge of official duties. Hon. William C. Dawson, of Georgia, was also a member of that committee, and appeared to take much interest in this claim. He was a man of much suavity of manner; one of that class of Southern statesmen who felt it necessary to carry every measure by the influence of personal kindness, and an expression of horror at all agitation of the slave question, under the apprehension that it might dissolve the Union.

Mr. Dawson was anxious to get this claim of Watson through Congress, and, not expecting the Chairman of the committee on Claims to favor its passage, requested the Author to examine and give support to it. It was that examination which gave him the first information as to the real cause of the Florida War. After a full and thorough investigation, he assured Mr. Dawson that he would be constrained to oppose the passage of any bill giving indemnity to Watson. At that time it was the usual practice for the committee on Claims to leave all petitions asking pay for slaves, or which involved the question of slavery, without reporting upon them, lest they should cause agitation. There being no prospect of obtaining from the committee a favorable report, the case was at the next session of Congress referred to the committee on Indian Affairs, who reported in its favor, providing for the payment of the full sum which Watson gave the Creeks, and interest thereon from the time of the contract up to the time of passing the bill.

1841.] This bill was placed on the calendar, and in 1841 the Author endeavored to call attention to it, in a speech made in the House of Representatives on the "Florida War." This led some members to examine it; and some of them, more independent than others, declared their hostility to its passage.

In the Twenty-eighth Congress, the Author, having become obnoxious to the slaveholders, was removed from the committee on Claims,[1] and Watson's petition was again referred to that committee, in order that it should receive the prestige of its influence; but it was reported upon late, and was so low on the calendar that it was not reached during that Congress.

1848.] In the Thirty-first Congress, Mr. Daniels, Chairman of the committee on Claims, reported it in February. But General Crowell, of Trumbull County, Ohio, being on the committee, opposed its passage, and caused a postponement for that session;

1849.] and at the next session it was, after a short discussion, passed over without any final action upon it.

At the Thirty-second Congress, the committee on Claims was yet more favorably constituted for the slave interest — Mr. Sacket, of New York, and Mr. Rantoul, of Massachusetts, being the only

---

(1) Hon. Elisha Whittlesey, the predecessor of Mr. Giddings, long and ably presided over the committee on Claims. He was a man of untiring industry; and when he found it necessary to report on a slave case, in 1835, he wrote the Register of the Treasury, inquiring if slaves had *ever* been paid for by the United States as property. The reply stated they had not; and the committee reported adversely to the case, although it was one of the strongest character possible. Francis Larche, living near New Orleans, owned a horse, cart and slave. The day before the battle below that city, in 1814, they were impressed into the service; and while thus held by the United States authorities, on the day of the battle, the horse and slave were killed by cannon shot, and Larche petitioned Congress for compensation for the loss of his slave. Mr. Whittlesey drew up an able report refusing such compensation.

At the commencement of the Twenty-seventh Congress, Mr. Giddings was placed at the head of that committee; but, being obnoxious to the advocates of slavery, he was removed from that position at the commencement of the Twenty-eighth Congress; yet there seemed to be an impression that his successor should be taken from Ohio, and Hon. Joseph Vance was made Chairman. He was a man at that time somewhat advanced in life, and not accustomed to legal investigations. Cases which required research, were usually consigned to some subordinate member of the committee. It was while he was acting as Chairman, that this case of Watson was first reported upon favorably by the committee on Claims, although it had never before been regarded by that committee as entitled to any encouragement.

two members upon it who openly resisted the slave power. Mr. Edgerton, of Ohio, Mr. Seymour, of Connecticut, and Mr. Curtis, of Pennsylvania, being Northern Democrats, remained silent during the discussion of this claim. It was however again reported by the Chairman, Mr. Daniels, of North Carolina, at an early day, and a full determination to carry it through was manifested by the slaveholders.

Both of the great political parties were at that time (1852) endeavoring to suppress all agitation of the slave question. Southern men, particularly, were horrified at every appearance of discussion in relation to the " pecculiar institution ; " and they hoped to pass this bill without even an examination of its merits before the House. But the opponents of slavery were not idle. Efforts were privately made to call attention of gentlemen to this claim, that they might examine its merits before it came up for discussion ; and on looking into it, a number of members prepared to oppose its passage.

1852.] After one or two postponements, it came on for discussion on the twentieth of February, 1852. Mr. Sacket, of New York, met the case at once, in a speech which showed that he had studied it very thoroughly, and understood it perfectly. He insisted that slaves were not *plunder*, and did not come within the contract of General Jessup, which gave to Creeks the " plunder" they might capture. 2d. That the whole transaction was one of *speculation* on the part of Watson, inasmuch as the report set forth that the negroes were worth at least sixty thousand dollars, while he paid only fourteen thousand and six hundred dollars — being less than one-fourth their value, evidently taking upon himself all risk of title and possession. 3d. That the officers of Government had no authority to involve the nation in this slave-dealing transaction. 4th. That those officers were not the Government, and could not bind the people to pay their funds for human flesh.

Mr. Abercrombie, of Alabama, was in favor of the claim. He declared that he was in Forida at the time of this contract, and knew all about it, and that it was well understood that the term "plunder" did include slaves.

Mr. Daniels, Chairman of the committee, felt called on by the effort of Mr. Sacket to speak early in the discussion. He insisted that General Jessup, the Commissioner of Indian Affairs and Secretary of War, fully understood the case; that it was understood by the parties that the term "plunder" *did* include slaves; that Watson was drawn into this matter, partly, to relieve the Government from the transaction in which it had become involved. He insisted that the negroes captured were *slaves* of the Seminoles; but when inquired of on that point, could only say, that officers engaged in the Florida War had spoken of them as such. He was much embarrassed by interrogatories propounded to him by Mr. Stanton, of Ohio, and other gentlemen.

Mr. Mace, of Indiana, a Democrat, took a short and comprehensive view of the case. He, nor any other man could tell whether these negroes were slaves or freemen. On the part of the officers of Government, there was not a single impulse of humanity manifested in regard to these people; but all their endeavors were put forth to *enslave* them. He was entirely opposed to the bill.

Hon. John W. Howe, of Pennsylvania, would never give his vote in favor of regarding men, and women, and children, as *plunder*. He commented with much force upon the contract, and the documentary evidence before the House, and would maintain the humanity of all prisoner captured in war. He sustained the position of General Gaines, that they were prisoners of war.

On the tenth of March the bill came up again for consideration, when Mr. Johnson, of Georgia, advocated its passage in a very elaborate speech. He differed from Mr. Sacket, Mr. Howe, and those who opposed the bill, mostly upon the great question—insisting that slaves were *property* under our Federal Constitution; that the people captured by the Creek Indians were not possessed of any rights; that they were to be regarded as mere chattels: indeed, this point lay at the foundation of the entire discussion. He however sought to add strength to the claim by reading letters from Mr. Crawford, Commissioner of Indian Affairs, and from Mr. Poinsett, Secretary of War, to show that they sympathized with the slave-dealer, and were desirous that this bill should pass.

Mr. Welch, of Ohio, in few words, declared his conviction that these negroes were prisoners of war, to be treated as such, and not to be regarded as slaves or chattels.

Mr. Evans, of Maryland, thought it difficult to understand the case, but would adopt the views of Judge Iverson, of Georgia; that gentleman had been a member of the House of Representatives, and his statements could be relied upon. He read a long affidavit showing the recollections of Mr. Iverson, and, as the United States had the *property in possession*, he would vote for the bill.

Mr. Stuart, of Michigan, now a Democratic Senator, thought the Government had been in great difficulty in getting these Seminoles to go West; they would not go without the negroes, many of whom had intermarried with the Seminoles. By the treaty which General Jessup made, in 1837, our Government was bound to send the negroes West, and having done so, was bound to pay Watson for his loss.

Mr. Skelton, of New Jersey, a Democrat, recognized no power in this or any other government to treat prisoners of war as *slaves*. The discussion had become interesting, and, in some degree, constituted an agitation of the slave question; and as the committee rose without taking a vote upon the bill, Mr. Orr, of South Carolina, moved a resolution precluding further debate upon it; but the House adjourned without taking a vote on the resolution.

The case came up again on the tenth of April, when a resolution to close debate in one hour was adopted. The House then resolved itself in committee; and Mr. Bartlett, of Vermont, a Democrat, took the position that the Government, nor its officers, had power to enter into any agreement with Indians or white men, by which they should enjoy any privilege, or receive any compensation, not authorized by law; that the contract between General Jessup and the Creeks was of no validity, but absolutely void; and every transaction touching the enslavement of the Exiles was without authority, and of no effect.

Mr. Walsh, of Maryland, insisted that the Indian tribes were not nations, and ought not to be treated as such; that it was not incumbent on the friends of the bill to show that slavery existed among the Seminoles; if they lived within a slave State, they might hold slaves; that the Government had the right to enslave the negroes when captured.

Mr. Sweetzer, of Ohio, Democrat, denied the authority of General Jessup to make any contract for the services of the Creek warriors other than the law had provided; nor could he have authority to make any stipulation as to the disposal of prisoners when captured.

Mr. Southerland, of New York, a Whig, thought the question of slavery was not necessarily involved in this case; that the United States, having sent the negroes West, were bound to indemnify Watson for his loss.

Mr. Daniels, by the rules of the House, had one hour to reply, after the expiration of the time for closing debate. He attempted to reply to some of the arguments offered against the bill, but advanced no new position. At the expiration of his speech the vote was taken, and the bill reported to the House as agreed to in committee. The previous question was then called, and under its operation the bill passed — seventy-nine members voting in favor of its passage, and fifty-three against it.

One member from the slave States, Williamson R. W. Cobb, of Alabama, voted against the bill. All the other members from the slave States voted for it; and were aided by the votes of members from the free States, as follows:

From *New Hampshire:* Harry Hibbard—1.

Massachusetts: Wm. Appleton, Zeno Scudder—2.

New York: Abram M. Schemmerhorn, James Brooks, Gilbert Dean, F. S. Martin, Abram P. Stevens, Joseph Southerland—6.

Connecticut: Collins M. Ingersoll—1

New Jersey: R. M. Price—1.

Pennsylvania: Joseph R. Chandler, Thomas Florence, Joseph H. Kuhns, Joseph McNair, Andrew Packer, John Robbins, Thomas Ross—7.

Ohio: John L Taylor—1.

Indiana: Sam'l W. Parker, Richard W. Thompson—2.

Michigan: E. S. Penniman, Charles E. Stuart—2.

Iowa: Lincoln Clark, Bernard Henn—2.

California: Joseph W. McCorkle—1. In all the free States twenty-five.

The vote against the bill was given by the following members, from the free States:

From *Maine:* E. K. Smart, Israel Washburn, jr.—2.

New Hampshire: Jared Perkins, Amos Tuck—2.

Massachusetts: Orrin Fowler, Z. Goodrich, Horace Mann—3.

New York: Henry Bennet, George Briggs, John G. Floyd, Timothy Jenkins, Daniel F. Jones, Preston King, William Murray, Joseph Russel, Wm. A. Sacket, W. W. Snow, Hiram S. Wallbridge, John Wells—12.

New Jersey: Charles Skelton, N. T. Stratton—2.

Vermont: Thomas W. Bartlett, James Meacham—2.

Connecticut: Charles Chapman—1.

Pennsylvania: James Allison, John L. Dawson, James Gamble, Galusha A. Grow, John W. Howe, Thomas M. Howe, Milo M. Dimmick, Thaddeus Stevens—8.

Ohio: Nelson Barrere, Joseph Cable, Alfred P. Edgerton, J. M. Gaylord, Alex. Harper, Wm. F. Hunter, John Johnson, Eben Newton, Edson B. Olds, Charles Sweetzer—10.

Indiana: Samuel Brenton, John G. Davis, Graham N. Fitch, Thomas A. Hendricks, Daniel Mace—5.

Illinois: Wyllis Allen, R. S. Molony—2.

Wisconsin: James D. Doty, Solomon Durkee, Ben. C. Eastman—3.

These fifty-two members, with Mr. Cobb, of Alabama, made up the entire opposition to the bill in the House of Representatives. In the Senate there was very little opposition to its passage; and after thirteen years, the people of the United States paid for the slaves whom Watson bought on speculation, but of whom he failed to obtain possession. The Northern advocates of the bill justified their support of it more generally upon the principle, that our officers sent the negroes West, and thereby rendered it difficult, if not impossible, for Watson to obtain possession of them; and they insisted that, in refunding to Watson his money, they did not pay him for human flesh, but for the money he had paid out at the instance of federal officers. This vote closed the controversy in regard to General Jessup's contract, to give the Creek warriors such *plunder* as they might capture from the enemy.

CHAPTER XVIII.

FURTHER DIFFICULTIES IN PROSECUTING THE WAR.

Emigrants under Captain Morrison — Feeling among the Regular Troops — They detest the practice of catching Negroes — Another party Emigrate — Still further Emigration — Situation of the Exiles — Deep depravity of the Administration — General McComb's Treaty — His general order — Peace cheers the Nation — Citizens of Florida return to their homes — Administration congratulates its friends — More murders perpetrated — Planters flee to villages for protection — Massacre of Colonel Harney's party — Indians seized at Fort Mellon — Exiles refuse to participate in these massacres — They would make no Treaty — Administration paralyzed — Report of Secretary of War — Its character — Barbarous sentiments of Governor Reid — Resolution of Legislature of Florida in favor of employing blood-hounds — Original object in obtaining them — The effort proves a failure — General Taylor retires from command of Army — Is succeeded by General Armistead.

WE now resume our chronological narration of events connected with the Exiles of Florida, during the year 1838.

On the fourteenth of June, Captain Morrison arrived at New Orleans from Tampa Bay in charge of some three hundred Indians and thirty negroes, on their way to the West; he having been assigned to that particular duty. These Indians and Exiles had most of them come to Fort Jupiter by advice of the Cherokees, and surrendered under the capitulation of March, 1837. At the time they reached New Orleans, Lieutenant Reynolds was absent with his first emigrating party; and the thirty-one negroes left at New Orleans were at that time in the hands of the Sheriff. Captain Morrison felt it his duty to hasten the emigration of those whom he had in charge, and on the sixteenth, he left that city with his prisoners for the Indian Country without waiting the return of Lieutenant Reynolds. On reaching Fort Gibson, he delivered them over to the officer acting as Seminole Agent for the Western Country, and they soon rejoined their friends who were located on the Cherokee lands.

It may not be improper to state, that, in several of our recent chapters, we have quoted from official documents pretty freely, for the reason that many living statesmen, as well as many who have passed to their final rest, were deeply involved in those transactions, and we desired to make them speak for themselves as far as the documents would enable us to do so. But as we have narrated most of the scenes involving individuals in transactions of such deep moral turpitude, we hope to be more brief in our future history.

When General Taylor assumed the command of the army, there was a feeling of deep disgust prevalent among the regular troops at the practice of seizing and enslaving the Exiles.

We have already noticed the fact, that the citizens of Florida supposed the war to have been commenced principally to enable them to get possession of negroes whom they might enslave. Indeed, they appear not to have regarded it as material, that the claimant should have previously owned the negro. If they once obtained control of his person, he was hurried into the interior of Georgia, Alabama, or South Carolina, where he was sold and held as a slave. And the Florida volunteers, while nominally in service, appear to have been far more anxious to catch negroes than to meet the enemy in battle.

This feelng was so general among the people and troops of Florida, that General Call, Governor of the Territory, recommended to the Secretary of War that military expeditions should be fitted out for the purpose of going into the Indian Country, in order to capture negroes, who, when captured, *should be sold, and the avails of such sales applied to defray the expenses of the war.*

It is easy to see that this feeling would lead the regular troops to entertain great contempt for the volunteers of Florida; and a corresponding feeling of hostility would arise on the part of such volunteers toward the regular troops.

These feelings operated upon President Jackson in ordering the withdrawal of General Scott; and General Jessup sought to appease this hostility by obeying the dictates of the slave power. Indeed, whatever appears like a violation of pledged faith, or bears the evidence of treachery on the part of General Jessup, may probably with great justice be attributed to the popular sentiment of the Territory. He had assiduously captured, and delivered over to bondage, hundreds of persons whom he had most solemnly covenanted to "*protect in their persons and property.*"

General Taylor discarded this entire policy. His first efforts were to make the Indians and Exiles understand that he sought their emigration to the Western Country, for the advancement of their own interest and happiness. Owing to these circumstances there was scarcely any blood shed in Florida while he had command. The army was no longer employed to hunt and to chase down women and children, who had been reared in freedom among the hommocks and everglades of that Territory.

There were yet remaining several small bands of Indians upon the Appalachicola River, and in its vicinity. Most of the Exiles who had a few years previously resided with these bands, had been captured by pirates from Georgia, and taken to the interior of that State and sold, as the reader has been already informed. Those of E-con-chattimico's and of Blunt's and of Walker's bands were nearly all kidnapped; but of the number of Exiles who remained with the other remnants of Indian Tribes, resident upon the Appalachicola River, we have no reliable information. We are left in doubt on this point, as General Taylor drew no distinctions among his prisoners; he neither constituted himself nor his officers a tribunal for examining the complexion or the pedigree of his captives. He denied the right of any citizen to inspect the people captured by the army under his command, or to interfere in any way with the disposal of his prisoners. He repaired to the Apalachee towns with a small force about the first of October. Neither the Indians nor Exiles made any resistance ; nor did they oppose emigration. They readily embarked for New Orleans on their way westward. Their emigration was not delayed in order to give planters an opportunity to examine the negroes. Under the general term of "Apalachees," two hundred and twenty persons were quietly emigrated to the Western Country; but, as we have already stated, how many of them were negroes, we have no information. These people were also delivered over to the agent, acting for the Western Indians, and settled with their brethren upon the Cherokee lands.

General Taylor now entered upon a new system for prosecuting the war, by establishing posts and manning them, and by assigning to each a particular district of country, over which their scouts and patroles were to extend their daily reconnoisances.

Small parties of Indians and negroes occasionally came in at different posts, and surrendered under the articles of capitulation of 1839.] March, 1837 ; and, on the twenty-fifth of February, one hundred and ninety-six Indians and *negroes* were embarked at Tampa Bay for the Western Conntry. But the proportion of negroes, compared with the whole number, is not stated in any official report. General Taylor, in his communications, speaks of them as *prisoners*, and occasionally uses the terms "Indians and negroes."

Thus, in less than a year, General Taylor shipped more than four hundred prisoners for the Western Country without bloodshed. These prisoners were also delivered over to the Indian Agent of the Western Country, and immediately reünited with their brethren already located on the Cherokee lands. There were, at that time, a colony of more than sixteen hundred of these people living upon the territory assigned to the Cherokees. They were without homes, or a country of their own : whereas the Government had constantly held out to them the assurance that, if they emigrated West, they should have a country assigned to their *separate use,* on which they could repose in safety.

At this point in our history, Mr. Van Buren's administration exhibited its deepest depravity. Since the ratification of the supplemental treaty of 1833, the Executive, through all its officers, had assured the Indians and Exiles that they should enjoy its full benefits, by having a territory set off to their separate use, where they could live independent of Creek laws. Under these assurances they had received the pledged faith of the nation, that they should be *protected* by the United States in their persons and property.

With these pledges, and with these expectations, a weak and friendless people had emigrated to that western region ; and when thus separated from their friends and country, with the slave-catching vultures of the Creek Nation watching and intending to make them their future victims, the President deliberately refused to abide by either the treaty or the articles of capitulation. He left them unprotected, without homes, and without a country which they could call their own. True, many of them had been betrayed, treacherously seized and compelled to emigrate ; but this was done in violation of the existing treaty and pledged faith of the nation, which they were constantly assured should be faithfully observed ; and these circumstances enhanced the guilt of those who wielded the Executive power to oppress them.

Major General McComb arrived in Florida (May 20) for the purpose of effecting a new treaty with the Seminoles upon the basis of *permitting them to remain in their native land.* The war had been waged with the intent and for the purpose of compelling the Indians to emigrate West and settle with the Creeks, and become subject to the Creek laws. It had continued three years at a vast expenditure of treasure and of national reputation. Many valuable lives had also been sacrificed ; and, although some two thousand Indians and Exiles had emigrated West, not one Exile had settled in the Creek Country, or become subject to Creek laws. Some hundreds had been enslaved and sold in Florida, Georgia, Alabama and South Carolina; but a remnant of that people, numbering some hundreds, yet maintained their liberties against all the machinations and efforts of Government to reënslave them.[1]

The vast expenditure of national treasure had called forth severe animadversion in Congress; while the entire policy of the slave power forbid all explanation of the real cause of this war, and of the objects for which its prosecution was continued.

Thus, while the nation was involved in a most expensive and disastrous contest for the benefit of slavery, the House of Representatives had adopted resolutions for suppressing all discussion and all agitation of questions relating to that institution.

General Scott, a veteran officer of our army, had exhausted his utmost science; had put forth all his efforts to conquer this indomitable people; or rather to subdue the love of liberty, the independence of thought and of feeling, which stimulated them to effort; but he had failed. The power of our army, aided by deception, fraud and perfidy, had been tried in vain. General Jessup, the most successful officer who had commanded in Florida, had advised peace upon the precise terms which the allies demanded at the commencement of the war; and General McComb, Commander-in-Chief of the army of the United States, was now commissioned to negotiate peace on those terms. But the first difficulty was to obtain a hearing with the chiefs who remained in Florida, in order to enter upon negotiations touching a pacification. To effect this object, recourse was had to a negro, one of the Exiles who knew General Taylor, and in whom General Taylor confided. At the request of General McComb, this man was dispatched with a friendly message to several chiefs, requesting them to come into the American Camp for the purpose of negotiation. His mission proved successful. A Council of several chiefs, and some forty head men and warriors, was convened at Fort King, on the sixteenth

---

(1) There is little doubt that the real number of Exiles was unknown to General Jackon, or to General Cass, at the commencement of the war. They appear to have regarded their number far less than it was estimated, during the first Seminole War of 1818.

of May, 1839, and the terms of peace agreed upon; but no treaty appears to have been drawn up in form. On the eighteenth of May, General McComb, at Fort King, his head-quarters, issued the following general orders:

"HEAD QUARTERS OF THE ARMY OF THE UNITED STATES,
Fort King, Florida, May 18, 1839.

"The Major General, commanding in chief, has the satisfaction "of announcing to the army in Florida, to the authorities of the "Territory, and to the citizens generally, that he has this day ter- "minated the war with the Seminole Indians by an agreement "entered into with Chitto-Tustenuggee, principal chief of the Sem- "inoles and successor to Arpeika, commonly called Sam. Jones, "brought to this post by Lieutenant Colonel Harney, 2d Dragoons, "from the southern part of the peninsula. The terms of the "agreement are — that hostilities immediately cease between the "parties; that the troops of the United States and the Semi- "nole and Mickasukie chiefs and warriors, now at a distance, be "made acquainted with the fact, that peace exists, and that all hos- "tilities are forthwith to cease on both sides — the Seminoles and "Mickasukies agreeing to retire into a district of country in Flori- "da, below Pease Creek, the boundaries of which are as follows: "viz, beginning at the most southern point of land between Char- "lotte Harbor and the Sanybel or Cooloosahatchee River, opposite "to Sanybel Island; thence into Charlotte Harbor by the southern "pass between Pine Island and that point along the eastern shore "of said harbor to Toalkchopko or Pease Creek; thence up said "creek to its source; thence easterly to the northern point of Lake "Istokopoga; thence along the eastern outlet of said lake, called "Istokopoga Creek, to the Kissimee River; thence southerly down "the Kissimee to Lake Okeechobee; thence south through said "lake to Ecahlahatohee or Shark River; thence down said river "westwardly to its mouth; thence along the seashore northwardly "to the place of beginning; that sixty days be allowed the In- "dians, north and east of that boundary, to remove their families

17

" and effects into said district, where they are to remain until further
" arrangements are made under the protection of the troops of the
" United States, who are to see that they are not molested by in-
" truders, citizens or foreigners ; and that said Indians do not pass
" the limits assigned them, except to visit the posts, which will be
" hereafter indicated to them.   All persons are, therefore, forbid-
" den to enter the district assigned to the Indians without written
" permission of some commanding officer of a military post.

 " By command of the General :   " ALEXANDER McCOMB,
                Major General Commanding.
  " EDMOND SHRIVER,
   " Captain and A. A. General."

The country now again rejoiced at what the people regarded as
the restoration of peace.   By the terms agreed upon, the Indians
retained as large a territory in proportion to the number left in
Florida as was held by them at the commencement of the war.

The people of Florida had originally petitioned General Jackson
for the forcible removal of the Indians, because they would not
seize and bring in their fugitive slaves.   They had protested against
peace upon any terms that should leave the negroes, whom they
claimed, in the Indian Country.   These citizens of Florida had
long since been driven from their homes and firesides by the enemy
whom they so much despised ; and they now desired peace.   The
Indians and Exiles were also anxious to cultivate corn and potatoes
for the coming winter, and were glad to be able to do so in peace.

Thus, the people of Florida, as they supposed, in perfect safety,
returned to their plantations, and resumed their former habits of
life.   And the political party in possession of the Government,
congratulated themselves and the country upon the fortunate conclusion of a war which had involved them in difficulties that were
inexplicable.

But this quiet continued for a short time only.   Early in July,
travelers and express-riders were killed by small parties of Indians ;
plantations were attacked and the occupants murdered ; buildings

burned and crops destroyed ; families fled from their homes, leaving all their property, in order to assemble in villages in such numbers as to insure safety to their persons ; and the Florida War again raged with accumulated horrors. As an illustration of the manner in which it was carried on, we quote the following :

"ASSISTANT ADJUTANT GENERAL'S OFFICE, ARMY OF THE SOUTH, }
Fort Brooke, East Florida, July 29, 1839. }

"SIR : It becomes my painful duty to inform you of the assas-
"sination of the greater part of Lieutenant Colonel Harney's
"detachment, by the Indians, on the morning of the 23d instant,
"on the Coloosahatchee River, where they had gone, in accordance
"with the treaty at Fort King, to establish a trading-house. The
"party consisted of about twenty-eight men, armed with Colt's
"rifles ; they were encamped on the river, *but unprotected by*
"*defenses of any kind*, and, it is said, without sentinels. The
"Indians, in large force, made the attack before the dawn of day,
"and before reveillé ; and it is supposed that thirteen of the men
"were killed, among whom were Major Dalham and Mr. Morgan,
"sutlers. The remainder, with Colonel Harney, escaped, sev-
"eral of them severely wounded. It was a complete surprise.
"The Commanding General, therefore, directs that you instantly
"take measures to place the defenses at Fort Mellon in the most
"complete state of repair, and be ready at all times to repel attack,
"should one be made. No portion of your command will, in
"future, be suffered to leave the garrison except under a strong
"escort. The detachment will be immediately withdrawn. Should
"Fort Mellon prove unhealthy, and the surgeon recommend its
"abandonment, you are authorized to transfer the garrison, and
"reinforce some of the neighboring posts.

"I am, Sir,   GEO. H. GRIFFIN,

"Lieutenant W. K. HANSON,   *Assistant Adjutant General.*
    "Commanding at Fort Mellon."

The Indians killed ten men belonging to the military service, and eight citizens, employed by the sutlers ; while Colonel Harney and fourteen others escaped. The Indians obtained fourteen rifles, six carbines, some three or four kegs of powder, and about three thousand dollars worth of goods.

Lieutenant Hanson, commanding at Fort Mellon, on receiving the order which we have quoted, seized some thirty Indians at that time visiting Fort Mellon, and sent them immediately to Charleston, South Carolina; whence they were embarked for the Indian Country, west of Arkansas, where they joined their brethren, who still resided upon the Cherokee Territory.

In these transactions, the Exiles who remained in Florida appear to have taken no part, at least so far as we are informed. They labored to obtain the treaty of peace; but such was the treachery with which they had been treated, that they would not subject themselves to the power of the white people, and were not of course present at the treaty; nor were they recognized by General McComb as a party to the treaty, or in any way interested in its provisions. Indeed, we are led to believe that General McComb adopted the policy on which General Taylor usually practiced, of recognizing no distinctions among prisoners or enemies.

The Administration appeared to be paralyzed under this new demonstration of the power and madness of the Seminoles. At the commencement of the war, some officers had estimated the whole number of Seminoles at fifteen hundred, and the negroes as low as four hundred. They had now sent some two thousand Indians and negroes to the Western Country; and yet those left in Florida, renewed the war with all the savage barbarity which had characterized the Seminoles in the days of their greatest power. Indeed, they exhibited no signs of humiliation.

The Secretary of War, Mr. Poinsett, a South Carolinian, probably exerted more influence with the President in regard to this war than any other officer of Government. His predecessor, General Cass, had treated the Exiles as mere chattels, having "no rights." He had advised the employment of Creek Indians, giving them such negroes as they might capture; he had officially approved the contract made with them by General Jessup. After he left the office, his successor, Mr. Poinsett, approved the order purchasing some ninety of them on account of Government. He had advised Watson to purchase them; had done all in his power to consign them to slavery in Georgia. He was, however, constrained to make an official report upon the state of this war, at the opening of the first session of the Twenty-sixth Congress, which assembled on the first Monday of December, 1839.

That report, when considered in connection with the events which gave character to the Florida War, constitutes a most extraordinary paper. Notwithstanding all the difficulties which he had encountered in his efforts to enslave the Exiles, to prevent at least ninety of them from going West, and the complaints of the Seminoles who had emigrated to the Western Country, at finding themselves destitute of homes and of territory on which to settle, he made no allusion to their troubles; nor did he give any intimation of the difficulties arising on account of the Exiles; nor did he even intimate that such a class of people existed in Florida.

1840.] He declared the result of General McComb's negotiation had been the loss of many valuable lives. "Our people "(said he) fell a sacrifice to their confidence in the good faith and "promises of the Indians, and were entrapped and murdered with "all the circumstances of cruelty and treachery which distinguish "Indian warfare. * * * The experience of the last summer "brings with it the painful conviction, that the war must be prose- "cuted until Florida is freed from these ruthless savages. Their "late cruel and treacherous conduct is too well known to require a "repetition of the revolting recital; it has been such as is calcula- "ted to deprive them of the sympathy of the humane, and convince "the most peaceable of the necessity of *subduing them by force.*"

It appeared necessary to raise the cry of treachery and cruelty against the Indians and Exiles. They had no friend who was acquainted with the facts, that could call attention of the nation to the treachery which had been practiced on them by the order, and with the approval, of the Secretary of War. No man was able to say how many fathers and mothers and children were, by the influence of that officer, consigned to a fate far more cruel than that which awaited the men, under Colonel Harney, at Coloosahatchee.

In his report the Secretary most truly remarked : "If the In- " dians of Florida had a country to retire to, they would have been " driven out of the Territory long ago ; but they are hemmed in " by the sea, and must defend themselves to the uttermost, or sur- " render to be transported beyond it." And he might well have added : *When they shall be thus transported, they will have no country — no home.* Indeed, the whole report shows that he relied on physical force to effect an extermination of the Indians and their allies ; he looked not to justice, nor to the power of truth, for carry- ing out the designs of the Executive.

Men in power appear to forget that justice sits enthroned above all human greatness ; that it is omnipotent, and will execute its appropriate work upon mankind. Thus, while the people of Florida and Georgia had provoked the war, by kidnapping and enslaving colored men and women, to whom they had no more claim than they had to the people of England ; while they had sent their peti- tion to General Jackson, asking him to compel the Indians to seize and bring in their negroes, and had protested against the peace negotiated by General Jessup, in 1837; — Mr. Reid, Governor of Florida, in an official Message to the Territorial Legislature, in December, 1839, used language so characteristic of those who sup- ported the Florida War, that we feel it just to him and his coadju- tors to give the following extract :

" The efforts of the General and Territorial Governments to quell " the Indian disturbances which have prevailed through four long " years, have been unavailing, and it would seem that the prophecy " of the most sagacious leader of the Indians will be more than " fulfilled ; the close of the fifth year will still find us struggling in " a contest remarkable for magnanimity, forbearance and credulity " on the one side, and ferocity and bad faith on the other. We

" are waging a war with beasts of prey; the tactics that belong to
" civilized nations are but shackles and fetters in its prosecution;
" we must fight ' fire with fire;' the white man must, in a great
" measure, adopt the mode of warfare pursued by the red man, and
" we can only hope for success by continually harrassing and pur-
" suing the enemy. If we drive him from hommock to hommock,
" from swamp to swamp, and penetrate the recesses where his
" women and children are; if, in self-defense, we show as little
" mercy to him as he has shown to us, the anxiety and surprise
" produced by such operations will not fail, it is believed, to pro-
" duce prosperous results. It is high time that sickly sentimen-
" tality should cease. ' Lo, the poor Indian !' is the exclamation
" of the fanatic, pseudo-philanthropist; ' Lo, the poor white man !'
" is the ejaculation which all will utter who have witnessed the
" inhuman butchery of women and children, and the massacres that
" have drenched the Territory in blood.

" In the future prosecution of the war, it is important that a
" generous confidence should be reposed in the General Govern-
" ment. It may be that mistakes and errors have been committed
" on all hands; but the peculiar adaptation of the country to the
" cowardly system of the foe, and its inaptitude to the operations
" of a regular army; the varying and often contradictory views and
" opinions of the best informed of our citizens, and the embarrass-
" ments which these cases must have produced to the authorities at
" Washington, furnish to the impartial mind some excuse, at least,
" for the failures which have hitherto occurred. It is our duty to
" be less mindful of the past than the future. Convinced that the
" present incumbent of the Presidential Chair regards with sincere
" and intense interest the afflictions we endure; relying upon the
" patriotism, talent and sound judgment of the distinguished Caro-
" linian who presides over the Department of War, and confident
" in the wisdom of Congress, let us prepare to second, with every
" nerve, the measures which may be devised for our relief. Feel-
" ing as we do the immediate pressure of circumstances, let us exert,

" to the extremest point, all our powers to rid us of the evil by
" which we are oppressed. Let us, by a conciliatory course, en-
" deavor to allay any unkindnesses of feeling which may exist
" between the United States army and the militia of Florida, and
" by union of sentiment among ourselves, advance the happy period
" when the Territory shall enjoy what she so much needs — a long
" season of peace and tranquillity."

Perhaps no vice is more general among mankind than a desire to
represent ourselves, and our country and government, to mankind
and to posterity as just and wise, whatever real truth may dictate.
Surely, if General Jessup's official reports be regarded as correct,
the people of Florida should have been the last of all who were
concerned in that war, to claim the virtue of magnanimity or forbearance, or to charge the Seminoles or Exiles with ferocity or bad
faith. The expression that " *it is high time that sickly sentimen-
tality should cease,*" manifests the ideas which he entertained of
strict, equal and impartial justice to all men.

This Message was an appropriate introduction to the legislative
action which immediately succeeded its publication. It was that
legislative body which first gave official sanction to the policy of
obtaining blood-hounds from Cuba to aid our troops in the prosecution of this war. Of this atrocious and barbarous policy much has
been said and written, and its authorship charged upon various men
and officers of Government. At the time of the transaction, it was
represented that the blood-hounds were obtained for the purpose of
trailing the Indians, and historians have so stated; [1] but for various
reasons, we are constrained to believe they were obtained for the
purpose of trailing *negroes*. It was well known that these animals
were trained to pursue *negroes*, and *only* negroes. They would no
more follow the track of a white man than they would that of a horse
or an ox. It was the peculiar scent of the negro that they had
been trained and accustomed to follow. No man concerned in
obtaining these animals, could have been ignorant that they had, in

(1) Captain Sprague's History of the Florida War so represents the subject.

all probability, never seen an Indian, or smelt the track of any son of the forest.

Every slaveholder well understood the habits of those ferocious dogs, and the manner of training them, and could not have supposed them capable of being rendered useful in capturing Indians. The people of Florida appear to have been stimulated in the commencement and continuance of this war solely by a desire to *obtain slaves*, rather than to *fight Indians;* and while acting as militia or as individuals, they were far more efficient in capturing negroes and claiming those captured by other troops than in facing them on the field of battle. Nor can we resist the conviction, that catching *negroes* constituted, in the mind of General Jessup, the object for which those animals were to be obtained. Such was evidently his purpose when he wrote Colonel Harney, as quoted in a former chapter, " If you see Powell (Osceola), tell him that I intend to send " exploring and surveying parties into every part of the country " during the summer; and that I shall send out and take *all the* " *negroes who belong to white people, and he must* not allow the " Indians or Indian negroes to mix with them. Tell him I am " sending to Cuba for blood-hounds to trail them, and I intend to " hang every one of them who does not come in."

We cannot close our eyes to the fact, that General Jessup intended the blood-hounds to be used in catching " the negroes belonging to the white people," as he said. Those white people were mostly slaveholders of Florida; those who proposed in the legislative assembly of that territory the obtaining of the animals, and adopted a resolution authorizing their purchase. They did not wait for the President to act, nor for the " Secretary of War," whom the Governor of Florida characterized as " that distinguished *Carolinian*" on whose judgment and patriotism the people of Florida so much relied.[1]

By resolution, Colonel Fitzpatrick was " authorized to proceed

[1] Not having the Statutes of Florida before us, we make this statement on the authority of Captain Sprague.

"to Havana, and procure a kennel of blood-hounds, noted for "tracking and pursuing negroes." He was fortunate in his mission. He not only obtained the animals, but he accomplished the journey, and reached St. Augustine as early as the sixth of January, 1840, with a reinforcement for the army of the United States of thirty-three blood-hounds well trained to the work of catching negroes. They cost precisely one hundred and fifty-one dollars seventy-two cents, each, when landed in Florida. He also procured five Spaniards who were accustomed to using the animals in capturing negroes; and as the dogs had been trained to the Spanish language, they would have been useless under the control of persons who could only speak the dialect of our own country.

The very general error that existed throughout the country, at the time of this transaction, arose from a misapprehension of the facts. There had been much said in regard to these blood-hounds before they were actually obtained. When the report of the War Department, under the resolution of the House of Representatives of the twenty-eighth of January, 1839, was published, containing the letter of General Jessup addressed to Colonel Harney, which we have quoted, many members of Congress appeared indignant at what they regarded as a stain upon our national honor in obtaining and employing blood-hounds to act in concert with our troops and our Indian allies in this war. Party feelings ran high, and southern members of Congress, who were acting with the Whig party, were willing to seize upon any circumstance that would reflect discreditably upon the then existing Administration.

On the twenty-seventh day of December, 1839, the Hon. Henry A. Wise, a member of the House of Representatives from Virginia, addressed a letter to the Secretary of War, inquiring as to facts relating to the employment of blood-hounds in aid of our troops.[1]

---

(1) We have no copy of Mr. Wise's letter, and have never seen the letter itself; but we state the fact that he wrote the Secretary of War by authority of that officer, who says in the letter quoted, ' I have the honor to acknowledge the receipt of *your letter of the 27th inst.*, inquiring," etc.

To this letter Mr. Poinsett, the Secretary of War, replied on the thirtieth of December, as follows :

"WAR DEPARTMENT, December 30, 1839.

" SIR : I have the honor to acknowledge the receipt of your let-
" ter of the twenty-seventh instant, inquiring into the truth of the
" assertion made by the public papers, that the Government had
" determined to use blood-hounds in the war against the Florida In-
" dians; and beg to assure you it will give me great pleasure to
" give you all the information on this subject in possession of the
" Department.

" From the time I first entered upon the duties of the War De-
" partment, I continued to receive letters from officers commanding
" in Florida, as well as from the most enlightened citizens in that
" Territory, urging the employment of blood-hounds as the most
" efficient means of terminating the atrocities daily perpetrated by
" the Indians on the settlers in that Territory. To these proposals
" no answer was given, until in the month of August, 1838, while
" at the Virginia Springs, there was referred to me, from the De-
" partment, a letter, addressed to the Adjutant General by the offi-
" cer commanding the forces in Florida (General Taylor), to the
" following effect :

"HEAD QUARTERS ARMY OF THE SOUTH, }
Fort Brooke, July 28, 1838. }

"SIR : I have the honor to inclose you a communication this moment received, on the subject of procuring blood-hounds from the Island of Cuba·to aid the army in its opera-tions against the hostiles in Florida. I am decidedly in favor of the measure, and beg leave to urge it as the only means of ridding the country of the Indians, who are now broken up into small parties that take shelter in swamps and hommocks, making it im-possible for us to follow or overtake them without the aid of such auxiliaries. Should this measure meet the approbation of the Department, and the necessary authority be granted, I will open a correspondence with Mr. Evertscn on the subject, through Major Hunt, As sistant Quarter Master at Savannah, and will authorize him, if it can be done on reasona-ble terms, to employ a few dogs with persons who understand their management.

" I wish it distinctly understood, that my object in employing dogs is only to ascertain where the Indians can be found, not to worry them.

" I have the honor to be, sir,
" Your obedient servant,
" Z. TAYLOR,
Brev. Brig. Gen. U. S. A. Commanding.

" General R. JONES,
" Washington, D. C."

"On this letter I indorsed the following decision, which was " communicated to General Taylor : ' I have always been of opin- " ion that dogs *ought* to be employed in this warfare to protect the " army from surprises and ambuscades, and to track the Indian to " his lurking place ; but supposed if the General believed them to " be necessary, he would not hesitate to take measures to secure " them.   The cold-blooded and inhuman murders lately perpetra- " ted upon helpless women and children by these ruthless savages, " render it expedient that every possible means should be resorted " to, in order to protect the people of Florida, and to enable the " United States forces to follow and capture or destroy the savage " and unrelenting foe.   General Taylor is therefore authorized to " procure such number of dogs as he may judge necessary : it be- " ing expressly understood that they are to be employed to track " and discover the Indians, not to worry or destroy them.'

" This is the only action or correspondence, on the part of the " Department, that has ever taken place in relation to the matter. " The General took no measures to carry into effect his own recom- " mendation, and this Department has never since renewed the sub- " ject.   I continue, however, to entertain the opinion expressed in " the above decision.   I do not believe that description of dog, " called the blood-hound, necessary to prevent surprise or track the " Indian murderer ; but still I think that every cabin, every mili- " tary post, and every detachment, should be attended by dogs. " That precaution might have saved Dade's command from massa- " cre, and by giving timely warning have prevented many of the " cruel murders which have been committed by the Indians in mid- " dle Florida.   The only successful pursuit of Indian murderers that " I know of, was, on a late occasion, when the pursuers were aided " by the sagacity of their dogs.   These savages had approached a " cabin of peaceful and industrious settlers so stealthily, that the " first notice of their presence was given by a volley from their " rifles, thrust between the logs of the house ; and the work of " death was finished by tomahawking the women, after tearing from

" them their infant children, and dashing their brains out against
" the door posts.

" Are these ruthless savages to escape and repeat such scenes of
" blood, because they can elude our fellow citizens in Florida, and
" our regular soldiers, and baffle their unaided efforts to overtake
" or discover them? On a late occasion, three of our estimable
" citizens were killed in the immediate neighborhood of St. Augus-
" tine, and one officer of distinguished merit mortally wounded. It
" is in evidence, that these murders were committed by two In-
" dians, who, after shooting down the father and beating out the
" son's brains with the butts of their rifles, upon hearing the ap-
" proach of the volunteers, retired a few yards into the woods and
" secreted themselves, until the troops returned to town with the
" dead bodies of those who had been thus inhumanly and wantonly
" butchered.

" It is to be regretted that this corps had not been accompanied
" with one or two hunters, who, with their dogs, might have tracked
" the blood-stained footsteps of these Indians; have restored to
" liberty the captives they were dragging away with them, and have
" prevented them from ever again repeating such atrocities; nor
" could the severest casuist object to our fellow citizens in Florida
" resorting to such measures, in order to protect the lives of their
" women and children.

" Very respectfully,

" Your most obedient servant,

" J. R. POINSETT.

" Hon. HENRY A. WISE,
" House of Representatives."

It is no part of our present duties to comment on the code of
morals which the Secretary of War had adopted. He undoubtedly
felt, that neither the Indians nor negroes " possessed any rights
which white men were bound to respect." He was not, he could
not, have been ignorant of the cold-blooded massacre of nearly three
hundred Exiles and Indians at Blount's Fort, in 1816; nor of the
manner in which the present war had been brought on; nor of the

objects for which it was prosecuted ; nor does it appear possible that he, a large slaveholder of South Carolina, could have expected these blood-hounds would follow the trail of Indians. But we must bear in mind that he had been exceedingly vexed with the indomitable resistance of the Exiles. They appeared perfectly determined not to be enslaved, and that determination had given him much trouble ; and he must have foreseen the defeat of his party in the next Presidential contest, should all these facts become known to the public. With these feelings, he was prepared to apply almost any epithets to the Indians, as the friends and allies of a people to whose real character he dared not publicly allude, although they were occasioning the Administration so much trouble.

Having shown that no blood-hounds had been previously employed, he proceeded to argue the propriety of employing them in future, by adopting the policy proposed by the Legislature of Florida, who, as we have already seen, had taken measures to obtain them some twenty days prior to the date of this communication.

The Secretary of War thus exonerated himself and the Federal Executive from the responsibility of employing blood-hounds, on the thirtieth of December ; and the animals arrived in Florida, under charge of Colonel Fitzpatrick, just one week *subsequently* to that date.

One feature was most obvious, in the commencement and prosecution of this war : we allude to the very respectful, almost obsequious obedience of the Executive to the popular feeling in favor of slavery, in every part of the country where that institution existed. This war had been commenced at the instance of the people of Florida. General Jessup attempted to change the articles of capitulation which he had signed, when the people of Florida protested against peace, unless attended by a restoration of slaves; and now, when the popular voice of the nation had paralyzed the Executive arm in regard to obtaining blood-hounds, the people of Florida, in their Legislature, took up the subject and carried the policy into practice, so far as to obtain the animals ; but that would be of no use unless they could be employed by the army of the United States. Preparatory to this adoption of the purchase made by the Legislature of Florida, Mr. Poinsett had argued the propriety of their employment, in his letter to Mr. Wise ; and twenty-six days afterwards, he wrote General Taylor as follows :

"WAR DEPARTMENT, Jan'y 26, 1840.

"SIR : It is understood by the Department, although not offi-
"cially informed of the fact, that the authorities of the Territory
"have imported a pack of blood-hounds from the Island of Cuba.
"And I think it proper to direct, in the event of those dogs being
"employed by any officer or officers under your command, that
"their use be confined altogether to tracking the Indians ; and in
"order to insure this, and to prevent the possibility of their injur-
"ing any person whatever, that they be muzzled and held with a
"leash while following the track of the enemy.
"Very respectfully,
"Your most obedient servant,
"J. R. POINSETT.
"Brig. Gen'l Z. TAYLOR,
"Com'd'g Army of the South, Florida."

From the commencement of this war, the officers of our army had found it necessary to employ persons who could communicate with the Indians in their own tongue. This was usually done through negroes, who could safely approach both Exiles and Indians ; they were, in fact, the only class of persons who could safely go from our posts to those of the enemy. No Indians could do it unless by arrangement made through those negroes ; inasmuch as Creeks, Chickasaws and Choctaws were employed to act with our troops in hunting down the Seminoles, who shot those Creeks, Choctaws and Chickasaws, when opportunity permitted, with just as little ceremony as they did white men.

When those negroes visited the Seminoles, they were supposed to convey to them as accurate intelligence in regard to our troops, as they brought back respecting the enemy's forces; they were, therefore, supposed to have put their brethren, the Exiles, upon their guard in respect to the blood-hounds. Understanding perfectly the nature and *education* of those animals, it does not appear very extraordinary to us that the Exiles remained for a time in the interior, where neither blood-hounds nor civilized troops were accustomed to penetrate. This policy of the Exiles rendered useless the whole expenditure of money and honor, made in the purchase of blood-hounds and Spaniards, with a view to their capture.

But the animals had been obtained, and authority given to our officers to employ them. The Spaniards attended them. The dogs were attached to different regiments, and fed liberally on bloody meat; young calves were provided, and driven with each scouting party, to supply food for them. The Spaniards were supplied with a sufficient number of assistants to keep the dogs in their leashes. Thus provided, several parties, composed of regular troops, militia, Indians, Spaniards, dogs and calves, started for the interior. Their marches continued in some instances for days before they found even the track of an enemy; but when they found foot-prints of Indians, and the dogs were looked to with confidence to lead on the warlike host, while some more humble officer, following the canine leaders, Spaniards and Indians, was expected to bear aloft the glorious stars and stripes, as they engaged in deadly conflict with the wily foe; — lo! just at that moment, when all hearts were palpitating; while hope was at its height; when the stern resolve clothed each brow with the dark scowl of battle, the dogs were blithe and frolicsome, but paid no more attention to the tracks of the Indians than to those of the ponies on which they sometimes rode.

This grand experiment for closing the Florida War was now pronounced a *dead failure;* and the use of dogs, and calves, and Spaniards, was discarded; and the whole affair served no other purpose than to bring odium upon the Administration, and ridicule upon the officers who proposed the employment of blood-hounds to act as allies of the American army.

General Taylor, having had command of the army in Florida nearly two years, and the sickly season having commenced, requested to be relieved from that responsible station. His request was granted, and he left Florida for his plantation in Louisiana. Brevet Brigadier General Armistead, by order of the War Department, assumed the position from which General Taylor retired.

18

CHAPTER XIX.

HOSTILITIES CONTINUED.

Presidential Election of 1840 — The War discussed as one of the issues — Effect on the Election — Publication of Jay's View — Action of the Executive paralyzed — Spanish Indians — Destruction of Indian Key — Troops inactive — Allies commit new depredations — New Expedient — Its failure — Chiefs invited to Fort King — Exiles refuse to treat — Massacre of Lieutenant Sherwood and party — Melancholy fate of Mrs. Montgomery — White men disguised as Indians — Murder of Cora Tustenuggee — Order of Secretary of War — Letter to General Armistead — Bribery of Indians — Mr. Thompson's Bill — Discussion of the causes of the War in Congress — Enemy find protection in large swamps — Their renewed depredations — General distress — People of Florida again driven from their homes — Employed in public service — Their Slaves employed — They become interested in continuing the War.

THE Presidential election of this year was conducted differently
1840.] from any that had preceded it. The opponents of Mr. Van Buren arraigned him before the people for his extravagance in the expenditure of the public treasure, and the immense losses which the nation sustained by the default and irresponsibility of officers appointed by him. It constitutes an era in our political history, from which we date the practice of calling directly upon the people to pass judgment of condemnation upon the action of our National Executive. Every honorable means was resorted to for the purpose of exposing the errors of the Administration during the previous four years.

Among the subjects made prominent before the country, was that of the extravagant expenditures in prosecuting the "Florida War." Speeches were made in Congress exposing the various practices by which the people's money was squandered in that unfortunate conflict; the policy of attempting to compel the Indians to emigrate, and the cruelty practiced towards them, were commented on with severity. These speeches were printed in pamphlet form, and sent to the people in vast numbers: but the real cause of the war, the deep depravity of that policy which sought the enslavement of the Exiles, was not mentioned; nor does it appear that any member of Congress was conscious, even, that such a people as the Exiles was living in Florida.[1] But, nevertheless, it is quite certain that this war proved one of the principal causes of Mr. Van Buren's defeat; and, during the pendency of the election, these complaints paralyzed the action of the Executive.

Another cause operated to call public attention to the war. Hon. William Jay, of New York, published a small book upon the action of our Government in regard to slavery. It was a work of much merit, and, coming from the pen of one so intimately associated with the best interests of the country, it exerted an influence upon the public mind. It had been published some two or three years; but at the time of which we are writing, it attracted attention in most of the free States, and gave public men to understand that their official acts were to be made known to coming generations.

The intimate relation which this war bore to slavery, rendered every movement in regard to it dangerous to the Executive character, and caused our army to be almost inactive for several months; but the allies, driven to desperation, prepared to wreak their vengeance on every white person who should venture within their reach. A small band, composed of Spanish negroes and Indians, among whom were said to be some maroons from Cuba, resided far down in the Peninsula of Florida. They were called Spanish Indians,

---

(1) The Author was at that time a member of the House of Representatives. He had then no conception of the real objects of this war: indeed, it had long been the practice for members to say nothing on the subject of slavery; and it was equally the practice for newspapers to print nothing on that delicate subject, as it was called. Of course the people knew very little concerning it.

and had remained neutral up to the period of which we are speaking ; but finding their brethren driven from their own possessions, and compelled to encroach upon the territory so long occupied by themselves, they took up arms against the United States. Every vessel that happened to be wrecked upon their coast was plundered, and the crews massacred.

On the morning of the seventh of August, a number of these people, said to have been led on by Spanish maroons, crossed over to a small island called "Indian Key," situated at some twenty miles distant from the main land, and attacked the dwellings, burned the storehouses, and destroyed most of the property belonging to the inhabitants. There were but four or five families resident on the island. Of these, Dr. Perrine, a man of some distinction, was murdered in his own house ; but, by his valor, he enabled the other members of his family to escape, amid the darkness of night. The allies obtained much plunder, but found no powder, which was said to have been the principal object of the foray.

During the summer and autumn, our troops in Florida were inactive. The season was sickly, and the officers and men lay supinely in their encampments. The enemy felt secure in their strongholds — sallying forth in occasional forays, murdering the people, and plundering the settlements with impunity. The Administration appeared astonished at the audacity with which a few Indians and negroes hurled defiance at our army and the nation. The expedient of employing savages to assist in the war had failed ; the more questionable policy of employing blood-hounds, had not only failed, but was supposed by many to reflect discredit upon the army and nation. Nearly five thousand troops were kept in Florida, maintained at vast expense ; but they could neither conquer the Indians, nor even protect the white people. Under these circumstances, the Executive saw but one resource ; of that he availed himself. By his direction, twelve Seminole and Mickasukie Indians, who had emigrated West, were induced by sufficient pecuniary considerations to leave their families in the Western Country and return to

Florida, for the purpose of persuading the Indians and Exiles to emigrate. Thus, after four years of war and constant expenditure of blood and treasure, the President discovered that moral power is greater and stronger than physical violence.

But this discovery came too late. He could no longer do justice to those fathers and mothers and children who had been slain, nor to those who had been enslaved; who had been taken far into the interior, sold and transferred from hand to hand like brutes. They had passed from Executive control. The crime now stained our national escutcheon, and no effort could wash it out. The very means which he adopted to close the war, operated to prolong it. These Seminoles and Mickasukies informed their brethren of their own condition, of the manner in which they were treated, and the violations of faith on the part of our Government in not giving them a territory for their separate use, as stipulated in the treaty, and constantly represented to them by our officers; that they were without a home and without a country, residing on Cherokee lands, under Cherokee protection, to prevent the Creeks from enslaving their friends, the Exiles. Many officers at the time doubted their desire to induce the emigration of their brethren.[1]

They, however, obtained an interview between the Commanding General and two Seminole chiefs at Fort King. The chiefs were attended by some forty warriors, who remained in that vicinity four or five days, receiving food and articles of clothing from the United States; but they suddenly disappeared, and it was believed they originally came with hostile, rather than pacific, intentions. When it was found they had left clandestinely, the troops attempted to follow them, but were unable to find any traces of their flight.

---

(1) Captain Sprague, in his history of the Florida War, says, "The truth, when made known to the Indians who remained in Florida, constituted the strongest argument why they should *not* emigrate. Had they (says that author) been kept in ignorance, better results might have been anticipated; but what they gathered from the honest confessions and silence of their brothers tended to make them venerate with more fidelity and increased love the soil which they had defended with heroic fortitude for five consecutive years."

While these things were transpiring, the army lay idle in their quarters; neither the Executive, nor the Secretary of War, nor the Commanding General, knowing what to do.

The Exiles learned from the Seminoles and Mickasukies, who visited them from the West, that many of their brethren who surrendered under the articles of capitulation, had been reënslaved, in violation of our plighted faith; and they refused to hold further intercourse with the agents of our Government. To them there appeared but one alternative — victory or death; and they greatly preferred the latter to slavery. Taking their families far into the interior, they hastened to renew the war with vigor and energy.

A party of some thirty Indians and Exiles were lurking about Micanopy, when, on the twenty-eighth of December, Lieutenant Sherwood, Lieutenant Hopson, Sergeant Major Carrol, and ten privates of the 7th Infantry, left Micanopy for the purpose of escorting Mrs. Montgomery, wife of a Lieutenant of that regiment, through the forest to Watkahoota, eight miles distant. The lady was on horseback, while others of the party rode in a wagon drawn by mules, and some marched on foot. The enemy having observed their movements, preceded them to a hommock, about four miles from Micanopy, where they secreted themselves, and awaited the approach of Mrs. Montgomery and party. When they were fairly within the hommock, through which the road passed, they were fired upon, and two privates fell dead. The war-whoop was raised, and the little party found themselves confronted by savages. Lieutenant Sherwood is said to have rallied his escort with promptness. Mrs. Montgomery, attempting to get into the wagon, was shot dead. Sherwood very discreetly retreated to the open forest, and dispatched Lieutenant Hopson to Micanopy for a reinforcement. Knowing the impossibility of retreating from Indians, and conscious that they gave no quarter, he bravely determined to defend himself or die on the field. But his assailants numbered three times as many warriors as he had. They out-flanked and surrounded his ill-fated party, all of whom with himself fell victims to that policy which had brought this war, with all its crimes, upon our nation.

We cannot withhold our sympathy from those patriotic men who enter the public service expecting to act in an honorable sphere in favor of just measures ; but who are often made the instruments of injustice, and their lives sacrificed to the spirit and policy of oppression. Our officers and soldiers, serving in this Florida War, were duly conscious of the dishonorable employment in which they were engaged ; that they were daily subjected to dangers and death for the purpose of enabling the people of Florida to seize men and women, and sell them into interminable bondage. Officers and men who would cheerfully meet danger and death upon the field of honorable warfare in defense of freedom, were compelled to meet death in all its various and revolting forms in Florida to uphold oppression, to sustain an institution which they abhorred ; nor can we wonder that the consciousness of these facts should have created a feeling of hostility between our regular troops and the slaveholders of Florida, who were constantly charging them with inefficiency and want of energy in the capture of negroes. This feeling ran so high that the white men of Florida were charged with disguising themselves as Indians, and actually committing murders and robberies upon mail carriers and express riders, in order to continue hostilities and keep up the war.[1] This feeling greatly increased the embarrassment of the Executive.

A chief named " Cora Tustenuggee," after due consultation with the interpreters sent to induce him to emigrate, concluded to surrender, and go West. He collected his band, numbering about one hundred in all. Among them were some half breeds, descendants of the pioneer Exiles. They had intermarried with Indians of this band, and were treated as Indians. While on their way to one of our posts, near Palaklikaha Lake, they were fired upon by a party

---

(1) Captain Sprague, in his history, declares, that it was proven in two instances that white men, disguised as Indians, actually committed depredations and murdered white people.

of dragoons who were said to have been conscious of the intentions of the Indians. This supposed violation of faith was greatly aggravated by the subsequent wanton murder of the chief, after he and his band had quietly submitted as prisoners. These people were immediately sent to Tampa Bay, and then embarked for the Western Country, where they joined their brethren, still resident on the Cherokee lands, and under Cherokee protection.

The Presidential election being past, the Executive felt more untrammeled; and Mr. Poinsett, Secretary of War, resisting the instruction which he might have drawn from four years of unfortunate experience, appears to have determined to leave this Florida War in as unpromising condition as he found it. He sent instructions to the Commanding General to renew the war with whatever force he could bring into the field.

It is a somewhat singular fact, that when the Secretary understood, and the country was fully informed, that he would leave the Department on the fourth of March, he wrote the commanding officer on the eighteenth of February, thirteen days prior to his own political dissolution, saying, "The Department entertains the well-" grounded hope that you will be able to bring the war to a close " upon the terms required by the treaty of Payne's Landing, and " by the *interests and feelings of the people of Florida.*"

The reader must be aware that the *feelings and interests* of the people of Florida *required* the capture and enslavement of the Exiles; for which the Secretary of War had so long labored, and which appeared to be his ruling passion—"strong in the hour of his political death."

To effect this object, recourse was had to the bribery of certain chiefs. Money was now offered certain influential men of the Seminoles and Exiles to induce them to exert their influence with their friends to emigrate. It was reported that slaves who had but a few years since left their masters, and intermarried with the Seminoles, dare not surrender, knowing that slavery awaited such act. Without them, their relatives and connexions would not remove. It was therefore proposed that Congress should make an appropriation for the purpose of purchasing such Exiles; yet the bill making it was general in its provisions, granting a hundred thousand dollars to be expended by the Secretary of War for the subsistence and *benefit* of certain chiefs and warriors of the Seminole Indians who wished to emigrate. The subsistence of such emigrants was provided for in other bills; but the *benefits* for which this money was to be expended was to purchase the pretended interest of certain white men to individual Exiles whom they claimed as property.

By thus disguising the real intention and object of the bill, it was evidently expected it would pass without scrutiny, under the rules which prohibited the discussion of all questions involving the subject of slavery. The better to carry out this design, Hon. Waddy Thompson of South Carolina, a Whig member of the House of Representatives, but fully sympathizing with the Executive in his policy of conducting the war in the manner "*required by the interests and feelings of the people of Florida*," was regarded as the proper agent to introduce the bill and superintend its passage.

The information found in the public documents had awakened previous investigation; and when this bill came up for action (Feb 9), the policy of this war, with the causes which led to its commencement, were exposed. Every effort was made by slaveholding members to prevent the public discussion of this subject. They insisted that the gag-rules, as they were called, prohibiting the discussion of slavery, forbid this exposure; but the presiding officer (Mr. Clifford of Maine) adhering to the parliamentary law, decided that an examination of the causes which led to the war was legitimate, and the discussion proceeded.

1841.]

This discussion was published and widely circulated among the people; and is supposed to have given to the public the first information touching the real causes of the war.[1]

---

(1) This first speech had been carefully prepared by the Author of this work, and contained little more than a collation of facts from public documents. It was

The bill passed by a large majority; and the report of the Secretary of War the next year, showing the expenditures of his department, exhibited the manner in which the money appropriated and entrusted to his care was expended. Another bill, however, making an appropriation of more than a million of dollars for suppressing Indian hostilities in Florida was passed, giving to the War Department all the powers desired for bribery, and tempting Indian chiefs to emigrate to the Western Country.

By reference to the map of Florida, it will be perceived that the great swamps, extensive everglades, hommocks, ponds and lakes, which spread over that Territoy, must present great difficulties in the progress of troops embodied in military force; while a small party, following the footsteps of their leader, would pass over, around or through them with facility. The Great Okefenoka Swamp, lying on the south line of Georgia and the northern portion of Florida, afforded a retreat for small parties of Indians and Exiles, from which they sallied forth and committed depredations upon the people of southern Georgia, murdering families, burning buildings and devastating plantations. The swamps bordering on the Withlacoochee, the Great Wahoo Swamp, and other fastnesses on the western portion of the Peninsula, gave shelter to other bands, who, in like manner, wreaked their vengeance upon the inhabitants of that portion of the Territory. So also the Big Cypress Swamp, lying farther south, afforded shelter for others, who laid waste the

---

made with the design of testing the application of the gag-rules more than for the purpose of exposing the character of the war. Hon. John Q. Adams, Wm. Slade, and the Author, often consulted with each other as to the best means for inducing the House to repeal those obnoxious rules. The Author suggested the plan of alluding to slavery while publicly discussing matters with which it was incidentally connected. Mr. Adams and Mr. Slade insisted that the Author should try his plan. Aware that appropriations for this war would be called for, he prepared this speech, showing the causes of the war; and when the bill above referred to came before the House. he proceeded to test his plan. He was frequently called to order, and great excitement was produced; but he succeeded in delivering the speech. When he was through, a southern member replied, declaring that the gag-rules may as well be repealed as kept in force, if they permitted such discussions. The position was evidently correct, and those disgraceful rules were repealed by the next Congress.

settlements along the St. John's River, and in the vicinity of the Atlantic Coast. From these, and numerous other strong-holds, the Indians and their allies came forth in small bands, spreading devastation and death throughout the Territory and the southern portion of Georgia.

The people of Florida who had sought this war, and protested against peace except on such terms as would secure them in the exercise of that oppression which they deemed so necessary to their happiness, now felt the full force of that appropriate penalty which some philosophers believe attaches to every violation of the law of righteousness. Some died by the hands of the very individuals whom they had oppressed, and whom they again sought to enslave; others were again driven from their homes, unable even to obtain food; their wives and children receiving rations from the public stores, and subsisting by the charity of the United States.

But this condition of things superinduced another most extraordinary feature of this war. Our officers, and the Executive, naturally feeling some degree of sympathy for a people thus driven from their homes, on whom the evils of war fell with so much force, extended to them every aid in their power. Some were employed in the Commissary's Department; some as contractors for transporting provisions; and others as attendants upon the army in all the various departments of service, so numerous in a time of war. Even the slaves who remained in the service of their masters were employed by the officers as guides, interpreters and employees at high wages. In this manner they earned for their owners far more than they could by labor upon plantations. This system was carried so far, that the war actually afforded to many greater profits than they could acquire in any other way; and consequently it became a matter of interest with such men to prolong hostilities, and they were said to exert all their influence to effect that object.

CHAPTER XX.

HOSTILITIES CONTINUED.

General Harrison assumes the duties of Chief Executive — Much expected of him — His sudden death — His successor — Political feeling — General Armistead retires — Is succeeded by General Worth — Instructions to General Worth — He discharges all unnecessary employees — Halec Tustenuggee — General Worth's attempt to capture him — Wild Cat — His character and adventures — General Worth sends message to him — He and some companions come in — His manner and bearing — Meets his daughter — Interesting scene — Is seized by Colonel Childs — Placed in irons and sent to New Orleans — General Worth orders his return — Meets him at Tampa Bay — Arrangements — Wild Cat sends messengers to his friends — Sympathy for him — Chief Micco — He brings in his people — Wild Cat's band comes in — He is released from his irons — Meets his friends — His wife and child — General Jessup's policy as to Exiles — Consults Wild Cat — Hospetarche and Tiger-tail — Otulke comes in — Hospetarche is suspicious — Wild Cat brings him in — Army suffers from sickness — General change of policy from that adopted at the commencement of the War — Army reduced — Wild Cat visits Tiger-tail — Singular adventure — Embarkation of Emigrants — Parting scene between Wild Cat and General Worth — The Emigrants reach Fort Gibson and join their friends — Wild Cat's position in his new home.

On the fourth of March, General Harrison was inaugurated President of the United States. Much was expected of him in regard to the war. The Whigs had condemned it throughout the Presidential struggle, and it was anticipated that he would bring it to a successful and honorable termination; but before he even entered upon the consideration of this subject, he was called from this to another sphere of existence, and was succeeded by the then Vice President, John Tyler, of Virginia. Nor is it easy to see what great reform General Harrison could have effected in regard to this war, had he lived to complete his term of service.

The policy of so directing the energies of the Federal Government as to support the interests of slavery, had long existed; he was not expected to make any substantial changes in that respect. But whatever may have been his designs, he had no opportunity to carry them into effect; and Mr. Tyler, after coming into office, soon ceased to enjoy the confidence of the Whig party, who generally declared themselves no longer responsible for his acts.

The new Administration soon identified itself with this war by the following order :

"ADJUTANT GENERAL'S OFFICE,
Washington City, May 19, 1841.

"SIR: Brigadier General Armistead, being about to relinquish "the command of the Florida Army, as you will see by the in-"structions communicated to him of this date, of which a copy is "herewith enclosed; as the officer next in rank, you will relieve "him and assume the command accordingly.

"I am directed, by the Secretary of War, to advise you of the "earnest desire of the Department to terminate, as speedily as pos-"sible, the protracted hostilities in Florida, and to cause the most "perfect protection and security to be given to the frontiers, and "to those citizens who may be disposed to penetrate the country, "for lawful purposes of trade or settlement. For the attainment "of these important objects, you are considered as being clothed "with all the powers of a commander in the field, under the laws "and regulations of the army.

"It is expected the troops under your command will be kept in "a perfect state of discipline, and that you make such disposition "of them as to be in readiness to meet any contingency that may "call for active and energetic movements, the execution of which "is left entirely at your own discretion.

"If you should deem it indispensable for the protection of the "frontier, the President directs that you make a requisition upon "the Governor of Florida for militia, not exceeding one regiment, "which, if called out, you will cause to be mustered into the service

" of the United States, in the manner prescribed by the regulations,
" for any period authorized by the constitution and laws.

" The Secretary of War, placing, as he does, entire confidence
" in your ability and patriotism, desires me to say, that every
" possible aid and support will be afforded to enable you to bring
" to a close this protracted and most embarrassing war.

" As the commander of Florida, you will exercise a sound dis-
" cretion in the use of the means placed at your disposal; and
" while these should be employed with the greatest efficiency, the
" Secretary of War directs that you will, consistently with the pri-
" mary object in view, diminish, in a spirit of sound economy, all
" unnecessary drains upon the Treasury, by discharging all persons
" employed in a civil capacity whose services you shall not deem
" indispensable to the duties of your command, and by regulating
" and reducing as far as practicable all other expenses, in accord-
" ance with the just expectations of the Government and the
" country.

" I am, Sir, your obedient servant,

" (Signed)   R. JONES, Adjutant General.

"Col. J. W. WORTH,
  "8th Infantry, Tampa, Florida."

General Worth now applied himself, with commendable zeal, to
the work assigned him.   His first object was to discharge all employees not necessary to the operations of the army, and in every
department to curtail the expenditures as far as possible ; thereby
rendering the war unprofitable to those who had been seeking to
prolong it.   Early in June he issued the following order :

"No. 1.]   " HEAD QUARTERS, ARMY OF THE SOUTH, }
                              Fort King, June 8, 1841. }

" I.   Hereafter no expenditures of money will be made on
" account of barracks-quarters, or other buildings at temporary
" posts, except for such slight covering as may be indispensably
" necessary for the protection of the sick and security of the public
" stores, without previous reference to, and authority obtained from,
" head-quarters.

" II. All safe-guards or passports granted to Indians prior to
" this date, are hereby revoked. Any Indian presenting himself
" at any post, will be seized and held in strict confinement, except
" when commanding officers may, in the exercise of sound discre-
" tion, deem it advisable to send out an individual runner to com-
" municate with others.

" III. When the garrisons are not too much reduced by sick-
" ness, detachments will be sent out as often as once in seven days,
" or more frequently if circumstances indicate a necessity, to scour
" and examine in all directions to the distance of eight or ten miles.

" IV. All restraints heretofore imposed upon district command-
" ers, in respect to offensive field operations, are hereby revoked ;
" on the contrary, the utmost activity and enterprise is enjoined.
" District commanders will give instructions to commanders of posts
" accordingly.

" V. Brief reports of the operations carried on under the fore-
" going orders, setting forth the strength of the detachments, and
" by whom commanded, with such observations as may be deemed
" useful or interesting to the service, will be made to district com-
" manders on the 10th, 20th, and last of every month, by whom
" they will be transmitted to these head-quarters.

" By order of Colonel WORTH :

"(Signed) G. WRIGHT,

" <i>Capt. 8th Infantry, and A. A. A. General.</i>"</div>

Halec Tustenuggee was regarded as the most active and vindictive of the hostile chiefs. Among his followers were some forty
Indian warriors and ten or twelve Exiles capable of bearing arms.
They and their families, numbering in all some two hundred souls,
were supposed to be somewhere in the neighborhood of Lake
" Fonee-Safakee," among the extensive swamps and hommocks of
that region. Some few of this band had surrendered and gone
West. Among those who came in to Fort Jupiter for the purpose
of emigrating, were several Exiles who had been born in that
region, and had ever been connected with this small tribe. Some

of those who had previously surrendered, were retained as guides and interpreters, with the expectation that they might be made useful in persuading their friends to emigrate also. It was thought very desirable to capture this band, if possible; and guides, and interpreters, and scouts were sent in every direction, where it was supposed they might be discovered, in order to open a communication with them. At length it was reported that a trail had been discovered leading to one of their favorite haunts, where it was believed they might be found.

We cannot better exhibit the dangers which constantly beset the Exiles who remained hostile, or the vigilance with which they and their friends watched for their own safety, than by giving a short account of Colonel Worth's expedition for the capture of this small party, which we copy from Sprague's History of the Florida War. Says that author:

" The negro guides, recently of the band, represented it as his
" favorite resort from its seclusion, where he held his green corn
" dances and councils. Measures were at once adopted to follow
" it up. Colonel Worth, with one hundred men of the 2d Infantry,
" accompanied by Lieutenant Colonel Riley and Major Plympton,
" together with Captain B. L. Beall's company 2d Dragoons, and
" forty men of the 8th Infantry, in command of First Lieutenant
" J. H. Harvil, moved from Fort King for Fort McClure or Warm
" Spring; thence, under the guidance of Indian negroes, to the
" neighborhood of the lake. At midnight, on the night of the
" tenth, the swamp was reached; the troops having marched forty-
" four miles. To surprise the Indian camp just at break of day,
" was the only chance of success. The guides represented it to be
" on the opposite side of the swamp, five or six miles through. The
" horses were picketed, and the baggage left with a small guard on
" the margin of the swamp. The soldier carried only a musket
" and his ammunition; the officers a rifle or sword. Quietly and
" resolutely the command moved, confident of success. The water
" became colder and deeper at every step; halts were frequently

" made to extricate the officers and soldiers from the mud. The
" night was dark, which added to the dismal gloomy shadows of a
" cypress swamp. The command could only follow by the splash-
" ing of water, and the calm but firm intonations of the word of
" command. The negroes in advance, followed closely by the most
" hardy and active, guided these two hundred men to what was be-
" lieved to be the stronghold of the enemy. Every hour and step
" confirmed this conviction. The advance reached the opposite
" side just before the break of day. Anxiously they awaited and
" greeted every officer and soldier as he emerged from the swamp,
" covered with mud and water. Day broke ; when silently the
" command was given — 'Fall in !' Eleven officers and thirty-
" five privates were present. Occasionally a straggler would arrive,
" and report those in the rear as coming. The Indian huts, by the
" gray dawn of morning (twenty-four in number), could be dis-
" cerned through the scrub, which separated the white and red man,
" three hundred yards distant. At this hour the Indian around
" his camp fire feels secure. From the number of huts, and their
" location, they outnumbered the asssailants. To await the arrival
" of the entire force, the 'day would be far advanced ; and discov-
" ery was a total defeat. It was determined with the number pres-
" ent to make a vigorous assault, and, if outnumbered, to rely upon
" those in the rear. Each man reprimed his musket, and cautious-
" ly, on his hands and knees, worked his way through the dense
" undergrowth to within a few yards of the cluster of huts and tem-
" porary sheds. Not a word was uttered. Eagerly each man
" grasped his musket, anxious for the first whoop, when he would
" be rewarded for his toil. A musket was discharged to arouse the
" inmates, and meet them on their retreat. It sent back its dull
" heavy reverberation, causing disppointment and chagrin. Not a
" human being occupied the huts, or was upon the ground."

Large fields of corn were before them ; they had been carefully
cultivated, and gave incontestable proof that the allies had just left.
This place had been the temporary residence of a strong force ; but

19

their patrols had discovered the approach of our troops, and communicated information to the party in time to enable them, with their wives and children, to escape from danger.

The officers and soldiers looked about a while with wonder, and then commenced the work of destroying the cabins and crops, which being effected, they retraced their steps to head-quarters, fully satisfied that a disciplined army was not adapted to the work of surprising Indians and Exiles.

Perhaps no act or policy of General Worth contributed so much to the favorable prosecution of the war, as his treatment of Coacoochee, or Wild Cat, as he was more recently called. This extraordinary personage became conspicuous in 1841. During the entire war he deeply sympathized with the Exiles — was always attended by some of his more dusky friends, in whose welfare he took a deep interest; nor has he yet forsaken them. Even at the time of writing this narrative, he is supposed to be with them; and a short notice of some of his more than romantic experience in this war may interest the reader in the fortunes of a man who may yet fill a large space in the history of our country.

He was the son of King Philip, a Seminole chief of some reputation. He is now (1857) about fifty years of age; five feet eight inches in height; well proportioned; exhibiting the most perfect symmetry in his physical form. His eye is dark, full and expressive; and his countenance youthful and pleasing. His voice is clear, soft and musical; his speech fluent; his gestures rapid and violent. His views are always ingenious and clearly expressed; and he never fails to infuse all his measures with spirit, and to exert a controlling influence over his followers. He was born near Ahapopka Lake, where he resided at the commencement of the Florida War; but soon after sought a more secure retreat in the large swamps, near Fort Mellon and Lake "Okeechobee." His band at that time numbered some two hundred souls, among whom were several families of Exiles. In these sable warriors he is said to have reposed much confidence. He accompanied them at the massacre of Major Dade and his battalion in December, 1835. Here he formed his acquaintance with Lewis Pacheco, who acted as guide to Major Dade. Lewis is said to have attended him, and to have shared in every battle in which Wild Cat participated, until the capitulation of 1837. After that capitulation had been agreed to, he visited General Jessup's camp with the apparent intention of emigrating West. He brought in some of his friends, among whom was Lewis Pacheco, whom he claimed as his slave, and declared that he had captured him at Dade's massacre. Lewis, being a negro, was placed within the stockade at Tampa Bay, but Wild Cat of course went among his friends in the vicinity. When he found that General Jessup was violating the articles of capitulation, and delivering over to slavery those Exiles who were claimed by the people of Florida, instead of securing them in their lives and property, for which the faith of the nation had been pledged, he became indignant, and insisted that every Indian and Exile who was enjoying his liberty, should leave the encampment where they were receiving food and raiment from the United States, and flee to their own homes. Micanopy, one of the most wealthy and influential chiefs, refused, and expressed his determination to emigrate. Wild Cat and Osceola (Powell), two young and daring chiefs, came to the tent of Micanopy, at midnight, and compelled him, at the peril of his life, to leave and flee to the Indian country. He did so, and with him every Indian and Exile, who was outside the stockade at Tampa Bay, made their escape.

At the battle of Fort Mellon, on the eighth of February, 1837, he is said to have commanded two hundred warriors, many of whom were Exiles. He was at the battle of "Okechobee," on the twenty-fifth of December, 1837 ; the severest battle ever fought in Florida. Nearly all his warriors were with him. He was posted on the left of the Indian line, occupying the hommock, when General Taylor approached. He declared that not an Indian gave way until the charge of Colonel Foster, although he said the fire of our men "sent a stream of bullets among his warriors." He stated the whole loss of the allied forces in that memorable conflict to be thirteen killed and nineteen wounded, being less than one-fourth of General Taylor's loss.

His father (King Philip) being imprisoned at St. Augustine in 1838, naturally felt desirous that his son should go with him to the Western Country, where he knew he must emigrate. He sent out a confidential friend with a message to Wild Cat, inviting him to come and see him. General Jessup also sent assurances of his perfect safety, if he wished to come and visit his father. The messenger found him, and faithfully delivered the message which his father sent. There were also other Indians and Exiles going to Fort Peyton, under the peaceful invitation and assurance of safety which General Jessup sent them. Wild Cat left his band; and, arrayed in his best robes, bearing a white flag, went with them and was betrayed, through the agency of General Hernandez, into the power of General Jessup, as we have heretofore shown. He was imprisoned in the castle at St. Augustine with his friend Talmas-Hadjo. Accustomed to roam in the forests at will, and enjoy the free air of Heaven, this confinement bore down their spirits and affected their physical health. He and his friend Talmas-Hadjo made their escape, an account of which was given in a former chapter.

His father remained with the other prisoners—was sent to Charleston; and subsequently died on his passage to Fort Gibson in 1837, with the first party of emigrants under Lieut. Reynolds.

Wild Cat now became one of the most active warriors in Florida. With his followers, he repaired to the Okefenoke Swamp, and, encamping in its fastnesses, sallied forth, as occasion permitted, and spread death and devastation in the southern settlements of Georgia. From thence he returned south, and committed constant depredations both east and west of the St. John's. In 1840, his daughter, an interesting girl of twelve years of age, fell into the hands of our troops, in a skirmish near Fort Mellon. This was regarded as a most fortunate circumstance, as it would be likely to procure an interview with the father. Micco, a sub-chief and friend of Wild Cat, was dispatched with a white flag, on which were drawn clasped hands in token of friendship, with a pipe and tobacco. He found Wild Cat, and delivered the message of the Commanding General, requesting an interview. Wild Cat agreed to come in, and gave Micco a bundle of eight sticks, denoting the days which would elapse before he appeared in camp. Micco returned, and made his report.

On the fifth of March, Wild Cat was announced as approaching the American camp with seven of his trusty companions. He came boldly within the line of sentinels, dressed in the most fantastic manner. He and his party had shortly before killed a company of strolling theatrical performers, near St. Augustine, and, having possessed themselves of the wardrobe which their victims had with them, he now decorated himself and followers in the most grotesque style. He approached the tent of General Worth, calm and self-possessed, and shook hands with the officers. He addressed the Commanding General in fluent and dignified language, saying, he had received the talk and white flag sent him; that, in pursuance of the invitation, he had come to visit the American camp with peaceful intentions; that, relying upon the good faith of the officer in command, he had entrusted himself to their power, in order to promote the designs of peace which had been tendered him. The dignity of his manner, the gracefulness of his gestures, the musical intonations of his voice, the blandness of his countenance, won the sympathy, and commanded the attention, of all around him.

At this moment his little daughter escaped from the tent, where it was intended she should remain until General Worth should feel that the proper time had arrived for him to present her to her father. With the feelings and habits of her race, she presented him musket balls and powder, which she had by some means obtained and secreted until his arrival. On seeing his child, he could no longer command that dignity of bearing so much the pride of every Indian chief. His self-possession gave way to parental emotions; the feelings of the father gushed forth; he averted his face and wept.

Having recovered his self-possession, he addressed Colonel Worth, saying, "The whites dealt unjustly by me. I came to "them, when they deceived me. I loved the land I was upon; "my body is made of its sands. The Great Spirit gave me legs "to walk over it; eyes to see it; hands to aid myself; a head with "which I think. The sun, which shines warm and bright, brings "forth our crops; and the moon brings back the spirits of our war- "riors, our fathers, our wives and children. The white man comes; "he grows pale and sickly; why can we not live in peace? They "steal our horses and cattle, cheat us, and take our lands. They "may shoot us—may chain our hands and feet; *but the red man's* "*heart will be free.* I have come to you in peace, and have taken "you all by the hand. I will sleep in your camp, though your "soldiers stand around me thick as pine trees. I am done: when "we know each other better, I will say more."

General Worth assured him of the good faith with which he should be treated; that the feelings which he had expressed were honorable to him and to his people; that the emotions manifested on seeing his child, were highly creditable to him as a father; assured him that his child should not be separated from him; that the American officers and soldiers highly respected the parental affection which he had exhibited. He then entered upon a consultation with him concerning the best mode of obtaining a peace.

Wild Cat spoke with great sincerity; frankly stated the condition and feelings of this people; stated the friendly attachment between the Exiles and Indians; said that they would not consent to be separated; that nothing could be done until their annual assemblage in June, to feast on the green corn; that, hard as the fate was, he would consent to emigrate, and would use his influence to induce his friends to do so.

After remaining four days in camp, he and his companions left, accompanied by his little daughter, whom he presented to her mother on reaching his own encampment.

Prompt to his engagement with General Worth, he returned on the tenth day after his departure. He stated that he could do nothing until June; but expressed his desire to see General Armistead, the former commander, who was yet at Tampa Bay. With that officer he also made arrangements to do whatever was in his power to induce his friends to emigrate.

There appears no good evidence on which to doubt the sincerity of Wild Cat; yet it appears that General Armistead, before leaving Florida, ordered Colonel Childs, commanding at Fort Pearce, to seize Wild Cat, if he should come within his power, with such followers as should attend him, and send them to Tampa Bay for emigration. General Armistead retired to Washington soon after issuing this order, leaving General Worth in command.

On the twenty-first of May, Wild Cat and his brother, together with an uncle, a brother of his father King Philip, and twelve other Indians and three Exiles, came into Fort Pearce, where Colonel Childs was in command. Wild Cat and his friends had reposed perfect confidence in the honor and good faith of General Worth. He had been betrayed by General Hernandez, acting under General Jessup's orders; had been imprisoned, and suffered much; but from the manner and bearing of General Worth, he had been led to repose the most implicit confidence in his sincerity. Colonel Childs, however, punctilious in his obedience to orders, at once seized and sent him and his companions in irons to Tampa Bay, where they were immediately placed on board a transport and sent to New Orleans, en route for Fort Gibson. The people of Florida heartily approved this transaction, feeling that the Territory was now rid of one of its most dangerous foes.

General Worth soon learned the manner in which Wild Cat had been again seized as a prisoner, in violation of the pledged faith of Government. Mortified and chagrined, he at once dispatched a faithful officer, with explicit directions, to bring Wild Cat and his friends back to Florida at the earliest moment at which he should be able. The officer found them at New Orleans, and forthwith started with them on his return to Tampa Bay.

This measure of General Worth, though bold, and in direct opposition to the popular sentiment of Florida, probably tended as much to the pacification of that Territory as any movement during the war.

General Worth set out to meet the distinguished chief, and reached Tampa Bay on the third of July. The next day he went on board the ship, where he met Wild Cat and his companions; they were yet in irons. As they met upon the deck, the General took him cordially by the hand; assured him of his sincere friendship; of the mistake by which he had been arrested; but assured him, that so great was his renown as a warrior, and such were the fears which the people entertained of him, that, as commanding General, he was constrained to hold him a prisoner.

Perhaps nothing so touches the vanity of a savage as an expression of his greatness; and the consummate policy of General Worth was never more apparent than in the manner of his treating this savage chief. After recounting the devastation and death which Wild Cat had scattered throughout the Territory, he told him, with great emphasis, that he had the power to put an end to the war. He then told him he was at liberty to select five of his most trusty friends, and send them to his band with such a message as would inform them of the precise state of facts, to name the time necessary to gather his band, and have them at Fort Brooke; that, if they failed to come in at the appointed time, he and his followers, who should remain with him, should be *hanged.*

Wild Cat listened with emotion; most of his followers wept. After General Worth had closed his remarks, he arose, and, with great force of eloquence and truth, portrayed the wrongs to which he and his friends had been subjected. He then added, that they had fought the white people bravely, had killed many, but they were too numerous and too strong for them to contend with; that they were compelled to submit. Then, in conclusion, he said he would send out his friends, and do what he could to induce his band to surrender, for emigration.

While he was speaking, the hour of twelve arrived, and an armed ship lying in port, opened her ports and commenced firing a national salute, in honor of the day. Wild Cat stopped, and, turning to General Worth, inquired the cause. It was explained to him, and he readily contrasted his own situation and that of his friends, who were sitting around him in irons, with the condition of the freemen to whom they were prisoners.

After he had concluded his remarks, he gathered around him his friends, and, having consulted with them, he selected his five messengers, one of whom was taken from the Exiles, and the other four from the Indians. The five messengers were brought together, and he addressed them in their own language, apparently with deep emotion; but when he came to inform them of the message they were to deliver to his wife and child, the feelings of the husband and father again overpowered him: he turned aside and wept; and such was the deep and thrilling interest which pervaded those around him, that the hardy sailors who had long been accustomed to danger, and the soldier who had become familiar with death in its various forms, were melted to tears. The sympathy became general; and all present seemed to acknowledge the reality of those holy affections of the human heart which God has implanted deep down in its core and center. Silence pervaded the whole assemblage. The order was given by General Worth in a low and solemn voice to remove the fetters from the limbs of the five messengers. It was done quietly, and all looked on with interest. After the irons had been taken from their limbs, and all was prepared for their departure, Wild Cat shook hands with each as they passed over the side of the ship. To the last he handed a silk handkerchief and a breast-pin, saying, "give them to my wife and child."

The time which Wild Cat had voluntarily set for their return, was forty days. The band was supposed to be on the Kissimee or

St. John's River; and much interest was felt by all in the result. They greatly feared that delay might take place in finding and communicating with them. Officers and soldiers participated in the excitement; and the messengers were instructed by them to inform the commanding officer at that post, if any great delay should occur.

The success of this mission was regarded as the turning point of the Florida War, and in its perfect success all felt a deep interest; as it was believed that his example would be followed by other chiefs of sufficient influence to bring this long protracted war to a close.

The officers visited Wild Cat and his friends, on board the ship, daily, and endeavored to cheer them by constantly expressing their confidence in the fidelity of the messengers. He endeavored to surmount the anxiety and apprehension which his situation naturally brought to his mind; but his care-worn countenance and anxious manner showed the corroding solicitude which he felt.

" Old Micco," the Indian chief who at first induced Wild Cat to come in to Fort Cummings, was at Tampa Bay at the time the messengers left. He was aged, but continued active. He had been the confidential friend of King Philip, the father of Wild Cat, and was now the warm friend of the son. He volunteered to accompany the messengers, assuring Wild Cat that he would himself return in ten days with such tidings as he should be able to gather in that time.

The old man, faithful to his engagement, on the tenth day appeared at Tampa Bay with six warriors and a number of women and children, and reported that others were on their way. The return of Micco with such intelligence cheered his followers and friends, and gave to our officers and soldiers confidence in the entire success of the plan; but the chief continued to exhibit gloom, and at times he evinced despondency of spirits.

In the meantime, his people continued to arrive daily, and in less than thirty days, his entire band were encamped at Tampa

Bay. He had informed General Worth of the precise number of his warriors by delivering to him a bundle containing one stick for each warrior. On the last day of July, it was found that the number of warriors, including Exiles, exactly corresponded with the number of sticks.

When informed that his warriors were all in, he resumed his natural cheerfulness; his countenance became lighted up with hope and intelligence; his bearing was lofty and independent. Several officers went on board to congratulate him. He was warmly greeted. He now, turning to the officer of the guard, in a tone of confident assurance, requested that his irons might be removed, and he permitted to address his warriors, as he said, "like a man." His shackles were taken off; and he then dressed himself in a manner which he deemed fitting the occasion. His turban was of crimson silk, from which three ostrich plumes were gracefully suspended; his breast was covered with glittering silver ornaments; his many-colored frock was fastened around his waist by a girdle of red silk, into which was thrust his scalping knife, enclosed in its appropriate scabbard. Red leggins and ornamented moccasins completed his attire. He was attended on shore by several officers, who took seats with him in the boat. As they approached the shore, and he saw his friends who had gathered at the landing to greet him, his heart seemed to swell with emotion; but gathering himself for the occasion he became dignified and haughty in his deportment, and as he stepped on shore he waived his hand, beckoning them all to stand back. They impulsively obeyed; and raising his form to its utmost height he sent forth a shrill war-whoop, which reached every ear in the vicinity, as the announcement of his freedom. A hearty response at once came back from every warrior of the band. The crowd simultaneously opened to the right and left, when, without noticing the presence of any person, he at once proceeded to the head-quarters, where he met General Worth, whom he saluted in the most respectful manner. He then turned to his people and addressed them, stating the arrangement with General Worth, thanking them for so cheerfully coming to him, declared they were now at peace with the white people. He then inquired for his wife and child, who had remained silent spectators of the whole scene. They at once came forward, and as he saw them, the feelings of the husband and father again overcame him for an instant; but resuming his lofty demeanor he mingled again with those faithful and tried followers, who had so often stood beside him in times of peril.

Such were the fortunes, and such the character, of one of those chieftains whom the incidents of the Florida War brought into public notice. He is now introduced to the reader, and will continue to receive occasional attention until the close of our narrative, and perhaps he may again appear in the future history of the people to whose trials and persecutions we are now directing attention.

We have felt this sketch due to the cause of truth, inasmuch as during the war, and even up to the present day, public newspapers have spoken of Wild Cat as a cruel and vindictive savage. His efforts in behalf of freedom have been represented by public officers as crimes, and he has been held up to the public as an unprincipled brigand. We would judge him, as we would all others, by his acts.

Wild Cat's band, now convened at Tampa Bay, had been previously diminished by emigration. It now numbered seventy-eight warriors, sixty-four women and forty-seven children — making in all one hundred and eighty-nine souls. We have no official statement of the number of Exiles who surrendered with this band. We suppose, however, from the warm interest which Wild Cat always took in behalf of the Exiles, that more would have flocked to his standard than to those of other chiefs; but we have no evidence that such was the fact. Probably the Exiles constituted about one-sixth of the band — that being the proportion of Exiles who accompanied him to Fort Cummings, and were seized with him by Colonel Childs. Indeed, we have had no official data by which to determine the proportion of Exiles who constituted the several parties that surrendered after General Jessup left the army. No subsequent commander in Florida appears to have drawn distinctions as to the color of his prisoners. They were all reported as *Seminoles*, and the term "negro" occurred only incidentally in their official reports, when speaking of the class of interpreters and agents who were employed ; nor do we find that General Worth made any effort to send any of his prisoners into slavery. So far as we are informed, like General Taylor, he treated them all as *prisoners of war*, entitled to the same rights, the same respect, and the same attentions, agreeably to the doctrine advanced by General Gaines at New Orleans.

General Worth appears to have felt authorized to send every Exile who surrendered, to the Western Country. If any of them were claimed by the slaveholders of Florida, he directed the proofs of ownership to be taken and the value of the negro estimated, and then, without waiting for further contest, the negro was treated as other prisoners, and sent West with his Seminole friends, leaving the Government to pay for the slave or not, as the Executive and Congress should determine.[1]

It was this policy which enabled General Worth to conduct the war with so much greater success than his predecessors. It enabled him to avail himself of all the influence of Wild Cat, now exerted in favor of emigration ; while General Jessup, by delivering over the Exiles to slavery, had induced the same chief to exert absolute violence to prevent emigration.[2]

General Worth, having secured the friendship and coöperation

(1) This statement is founded upon the authority of Captain Sprague. It is however certain, that many of the claimants actually received compensation from the public treasury for the loss of their slaves. The power to pay for them was assumed by Executive officers, under the appropriation act of March, 1841, without reference to Congress.

(2) Captain Sprague, in his history, enters into a somewhat lengthened apology for this practice of General Worth, by saying, the negroes were the most active and vindictive of the hostile forces ; that, from the peculiar situation of the country, ten negroes could keep it in a state of constant alarm ; that many of them had intermarried with the Seminoles and become identified with them, had acquired their habits, and would have been useless to their owners had they been delivered to them ; that the negro would have remained in service but a few days, when he would have again taken to the swamps and hommocks, where he could elude pursuit, and would have been more vindictive than before.

of Wild Cat, entered into consultation with him as to the best method of carrying out his plan of peaceful surrender of the Indians and Exiles, and their emigration West. Those in the eastern part of the Territory, under Hospetarche and Tiger-tail and Sam Jones, were bitterly opposed to emigration. They determined, in council, to kill any messenger sent to them for the purpose of persuading them to surrender, or any one who should attempt to leave them for the purposes of emigration.

Notwithstanding this determination, some three or four families, numbering in all about twenty souls, made their escape (Aug. 10), and, though closely pursued, reached the military post on Pease Creek, and were sent to Tampa Bay, where they joined Wild Cat's band. Otulke, a brother of Wild Cat, lived in the vicinity of those people who had become so indignant, and it was deemed important to inform him of Wild Cat's determination to go West. The chief had also a younger brother, now with the band at Tampa Bay, who volunteered to perform the hazardous duty of carrying a message to Otulke. Much solicitude was felt for his safety, but he accomplished his mission successfully. Otulke, with some six warriors and their families, obeyed the call, and came to Tampa Bay and joined the party destined for emigration.

Otulke also brought a message from Hospetarche, an aged chief, the head of a small band numbering nearly one hundred souls. He was said to be eighty-five years of age; but was yet active, and possessed great energy. He sent a message to Wild Cat that he, too, was coming in to see him. He was from the "Great Cypress Swamp," whose inhabitants were regarded as very treacherous, and altogether destitute of integrity.

A few days after Otulke arrived, Hospetarche sent a boy with a white flag to Tampa Bay, saying, he was old and fatigued, and wanted whisky and provisions to enable him to reach Fort Brooke. These were sent him; but the next day another message of the same character was received, and complied with. This practice continued for five days. And such was the desperate character of the old chief, that none of the friendly Indians dared go out to meet him, particularly as they learned that he was attended only by warriors; they believed he was intent on hostility rather than peace, and they feared him.

Wild Cat had been absent for some days. When he returned, he ascertained the situation of Hospetarche, with whom he had long been acquainted. The next morning he dressed himself in his gayest attire, and, taking his rifle, mounted his favorite horse, which had been brought to Tampa Bay by his followers.

The officers who witnessed his departure, declared that the noble animal exhibited evidence of having recognized his master. No sooner had Wild Cat mounted, than he began to champ his bit and paw the earth, as if impatient to bear forth his rider to the hunting grounds. Wild Cat, sitting upon his spirited horse, shook hands with General Worth and the other officers, and then dashed into the forest; and before sunset, returned with his venerable friend, Hospetarche, and eighteen warriors.

After they arrived, they were treated kindly, but placed under a strong guard. They sent confidential friends however to their homes, who in a few days returned, bringing with them the women and children of the whole band. There were now at Tampa Bay nearly three hundred prisoners ready for emigration, including Exiles, supposed to be about sixty· in number.

While General Worth was thus successful in his efforts to induce the Indians and their allies peacefully to emigrate, he was pained to witness the sufferings to which his army were subjected. As an illustration of the sacrifice which our nation made in this effort to enslave the Exiles, we would state, that the 1st regiment of Infantry, under Colonel Miller, came to Florida in 1838, and left in August, 1841. It numbered some six hundred men, and during the three years of its residence in Florida, one hundred and thirty-five soldiers and six commissioned officers died of sicknes. This we believe to be nothing more than the average loss of the troops who served in that war, in proportion to the time of service. The official reports for July, 1841, showed two thousand four hundred and twenty-eight men on the sick list, unfit for duty, being considerably more than one half of the whole army.

A few Indians and Exiles, from various bands, occasionally arrived at Tampa Bay, and joined the emigrating party. Throughout the different families, they appeared to believe that General Worth was acting in good faith. The whole character of the war had undergone a change. It had originally been commenced and prosecuted for the purpose of reënslaving Exiles: now that object, so far as they could discover, appeared to have been given up. Exiles and Indians were treated alike. Wild Cat, their most active and popular chief, and the leading Exiles with him, were acting with sincerity in favor of emigration. The war was in fact suspended, for the adoption of a more pacific policy, which seemed to promise success.

Tiger-tail was yet inexorable and inveterate. He was said to have murdered his own sister for proposing to surrender; yet a small party from his band escaped to Tampa Bay, and were protected. A few other Indians and Exiles were captured without bloodshed; and such were the prospects of returning peace, that by the commencement of September, General Worth informed the War Department that the 3d regiment of Artillery could be spared from the service in Florida; and that he hoped, within a month, to discharge the 4th and 5th Infantry, and the 3d Dragoons.

Wild Cat visited Tiger-tail in his retreat, which was regarded as a most hazardous undertaking. With six followers he started on a visit to this barbarous chief. He reached the vicinity of his camp near nightfall, but deemed it prudent not to approach at that late hour of the day. He and his friends fearing discovery, bivouacked in a grove, supposing they had not been noticed by any one. In the darkness of the night, they heard slight movements near them. Wild Cat suspected it was the wary chief, preparing to massacre himself and friends. He boldly called out, announcing his own name, and telling Tiger-tail not to come upon him like a coward,

Thlocklo Tustenuggee, (Tiger Tail.)

by stealth, but to speak frankly, or come up boldly to a personal conflict. Tiger-tail, surprised and astonished at this course, commenced conversation. Wild Cat, referring to their former friendship, avowed his desire to renew the attachment; or, if Tiger-tail insisted on fighting, then he would meet him in a manner becoming a bold warrior. The ferocity of Tiger-tail gave way. They agreed to meet next day, when a long consultation was held. The savage chief gave assurances of his peaceful disposition, and promised to reflect upon the propriety of emigrating. Wild Cat also sent to other chiefs messages, assuring them of his intention to emigrate; that his band, and that of Hospetarche, with individuals from other villages, were at Tampa Bay with the intention of soon embarking for the Western Country.

Tiger-tail insisted on seeing Alligator, a Seminole chief, who emigrated in 1837, saying, if Alligator would come back and advise him to go West, he would comply with such advice. A messenger was accordingly sent West to bring Alligator to Florida.

In the meantime, Wild Cat declared to General Worth that he desired to see his own people on their way; and assigned as the reason for such desire, that Indians were a restless people, and could not be long kept inactive, with no employment for either body or mind. The advice was received by General Worth with respect, and he at once gave orders to prepare for the journey. Transports had been employed, and were then in waiting. The women and children were engaged in cracking corn, to serve as food for their journey. Amid all the cares which surrounded him, General Worth endeavored to make both Indians and Exiles comfortable, and render them cheerful. They were a wronged and persecuted people, about to leave their homes, their native country, and go to a distant region, of which they were ignorant. Driven from the graves of their fathers, they were about to be separated from scenes which had been familiar to them from childhood.

Of those who had come in for emigration, fifteen had died. Wild Cat detailed from his band seven, and Hospetarche detailed ten war-

20

riors, who, with their families, making some eighty souls in all, were
to remain with General Worth for a while in order to exert what
influence they could with their friends in favor of emigrating to the
West. The number who actually embarked was little more than
two hundred and fifty, exclusive of fourteen Mickasukies, who per-
sisted in drawing their rations, and in all things being separated
from the others. Some fifty Exiles are supposed to have been
among those who embarked, and two of the seventeen families who
remained at Tampa Bay were of mixed blood. The emigrants were
all on board the transports, when General Worth and staff paid
them a last visit. The scene was said to be affecting. Hospetarche,
venerable for his years, sat in silence, resting his head upon his
hands, and looking back upon his native land. He appeared dis-
qualified for holding conversation with any one, and none appeared
willing to disturb his seeming melancholy reflections. The women
— both Exiles and Indians — were weeping and sighing, unre-
strained by that dignity so much cultivated by savages of the other
sex. The warriors — black and red — were solemn and silent.
This appeared to give Wild Cat pain. He stood upon the quarter
deck with his sub-chiefs around him. As General Worth was
about to take leave, "I am looking (said Wild Cat) at the last
" pine tree of my native land. I am about to leave Florida for
" ever; and I can say that I have never done anything to disgrace
" the land of my birth. It was my home : I loved it as I loved
" my wife and child. To part from it, is like separating from my
" own kindred. But I have thrown away the rifle ; I have shaken
" hands with the white man, and I look to him for protection."
He then addressed General Worth, thanked him for all his kindness and confidence ; and on behalf of his people he expressed a
high sense of gatitude for the humanity and friendship extended to
them. Then extending his hand to the General he bade him fare-
well. General Worth, in taking leave, expressed the hope that
they would have a pleasant journey, and find themselves happy in
their western homes. They parted ; the anchor was hauled up,

the sails hoisted; and the unhappy emigrants soon cast their last lingering look upon the long-loved scenes of their childhood.

They were hurried on their way as rapidly as wind and steam could propel the ships in which they embarked. They made a short stay at New Orleans; and in two weeks from the time they left Tampa Bay, they landed at Fort Gibson, and were conducted to the settlement made by their brethren who had previously emigrated. Here Wild Cat found himself in a new sphere. Respected and beloved by his followers for his gallant bearing; his undoubted courage; his devotion to the interests of his people; his truth and justice — distinguished above all others of his tribe by his warlike exploits, he was qualified and prepared to enter upon the trying scenes which awaited his future life.

CHAPTER XXI.

CLOSE OF THE WAR.

Delegation from Emigrants return to Florida — Their efforts in favor of Peace — Pacific indications — Troops discharged — Indians and Negroes surrender — Foray of Captain Wade — Waxe Hadjo surrenders — Massacre at Mandarin — People of Georgia and Florida dissatisfied with General Worth — They insist on furnishing Troops — Gen. Worth refuses to employ Militia — General McDonald and Volunteers from Georgia take the field — Demand the withdrawal of the Regular Troops — They are withdrawn — Call for Provisions — General Worth refuses to furnish them — Militia disband — Tustenuggee Chapco surrenders — More Troops discharged — General Worth states the number of Enemy, and recommends cessation of Hostilities — Propositions rejected by Executive — Battle with Halec Tustenuggee — His character — His capture — He and his people sent West — President reconsiders General Worth's advice — Adopts the proposed policy — General Worth calls Council — Terms of Peace agreed upon — General Order — General Worth retires — War ended — Its object — Its cost — Number of lives sacrificed — Character of Indians and Exiles who remained in Florida.

On the fourteenth of October, Alligator, with two other chiefs, and one of the leading Exiles, named James, reached Fort Brooke, on their return from the Western Country. They came at the request of General Worth to exert their influence with Tiger-tail and others in favor of emigration. The next day they left for the interior, and after an absence of seven days returned with Tiger-tail. The General held several conversations with him, and kindly expressed his sympathy for the Indians, explaining his own situation and duty, and advising the Indians to emigrate as their best policy. Tiger-tail, after remaining in camp four days, returned for his band; and friendly Indians were dispatched by

1841.]

General Worth to Sam Jones and other chiefs to induce them also to come in. Some thirty Indians deserted Halec Tustenuggee (Nov. 10), and came to Fort Brooke. The appearance of Indians and Exiles was so pacific that the Commanding General discharged from further service in Florida five companies of dragoons, who were ordered to the western frontier. The Indians and Exiles who remained at Fort Brooke when Wild Cat and his party left for the West, were active in their endeavors to induce their other friends to emigrate. In these efforts they were at least partially successful. Small parties from the bands of Tiger-tail and Nethloke-Mathla arrived occasionally, and with the apparent consent of those chiefs; but Tiger-tail himself appeared suspicious and wary. He would not come in then, but promised to do so at some future day. The influence of most of the Exiles now remaining in Florida was exerted in favor of emigration. It is believed that nearly every family of pure Exile blood had left; that the last of that class had departed with Wild Cat, particularly all of the descendants of those pioneers who remained unconnected with the Indians by marriage. There were yet remaining a few who had more recently fled from their masters in Florida and Georgia. They dared not trust themselves within the power of our troops, lest they should be reconsigned to slavery. They exerted a strong influence with the Indians against emigration. There were also, in almost every band and small village of Indians, Exiles who had intermarried with Indian families. They could not well separate from their family connexions, and therefore refused to surrender for emigration, until those relatives would go with them. By the twentieth of November, fifty-two warriors and a hundred and ten women and children — making in all one hundred and sixty-two people — were gathered from the bands of Tiger-tail and Nethloke-Mathla; some thirty of whom were Exiles, intermarried with the Indians and half-breeds.

Captain Wade made a foray into the Indian Country, and captured some sixty-five Indians and Exiles of two different bands, by surprise, and without bloodshed. They were mostly women and children, and were at once sent forward to Tampa Bay for emigration.

About the close of November, "Waxe-Hadjo," a young chief from the Cypress Swamp, with seventeen warriors and more than thirty women and children — some ten or twelve of whom were half-breeds, descendants of Exiles and Seminoles — surrendered, and were sent to Fort Brooke for emigration.

While everything thus wore the appearance of peace, and all were regarding the war as near its close, a small settlement of white people, at a place called Mandarin, twenty-two miles from Jacksonville, was assailed in open day, and five of the people murdered. This attack was conducted by a small party of Indians, less than twenty in number, who had come from the interior, and in a stealthy manner approached this settlement, committed the murders, and retired before any troops could be brought to the scene of slaughter.

Near the close of the year, the authorities of Georgia and Florida gave evidence of their dissatisfaction of the manner in which General Worth was conducting the war. The militia of neither Florida nor Georgia were called on to participate in the war. No opportunities were afforded them of seizing negroes and selling them into slavery; none but the regular sutlers were permitted to encamp with or near the troops; in short, the war, as then conducted, afforded them but little profit. General Worth had encouraged the return of the people to their homes and plantations, and very few of them now drew rations from the public stores for their support. He had discharged citizens and their slaves from public employment, and the war was carried on without permitting the people, or politicians of Georgia or Florida, to interfere or dictate the manner of its prosecution.

This proceeding of General Worth greatly excited the people and Executive of Georgia, who insisted upon furnishing militia to carry on the war. The Secretary of War referred the matter at once to General Worth, and a most interesting and amusing correspondence followed between the Executive of Georgia and the Commanding General. The latter refusing to call for militia from that State, they were mustered without his authority, and he was requested by Governor McDonald to withdraw the United States forces from the Georgia frontiers.

As there was then no enemy near that State, and no danger to the inhabitants, he removed the troops, and the Georgia militia were ordered by the Governor to take their place. They did so with the confident expectation that General Worth would furnish rations and hospital supplies and arms from the United States stores. But he refused to do this, and the gallant militia of that State immediately retired to their homes in order to dine.

The correspondence on this subject continued until May, 1842, and shows the skillful management of individuals to get up alarms in regard to the supposed presence of hostile Indians, and thereby manifest the necessity of posting troops in certain localities, where there had probably never been an enemy. To give importance to these counterfeited alarms, letters were written, and presentments were made by Grand Juries. The Delegate from the Territory of Florida demanded of the Executive the employment of militia for the protection of the frontier, and that such militia be authorized to act independently of the Commanding General.

Hon. John C. Spencer, Secretary of War, replied, that the Department could see no particular advantage to be derived from such a division of the duties of the Commanding General; and, as he had no doubt General Worth would do whatever was proper, he referred the whole matter to his consideration.

Had General Jessup, in 1836 and '37, adopted the policy which guided General Worth; had he sent his prisoners to the Western Country without permitting the militia, or the people of Florida, to seize and enslave those whom he had engaged to protect and defend, there is little doubt that the war would have been closed during the time he was employed in Florida.

During the last days of December, Tustenuggee Chopco, a sub-chief, and about seventy followers, consisting of warriors, women and children, a proportion of whom were Exiles and half-breeds, surrendered near the Great Cypress Swamp, and were also sent to Fort Brooke for emigration.

1843.]   At the commencement of this year several more companies of troops were discharged, the number of the enemy being so far diminished as to render their presence useless.

On the fifth of February, some three hundred and fifty Indians and Exiles were embarked at Tampa Bay for the Western Country. They in due time reached Fort Gibson, and took up their residence with those who had gone before them, and were still residing upon the lands of the Cherokees.

On the fourteenth of February, General Worth addressed the Commanding General of our army, at Washington City, a communication, giving a detailed statement of the number of Indians yet remaining in Florida — amounting in all to three hundred, according to the best information he had been able to obtain. He also stated the impossibility of capturing these individuals, scattered as they were over a vast extent of country, and advising that they be dealt with, henceforth, in a peaceful manner; and that at least five-sixths of the troops then employed in Florida be withdrawn, and an equal proportion of the expenses of the war be curtailed. He proposed sending a portion of those friendly Indians who remained at Fort Brooke, among the hostiles, to continue with them, and exert what influence they could in favor of peace and of emigration; with the assurance, that no further hostilities would be prosecuted by the United States while the Indians remained peaceful.

The proposition, however, was rejected by the Executive; and General Worth continued to carry forward the work which he had prosecuted thus far with such signal success. He dismissed more troops from service in Florida; discharged employees in the various departments under his command, and made such retrenchment; as he was able to effect, without detracting from the efficiency of the public service.

On the sixteenth of April, the troops fell in with Hallec Tustenuggee, who, with some seventy warriors of his own and other bands, was encamped upon an island in the Great Wahoo Swamp, and after an irregular fight of two hours, routed them. The loss was slight on both sides. Our troops had one man killed, and four wounded; the allies three wounded, whom they carried from the field. This was the last battle fought in the Florida War. The Indians scattered in various directions, and in that way evaded pursuit.

Halec Tustenuggee was a most skillful warrior: bold and daring in his policy, yet capable of dissimulation and treachery. He had been the object of pursuit for two years. His unceasing vigilance had enabled him to bid defiance to civilized troops. He was now nearly destitute of powder and provisions, and, as an alternative, professed a desire for peace. He came into the American camp boldly, shook hands with General Worth, and proclaimed his pacific purpose. His professions were treated with great apparent respect. He wanted provisions for his band. They were encamped within three miles of General Worth's head-quarters, and were fed at public expense. And when the whole band had come within the lines, for the purpose of attending a feast, they were secured as prisoners, and immediately sent to Tampa Bay for emigration; and, on the fourteenth of July, this entire band, consisting of one hundred and twenty persons, embarked for Fort Gibson, by way of New Orleans. They reached their destination in safety; and most of them took up their residence with their brethren, the Seminoles; while others joined the Creeks.

The Federal Executive, having more maturely considered the suggestions of General Worth, at length concluded to accede to his propositions for a pacification with the remaining hostiles in Florida. That officer, having secured Halec Tustenuggee and his band, and sent them West, now dispatched his messengers to those small bands of hostiles which remained, inviting them to hold a council and enter into an arrangement, based upon the condition, that the allies should remain in the southern portion of the Peninsula of Florida, confined to certain limits, and abstain from all acts of aggression upon their white neighbors.

Most of these small bands sent chiefs, or sub-chiefs, to attend the council; and terms of peace were agreed to, and the following General Order was issued:

"ORDER, ⎞   HEAD QUARTERS NINTH MILITARY DEPARTMENT, ⎞
  No. 28. ⎠   *Cedar Key, Florida*, August 14, 1843.   ⎠

" It is hereby announced, that hostilities with the Indians within
" this Territory have ceased.   Measures are taken to pass the few
" remaining Indians within certain limits — those in the far south
" immediately; those west of the Suwanee in a few days, who,
" meantime, there is every reasonable assurance, will conduct in-
" offensively if unmolested in their haunts.   The lands thus tem-
" porarily assigned, as their planting and hunting grounds, are
" within the following boundaries, to wit: From the mouth of
" Talockchopco, or Pease Creek, up the left bank of that stream to
" the fork of the southern branch, and, following that branch, to
" the head or northern edge of Lake Istokpoga; thence down the
" eastern margin of that lake to the stream which empties into the
" Kissimee River, following the left bank of the said stream and
" river to where the latter empties into Lake Okeechobee; thence
" down, due south, through said lake and everglades to Shark
" River, following the right bank of that river to the Gulf; thence
" along the Gulf shore (excluding all islands between Punta Rosa
" and the head of Charlotte's Harbor) to the place of beginning.

" The foregoing arrangements are in accordance with the instruc-
" tions of the President of the United States.

" By order of Col. WORTH :

"S. COOPER, A. A. General."

Most of the troops were now withdrawn from Florida.   General Worth retired from the command, and the Florida War was supposed to have ended.   It had been commenced with a determination to reënslave the Exiles.   That object was, in part, attained.   More than five hundred persons were seized and enslaved, between the first of January, 1835, and the fourteenth of August, 1843. Probably one half of them had been born free; the others had themselves escaped from slavery. To effect this object, forty millions of dollars were supposed to have been expended. Eighty thousand dollars was paid from the public treasury for the enslavement of each person, and the lives of at least three white men were sacrificed to insure the enslavement of each black man. The deterioration of our national morality was beyond estimate, and the disgrace of our nation and government are matters incapable of computation. The suffering of the Indians and Exiles amidst such prolonged persecution, such loss of lives and property, we cannot estimate. The friends and families who were separated, the number of those who were made wretched for life, the broken hearts, we will not attempt to enumerate. Nearly one half of the whole number were consigned to the moral death of slavery, and many to that physical death which was dreaded far less than slavery. After wandering in the wilderness thrice forty years, they fell under the oppression, the persecution, the power of a mighty nation, which boasts of its justice, its honor, and love of liberty. We lament the sad fate of those who died in that struggle; but with deeper anguish, and far keener mortification, we deplore the unhappy lot of those who were doomed to drag out a miserable existence, amidst chains and wretchedness, surrounded by that moral darkness which broods over the enslaved portion of our fellow-beings in the Southern States.

There are yet remaining in Florida a few descendants of the pioneer Exiles. They are intermarried with the bands of " Billy Bowlegs," and of " Sam Jones," sometimes called Aripeka; they are now mostly half-breeds, and are rapidly becoming amalgamated with the Indian race.

Besides these, there are a number of Spanish Refugees, or colored people who fled from Spanish masters and took up their residence with those called " Spanish Indians." These did not engage in the war until 1840 : nor did they then engage in any of the battles with our army ; they contented themselves with plundering ships wrecked on their coast, and the foray upon Indian Key. They refused to send delegates to the council summoned by General Worth, to establish terms of pacification. They live independent of the white people, subsisting mostly on fish and the natural products of the soil, holding very little intercourse with either white men or other Indians. Descendants of Exile parents, they have the complexion and appearance of pure Spaniards ; but they are rapidly blending with the Indians, and forming a mixed race. ·

These different bands, remaining in Florida, and aggregating into a distinct people, have on several occasions since 1843, given evidence of implacable hostility to the whites. And at the time of writing this narrative, they are engaged in open war ; while the Government of the United States is endeavoring to secure peace in the same manner and upon the same terms on which General Worth obtained it, in 1843. Their future history may, hereafter, occupy the pen of some other historian.

CHAPTER XXII.

HISTORY OF EXILES CONTINUED.

Character of Abraham — His knowledge of the Treaty of Payne's Landing — Its stipulations — General Jessup's assurances — Confirmed by other Officers of Government — Disappointment of Exiles on reaching Western Country — They refuse to enter Creek jurisdiction — Creeks disappointed — General Cass's policy of reuniting Tribes — Agent attempts to pacify Exiles — Hospitality of Cherokees — Discontent of all the Tribes — Seminoles loud in their complaints — Hostilities apprehended — Conduct of Executive — Agents selected to negotiate another Treaty — Treaty stipulations — Attempts to falsify history — Executive action unknown to the people.

THE Exiles were now all located on the Cherokee lands, west of the State of Arkansas. They had been removed from Florida at great expense of blood and treasure; but they were yet free, and the object of the Administration had not been attained. Conscious of the designs of the Creeks, the Seminoles and Exiles refused to trust themselves within Creek jurisdiction. They were tenants at will of the Cherokees, whose hospitality had furnished them with temporary homes until the Government should fulfill its treaty stipulations, in furnishing them a territory to their separate use.

Abraham was, perhaps, the most influential man among the Exiles. He had been a witness and interpreter in making the treaty of Payne's Landing, and had dictated the important provision in the supplemental treaty; he had exerted his influence in favor of emigration; to him, therefore, his people looked with more confidence than to any other individual. In all his intercourse with our officers, he had been assured of the intention to fulfill those treaties; and when he found the Government hesitating on that point, he became indignant, and so did others of his band. But he could only express his indignation to the Agent appointed to superintend their affairs and supply their wants. These complaints were made known to the Indian Bureau, at Washington; but they were unheeded, and the Exiles and their friends lived on in the vain hope that the Administration would at some day redeem the pledged faith of the nation, and assign them a territory for their separate use, where they could live independent of the Creeks, as they had done for nearly a century past.

Nor is it easy for men at this day to appreciate that feeling which so stubbornly sought their enslavement; we can only account for this unyielding purpose, from the long-established practice of so wielding the power and influence of the nation as best to promote the interests of slavery. It is certain, that it would have cost the United States no more to set off to the Exiles and Seminole Indians a separate territory, on which they could live free and independent, than it would to constrain them to settle on the Creek lands, and subject them to Creek laws, and Creek despotism, and Creek servitude.

General Jackson, in 1816, had ordered Blount's Fort to be destroyed and the negroes returned to those who owned them. To effect this latter object, in 1822, he proposed to compel the Seminole Indians to return and reünite with the Creeks. If at any time there were other reasons for the frauds committed upon the Exiles and Indians—for the violations of the pledged faith of the nation—it is hoped that some of the officers who acted a prominent part in those scenes of treachery and turpitude, or their biographers, will yet inform the public of their existence.

Settled, as the Seminoles and Exiles now were on the Cherokee lands, all parties concerned were necessarily dissatisfied. The Creeks were disappointed, and greatly dissatisfied at not having the Exiles in their power, and charged our Government with bad faith in not delivering that extraordinary people into their hands. The Cherokees had assured the Seminoles and Exiles that our Government would deal honorably with them, and would faithfully carry out the treaty of Payne's Landing, with the proviso contained in the supplemental treaty; and they were now greatly dissatisfied at the refusal of the Executive to observe this solemn stipulation; while the Seminoles and Exiles were indignant at the deception, fraud and perfidy practiced upon them.

Complaints against the Government now became general among all these tribes. All had been deceived; all had been wronged; and all became loud in their denunciations of the Government. This feeling became more intense as time passed away. It was in vain that our Indian agents and military officers at the West endeavored to quiet this state of general discontent. The newspapers of that day gave intimations of difficulties among the Indians at the West; they stated, in general terms, the danger of hostilities, but omitted all allusion to the cause of this disquietude.

The Executive appeared to be paralyzed with the difficulties now thrown in his way. He urged upon the Indian agents and military officers to use all possible efforts to suppress these feelings of hostility, which now appeared ready to burst forth upon the first occasion; coolly insisting that, at some future day, the Seminoles and Exiles would consent to remove on to the Creek territory.

At length the danger of hostilities became so imminent, that the Executive deemed it necessary to enter upon further negotiation in order to effect the long cherished purpose of subjecting the Exiles to Creek jurisdiction and consequent slavery. To effect this object it was necessary to select suitable instruments. Four Indian Agents, holding their offices by the Executive favor, were appointed to hold a Council with their discontented tribes, and if possible to negotiate a new treaty with them. It is somewhat singular that no statesman, no person favorably known to the public, or possessing public confidence, was selected for so important a service.

Of course any treaty formed under such circumstances and by

1845.] such agents would conform to the Executive will. The treaty bears date on the twenty-fifth of January; and we insert the preamble and those articles which have particular relation to the subject matter of which we are speaking. They are as follows:

" Articles of a Treaty made by Wm. Armstrong, P. M. Butler, James Segan and Thomas S. Judge, Commissioners in behalf of the United States, of the first part; the Creek Tribe of Indians of the second part, and the Seminole Indians of the third part:

" WHEREAS, It was stipulated in the fourth article of the Creek " Treaty of 1833, that the Seminoles should thence forward be " considered a constituent part of the Creek nation, and that a per- " manent and comfortable home should be secured for them on the " lands set apart in said treaty as the country of the Creeks; and " whereas, many of the Seminoles have settled and are now living " in the Creek Country, while others, constituting a large portion " of the tribe, have refused to make their homes in any part there- " of, assigning, as a reason, that *they are unwilling to submit to* " *Creek laws and Government, and that they are apprehensive of* " *being deprived by the Creek authorities of their property;* and " whereas, repeated complaints have been made to the United States " Government, that those of the Seminoles who refuse to go into " the Creek Country have, without authority or right, settled upon " lands secured to other tribes, and that they have committed nu- " merous and extensive depredations upon the property of those " upon whose lands they have intruded:

" Now, therefore, in order to reconcile all difficulties respecting " location and jurisdiction; to settle all disputed questions which " have arisen, or may hereafter arise, in regard to rights of prop- " erty; and, especially, to preserve the peace of the frontier, seri- " ously endangered by the restless and warlike spirit of the intru- " ding Seminoles, the parties to this treaty have agreed to the fol- " lowing stipulations:

" Article 1. The Creeks agree that the Seminoles shall be
" entitled to settle in a body, or separately, as they please, in any
" part of the Creek Country; that they shall make their own town
" regulations, subject, however, to the general control of the Creek
" Council in which they shall be represented; and, in short, that
" no distinction shall be made between the two tribes in any re-
" spect, except in the management of their pecuniary affairs; in
" which neither shall interfere with the *other*.

" Art 2. The Seminoles agree that those of their tribe who
" have not done so before the ratification of this treaty, shall imme-
" diately thereafter remove to, and permanently settle in, the Creek
" Country.

" Art. 3. It is mutually agreed by the Creeks and Seminoles
" that all contested cases between the two tribes, concerning the
" right of property growing out of sales or transactions that may
" have occurred previous to the ratification of this treaty, shall be
" subject to the decision of the President of the United States."

The leading feature of this treaty, is a studied effort to make no
allusion to the Exiles, or to recognize their existence in any way.
General Jessup, in the articles of capitulation, had expressly stipulated for the protection of the persons and property of the " allies "
of the Seminoles; but for half a century efforts had been made to
exclude them from the page of our national history, and never was
that policy more strikingly illustrated than in this treaty.

As heretofore stated, the Seminoles were said to own some forty
slaves; but the Author has been unable to find any hint or intimation that any one of those slaves was claimed by the Creeks: yet
efforts were made to falsify the truth of history by representing the
four or five hundred Exiles now living with the Seminoles to be
slaves to their friends and " *allies*."

· The next extraordinary feature of the treaty, is the recital of the
Creek treaty as binding upon the Seminoles, when they had been
no party to it, nor even had knowledge of its existence.

21

But the third article is that on which both Exiles and Seminoles appear to have relied. Thinking the President would do justice; feeling themselves subject to the power of the Executive, and pressed on all sides to accede to terms of pacification, they signed the treaty as the best alternative that lay before them.

In accordance with the past policy of the Administration, this treaty was withheld from publication. It was of course submitted to the Senate in secret session for approval. It was then amended, and still kept from the public for nearly two years after its negotiation.

NOTE.—At the session of Congress, 1845-6, a bill containing, among many other things, an appropriation to carry out this treaty, was reported by the committee on Ways and Means, of the House of Representatives. The treaty itself yet lay concealed in the office of the Secretary of the Senate, where it had been ratified in secret session, and not a member of the House of Representatives had seen it, unless it was the Chairman of the committee of Ways and Means, or other confidential friends of the Executive, to whom it was given for personal examination.

The bill was printed, and the Author seeing this provision, determined to know something of the treaty, before voting money to carry it into effect. For this purpose, he called on one of the Senators from Ohio (Hon. Thomas Corwin), to get a copy of the treaty. Mr. Corwin went with him to the office of the Secretary of the Senate, and after much inquiry, and passing from one clerk to another, a copy was obtained.

When the bill came up for discussion, inquiry was made as to the treaty, its character and object. No member appeared to have any knowledge of it, save the Chairman of the committee of Ways and Means, (Mr. McKay of North Carolina.) The Author of this work endeavored to give the House some idea of its origin, and, in the course of his remarks, referred to the manner in which the State of Georgia had been implicated in the persecution of the Exiles. This reference to the State of Georgia awakened the ire of Mr. Black, a Representative from that State, who advanced toward the Author with uplifted cane, as if to inflict personal chastisement, and quite a *scene* followed, which at the time created some sensation in the country.

CHAPTER XXIII.

THE REUNION AND FINAL EXODUS.

Difficulties in effecting a reunion of Tribes — Its objects — Exiles and Seminoles move on to Creek Lands — They settle in separate Villages — Creeks demand Exiles as Slaves — Exiles arm themselves — They flee to Fort Gibson — Demand protection of the United States — General Arbuckle protects them — Reports facts to Department — Administration embarrassed — Call on General Jessup for facts — He writes General Arbuckle — Reports facts to the President — President hesitates — Refers question to Attorney General — Extraordinary opinion of that Officer — Manner in which Mr. Mason was placed in office — Exiles return to their Village — Slaveholders dissatisfied —Slave-dealer among the Creeks — His offer — They capture near one hundred Exiles — They are delivered to the Slave-dealer — Habeas Corpus in Arkansas — Decision of Judge — Exiles hurried to New Orleans and sold as Slaves — Events of 1850 — Exiles depart for Mexico — Are pursued by Creeks — Battle — The Exiles continue their journey — They settle near Santa Rosa — The fate which different portions of the Exiles met — Incidents which occurred after their settlement in Mexico — Conclusion.

THE Creeks and Seminoles had been separated for nearly a century. They had most of that time lived under separate governments. Each Tribe had been controlled by their own laws; and each had been independent of the other. They had often been at war with each other; and the most deadly feuds had been engendered and still subsisted among them. To unite them with the Creeks, and blot the name of "Seminole" from the page of their future history, in order to involve the Exiles in slavery, had long been a cherished object with the administration of our Government. It was now fondly hoped, that that object would be accomplished without further difficulty.

1846.]

But at no period had the Seminole Indians regarded the Exiles with greater favor than they did when removing on to the territory assigned to the Creeks. Although many of them had intermarried with the Seminoles, and half-breeds were now common among the Indians; yet most of the descendants of the pioneers who fled from South Carolina and Georgia maintained their identity of character, living by themselves, and maintaining the purity of the African race. They yet cherished this love of their own kindred and color; and when they removed on to the Creek lands, they settled in separate villages: and the Seminole Indians appeared generally to coincide with the Exiles in the propriety of each maintaining their distinctive character.

During the summer and autumn both Indians and Exiles became residents within Creek jurisdiction; and the Executive seemed to regard the trust held under the assignment made at Indian Spring, twenty-four years previously, as now fulfilled. Regarding the Creeks as holding the equitable or beneficial interest in the bodies of the Exiles, under the assignment from their owners to the United States, and they being now brought under Creek jurisdiction, subject to Creek laws, the Executive felt that his obligations were discharged, and the whole matter left with the Creeks.

This opinion appears also to have been entertained by the Creek Indians; for no sooner had the Exiles and Seminoles located themselves within Creek jurisdiction, than the Exiles were claimed as the legitimate slaves of the Creeks. To these demands the Exiles and Seminoles replied, that the President, under the treaty of 1845, was bound to hear and determine all questions arising between them. The demands were, therefore, certified to the proper department for decision. But this setting in judgment upon the heaven-endowed right of man to his liberty, seemed to involve more personal and moral responsibility than was desirable for the Executive to assume, and the claims remained undecided.

The Creeks became impatient at delay; they were a slaveholding people, as well as their more civilized but more infidel brethren, of the slave States. The Exiles, living in their own villages in the enjoyment of perfect freedom, had already excited discontent among the slaves of the Creek and Choctaw Tribes, and those of Arkansas. The Creeks appeared to feel that it had been far better for them to have kept the Exiles in Florida, than to bring them to the Western Country to live in freedom. Yet their claims under the treaty of 1845, thus far, appeared to have been disregarded by the President; they had been unable to obtain a decision on them; and they now threatened violence for the purpose of enslaving the Exiles, unless their demands were peacefully conceded.

The Exiles, yet confident that the Government would fulfill its stipulations to protect them and their property, repaired in a body to Fort Gibson, and demanded protection of General Arbuckle, the officer in command. He had no doubt of the obligation of the United States to lend them protection, according to the express language of the articles of capitulation entered into with General Jessup, in March, 1837. He, therefore, directed the whole body of Exiles to encamp and remain upon the lands reserved by the United States, near the fort, and under their exclusive jurisdiction, assuring them that no Creek would dare set foot upon that reservation with intentions of violence towards any person. Accordingly the Exiles, who yet remained free, now encamped around Fort Gibson, and were supported by rations dealt out from the public stores.

Soon as he could ascertain all the facts, General Arbuckle made report to the War Department relative to their situation, and the claims which they made to protection under the articles of capitulation, together with the rights which the Creeks set up to reënslave them.

This state of circumstances appears to have been unexpected by the Executive. Indeed, he appears from the commencement to have under-rated the difficulties which beset the enslavement of a people who were determined upon the enjoyment of freedom; he seems to have expected the negroes, when once placed within Creek jurisdiction, would have yielded without further effort. But he was now placed in a position which constrained him either to repudiate the pledged faith of the nation, or to protect the Exiles in their *persons and property*, according to the solemn covenants which General Jessup had entered into with them.

Yet the President was disposed to make further efforts to avoid the responsibility of deciding the question before him. General Jessup had entered into the articles of capitulation, and the President appeared to think he was competent to give construction to them; he therefore referred the subject to that officer, stating the circumstances, and demanding of him the substance of *his undertaking* in regard to the articles of capitulation with the Exiles.

General Jessup appears to have now felt a desire to do justice to that friendless and persecuted people. Without waiting to answer the President, he at once wrote General Arbuckle, saying, "The "case of the Seminole negroes is now before the President. By "my proclamation and the convention made with them, when they "separated from the Indians and surrendered, *they are free*. The "question is, whether they shall be separated from the Seminoles "and removed to another country; or be allowed to occupy, as they "did, in Florida, separate villages in the Seminole Country, west "of Arkansas? The latter is what *I promised them*. I hope, "General, you will prevent any interference with them at Fort "Gibson, until the President determines whether they shall remain "in the Seminole Country, or be allowed to remove to some "other."

General Arbuckle, faithful to the honor of his Government, continued to protect the Exiles. He fed them from the public stores, not doubting that the Executive would redeem the pledge of the nation given by General Jessup, its authorized agent. But the President (Mr. Polk) himself a slaveholder, with his prejudices and sympathies in favor of the institution, did not understand the articles of capitulation according to the construction put upon them by General Jessup; he appears, therefore, to have called on the

General for a more explicit report of facts. In reply to this call, he reported, saying, "At a meeting with the three Indian " chiefs, and the negro chiefs, Auguste and Carollo, I stipulated " to recommend to the President to grant the Indians a small " tract of country in the south-eastern part of the Peninsula; but " it was distinctly understood that the negroes were to be separated " from them at once, and sent West, whether the Indians were " permitted to remain in Florida or not. With the negroes, it was " stipulated that they should be sent West, as a part of the Semi-" nole nation, and be *settled in a separate village, under the* PRO-" TECTION OF THE UNITED STATES." In another letter, addressed to the Secretary of War, he says: " A very *small portion* of the " Seminole negroes who went to the West, were brought in and " surrendered by their owners, under the capitulation of Fort Dade. " Over these negroes the Indians have all the rights of masters; " but all the other negroes, making more than *nine-tenths of the* " *whole number*, either separated from the Indians and surrendered " to me, or were captured by the troops under my command. I, " as commander of the army, and in the capacity of representative " of my country, *solemnly pledged the national faith that they* " *should not be separated, nor any of them sold to white men or* " *others*, but be allowed to settle and remain in separate villages, " UNDER THE PROTECTION OF THE UNITED STATES."

But even with these explicit statements before him, the President appears to have been unable to form an opinion; and he referred the matter to the Attorney General, Hon. John Y. Mason, of Virginia, who had been bred a slaveholder, and fully sympathized with the slave power. He, having examined the whole subject, delivered a very elaborate opinion, embracing seven documentary pages;[1] but concluding with the opinion, that although the Exiles

---

(1) Vide opinions of the Attorney Generals, from 1838 to 1851, page 1944, Senate Doc 55. It is a singular fact that, in the whole of this elaborate opinion, no allusion is made to the real condition of the Exiles; nor would any person suspect, from reading it, that the Attorney General had any knowledge of the claim which the Creeks preferred. Although he

were entitled to their freedom, the Executive *could not interfere in
any manner to protect them*, as stipulated by General Jessup, but
must leave them to retire to their Towns in the Indian Territory,
where *they had a right to remain.*

1848.]   We should be unfaithful to our pledged purpose, were
we to omit certain important facts connected with this
opinion of the Attorney General.   Nathan Clifford, of Maine, was
appointed Attorney General of the United States in 1846, soon
after the report of General Arbuckle concerning the situation of the
Exiles reached Washington.   The subject was before the President
more than two years.   This delay we cannot account for, unless it
were to save Mr. Clifford (being a Northern man) from the responsibility of deciding this question, involving important interests of
the slaveholding portion of our Union.   In 1848 Mr. Clifford was
appointed Minister to Mexico, and Hon. Isaac Toucey, of Connecticut, was appointed Attorney General.   But he, too, was from a
free State, and it would throw upon him great responsibility were
he constrained to act upon this subject.   Were he to decide in favor
of the Exiles, it might ruin his popularity at the South ; and if
against them, it would have an equally fatal effect at the North.

Under these circumstances, recourse was had to an expedient.
Before Mr. Toucey entered upon the discharge of his official duties,
Mr. Mason, himself a slaveholder, was appointed to discharge the
duties *ad interim.*   He entered the office, wrote out the opinion
referred to, and then resigned the office and emoluments to Mr.
Toucey ; having decided no other question, nor discharged any
other duty, than this exercise of official influence for the enslavement of the Exiles.

---

quotes the clause in the articles of capitulation, which expressly and emphatically declares
that "Major General Jessup, in behalf of the United States, agrees that the Seminoles *and
their allies, who come in and emigrate, sha'l be protected in their lives and property ;*" yet
he appears never to have conceived the idea that such a stipulation could impose any
duties upon our Government in favor of negroes ; nor does he attempt to define the meaning of this most explicit covenant.

The President affirmed the principles decided by the Attorney General, and the Exiles were informed that they *had the right to remain in their villages, free from all interference, or interruption from the Creeks.* They had no other lands, no other country, no other homes. Many of their families were connected by marriage with the Seminoles They and the Seminole Indians had, through several generations, been acquainted with each other; they had stood beside each other on many a battle field. Seminoles and Exiles had fallen beside each other, and were buried in the same grave; they had often sat in council together, and the Exiles were unwilling to separate from their friends. Wild Cat and Abraham and Louis, and many leading men and warriors of the Exiles and Seminoles, having deliberated upon the subject, united in the opinion, that the Exiles should return to their villages and reside upon the lands to which they were entitled.

In accordance with this decision, they returned to their new homes, resumed their habits of agriculture, and for a time all was quiet and peaceful; but their example was soon felt among the slaves of Arkansas, and of the surrounding Indian tribes. Nor is it to be supposed that the holders of slaves in any State of the Union, would be willing to admit that so large a body of servants could, by any effort, separate from their masters, for a century and a half maintain their liberty, and after so much effort to reënslave them, be permitted to enjoy liberty in peace.

Hundreds of them had been seized in Florida and enslaved. The laws of slave States presumed every black person to be a slave; and it was evident, that if they could once be subjected to the will of some white man, the laws of Arkansas would enable him to hold them in bondage.[1]

An individual, a slave-dealer, appeared among the Creeks and

---

[1] Under this law, which is general in all slave States, free colored citizens of nearly every free State of the Union have been seized and enslaved, and are now toiling in chains.

offered to pay them one hundred dollars for each Exile they would seize and deliver to him ; he stipulating to take all risk of title.[1]

1849.]   This temptation was too great for the integrity of the Creeks, who were smarting under their disappointment, and the defeat of their long cherished schemes, of reënslaving the Exiles. Some two hundred Creek warriors collected together, armed themselves, and, making a sudden descent upon the Exiles, seized such as they could lay their hands upon. The men and most of the women and children fled ; but those who had arms collected, and presenting themselves between their brethren and the Creeks who were pursuing them, prepared to defend themselves and friends.[2] The Creeks, unwilling to encounter the danger which threatened them, ceased from further pursuit, but, turning back, dragged their frightened victims, who had been already captured, to the Creek villages, and delivered them over to the slavedealer, who paid them the stipulated price.

(1) Hon. R. W. Johnson, a Representative from Arkansas, spoke of this wretch as having come from Louisiana ; but from manuscript letters on file in the War Department, the Author is led to think he came from Florida, and had previously participated in kidnapping Exiles in that Territory.

(2) The Author, being unable to obtain a publication of the documents showing these facts, states them upon the best authority he possesses. During the discussions upon what is called the Indian Appropriation Bill for 1852, in the House of Representatives of the United States, the following colloquial debate occurred, and is now cited as a part of the evidence on which these facts are stated. It will be found in the Congressional Globe of 1852, vol. 24, part 3d, pages 1804, 1805 :

"Mr. GIDDINGS. I rise for a different purpose than that of expressing my approbation of the amendment which has just been read. I ask the especial attention of gentlemen to some interrogatories which I desire to propound for the purpose of obtaining information ; and that the information may go to the country, I will observe, that I desire to have the experience of the able Chairman of the committee on Indian Affairs (Mr. Johnson of Arkansas), to obtain this intelligence. According to reliable information which I received in the summer of 1850, these Creek Indians, to whom attention has been turned, with force and violence, seized from seventy to one hundred free persons of color in the Indian Territory, or at least those claiming to be free, and enslaved, sold and transported them to the State of Louisiana, where they are now in servitude as slaves. I will state that this was done in violation of the treaty entered into in 1845, and in subversion of our solemn faith, entered into with these negroes during the Seminole War, in 1837. The official information upon this subject is in the Indian Department, where it has been received ; and from which

1850.] The Seminole Agent, learning the outrage, at once repaired to the nearest Judge in Arkansas, and obtained a writ of habeas corpus. The Exiles were brought before him in obedience to the command of the writ, and a hearing was had. The Agent showed the action of General Jessup; the sanction of the capitulation of March, 1837, by the Executive; the opinion of the Attorney General, and action of the President, deciding the Exiles to be free, and in all respects entitled to their liberty. But the Judge decided that the Creeks had obtained title by virtue of their contract with General Jessup; that neither General Jessup, nor the President, had power to emancipate the Exiles, even in time of war; that the Attorney General had misunderstood the law; that the title of the Creek Indians was legal and perfect; and they, having sold them to the claimant, his title must be good and perfect.[1]

that we have not been able to obtain any intelligence by resolution, although a resolution for that purpose has been in my desk since the first day of the session. The questions I desire to propound to those gentlemen are — First, Is it a fact that those persons of color were seized and sold into slavery; and, second, by what claim of right or pretended title did these Creek Indians enslave and sell those people?

"Mr. JOHNSON. I have no official knowledge in the matter at all. Then as to the knowledge I have obtained incidentally, I do know that there has been a great contest in relation to a portion of these Creek Indian negroes; I do know that the matter has been looked into here in the Executive Departments; I do know that the matter has never been before the House at all, unless it has strangely escaped my notice; I know it has not been before my committee; I know the Attorney General of the United States has declared his opinion as to the title of these negroes: I think there were seventy of them, though it might have been more or less. So, then, I have no official information on the subject to which the gentleman alludes.

"Some two or three years ago, I knew of a contest going on about the title to these negroes, and that it was decided that they belonged to those Indians. They had established themselves in a free town, which they maintained with force and arms. There were heavy disturbances existing there in the Indian nation, amounting at times almost to civil war: I believe before it was done with, it was quite civil war. I know they were taken; but what was done with them, I do not know. They were taken, and carried out of the nation, with the design of holding them as property, when they could not hold them in the nation on account of the disturbance which they created. I know the decision of the Attorney General of the United States, as to the title to these negroes; and that is the whole statement in regard to the matter as far as I can give it."

(1) The Author has written many letters, and made frequent efforts, to obtain a copy of

No sooner was the decision announced, than the manacled victims were hurried from their friends and the scenes of such transcendent crimes and guilt. They were placed on board a steamboat, and carried to New Orleans. There they were sold to different purchasers, taken to different estates, and mingling with the tide of human victims who are septennially murdered upon the cotton and sugar plantations of that State, they now rest in their quiet graves, or perhaps have shared the more unhappy fate of living and suffering tortures incomparably worse than death.

The year 1850 was distinguished by a succession of triumphs on the part of the slave power. While the President and his Cabinet, and members of the Senate and of the House of Representatives, were seeking the passage of the Fugitive Slave Law; while slaveholders and their northern allies appeared to be aroused in favor of oppression within the States of our Union, their savage coadjutors of the Indian territory were equally active.

There yet remained some hundreds of Exiles in that far-distant territory unsubdued, and enjoying liberty. They had witnessed the duplicity, the treachery of our Government often repeated, toward themselves and their friends — they had, most of them, been born in freedom — they had grown to manhood, had become aged amidst persecutions, dangers and death — they had experienced the constant and repeated violations of our national faith : its perfidy was no longer disguised ; if they remained, death or slavery would constitute their only alternative. One, and only one, mode of avoiding such a fate remained — that was, to leave the territory, the jurisdiction of the United States, and flee beyond its power and influence.

Mexico was *free!* No slave clanked his chains under its government. Could they reach the Rio Grande ? Could they place

the record of this writ, if any had been kept, and the proceedings, together with the opinion of the Judge thereon, but has not succeeded. The statement, therefore, rests on the verbal reports, current at the time in the Indian Country, and communicated to the Author by individuals who happened to be there at the time.

themselves safely on Mexican soil, they might hope yet to be free. A Council was held. Some were connected with Seminoles of influence. Those who were intimately connected with Indian families of influence, and most of the half-breeds, feeling they could safely remain in the Indian territory, preferred to stay with their friends and companions. Of the precise number who thus continued in the Indian Country, we have no certain information ;[1] but some three hundred are supposed to have determined on going to Mexico, and perhaps from one to two hundred concluded to remain with their connexions in the Indian Country.

Abraham had reached a mature age ; had great experience, and retained influence with his people. Louis Pacheco, of whom we spoke in a former chapter, with his learning, his shrewdness and tact, was still with them, and so were many able and experienced warriors. Wild Cat, the most active and energetic chief of the Seminole Tribe, declared his unalterable purpose to accompany the Exiles; to assist them in their journey, and defend them, if assailed. Other Seminoles volunteered to go with them. Their arrangements were speedily made. Such property as they had was collected together, and packed for transportation. They owned a few Western ponies. Their blankets, which constituted their beds, and some few cooking utensils and agricultural implements, were placed upon their ponies, or carried by the females and children ; while the warriors, carrying only their weapons and ammunition, marched, unencumbered even by any unnecessary article of clothing, prepared for battle at every step of their journey.

After the sun had gone down (Sept. 10), their spies and patrols, who had been sent out for that purpose, returned, and reported that all was quiet ; that no slave-hunters were to be seen. As the darkness of night was closing around them, they commenced their journey westwardly. Amid the gloom of the evening, silent and sad they took leave of their western homes, and fled from the jurisdic-

(1) The Author has been unable to obtain official data of the number of Exiles who remained in the Indian Country.

tion of a people who had centuries previously kidnapped their
ancestors in their native homes, brought them to this country, enslaved them, and during many generations had persecuted them.
Many of their friends and relatives had been murdered for their
love of liberty by our Government; others had been doomed to
suffer and languish in slavery—a fate far more dreaded than death.
At the period of this exodus, their number was probably less than
at the close of the Revolution.

When the slaveholding Creeks learned that the Exiles had left,
they collected together and sent a war party in pursuit, for the purpose of capturing as many as they could, in order to sell them to
the slave-dealers from Louisiana and Arkansas, who were then
present among the Creeks, encouraging them to make another
piratical descent upon the Exiles for the capture of slaves.

This war party came up with the emigrants on the third day after
leaving their homes. But Wild Cat and Abraham, and their experienced warriors, were not to be surprised. They were prepared
and ready for the conflict. With them it was death or victory.
They boldly faced their foes. Their wives and children were looking on with emotions not to be described. With the coolness of
desperation, they firmly resolved on dying, or on driving back the
slave-catching Creeks from the field of conflict. Their nerves were
steady, and their aim fatal. Their enemies soon learned the danger
and folly of attempting to capture armed men who were fighting for
freedom. They fled, leaving their dead upon the field; which is
always regarded by savages as dishonorable defeat.[1]

The Exiles resumed their journey, still maintaining their warlike
arrangement. Directing their course south-westerly, they crossed the
Rio Grande, and continuing nearly in the same direction, they proceeded into Mexico, until they reached the vicinity of the ancient but

(1) The Author has been compelled to rely on verbal reports received from individuals
for these facts. He also understood Mr Johnston, the Representative from Arkansas, in
the debate referred to in a former note, to say distinctly, that the Creeks pursued the Exiles, and that a *battle was fought*, but he was unable to state particulars.

now deserted town of Santa Rosa.[1] In that beautiful climate, they found a rich, productive soil. Here they halted, examined the country, and finally determined to locate their new homes in this most romantic portion of Mexico. Here they erected their cabins, planted their gardens, commenced plantations, and resumed their former habits of agricultural life. There they yet remain. Forcibly torn from their native land, oppressed, wronged, and degraded, they became voluntary Exiles from South Carolina and Georgia. More recently exiled from Florida and from the territory of the United States — they are yet *free!* After the struggles and persecutions of a hundred and fifty years, they repose in comparative quiet under a government which repudiates slavery. To the pen of some future historian we consign their subsequent history.

Before taking leave of the reader, we would call his attention to a review of the fate which attended different portions of the Exiles, and to a few further incidents, for some of which we have only newspaper authority ; but from all the circumstances we have no doubt they actually transpired.

Of the Exiles and their descendants, twelve were delivered up at the treaty of Colerain in 1796, and consigned to slavery; two hundred and seventy were massacred at Blount's Fort in 1816 ; thirty were taken prisoners — these all died of wounds or were enslaved. At the different battles in the first Seminole War in 1818, it is believed that at least four hundred were slain, including those who fell at Blount's Fort.

In the Second Seminole War, probably seventy-five were slain in battle, and five hundred were enslaved; and at least seventy-five were seized by the Creek Indians, in 1850, and enslaved. Probably a hundred and fifty connected with the Seminoles now reside in the Western Country, and will soon become amalgamated with the Indians ; while three hundred have found their way to Mexico,

(1) Vide Official Report of Major Emory, in regard to the boundary line between the United States and Mexico. He states the location of Wild Cat and the Seminole Indians, but omits all reference to the Exiles.

and are free.[1] Making, in all, thirteen hundred and fifty souls; being some hundreds less than was reported by the officers of Government, in 1836. This discrepancy is accounted for by the fact, that the Exiles captured by individual enterprise, and by the Georgia and Florida militia, were never officially reported to the War Department, and we have no reliable data on which we can fix an estimate of the number thus piratically enslaved. There are also a few yet in Florida, not included in the above estimate.

As to their present situation, we can give the reader but little further information. In the summer of 1852, Wild Cat suddenly appeared among his friends, the Seminoles, who yet remained in the Indian Country. His appearance excited surprise among the Creeks. They at that time maintained a guard, composed of mounted men: these were at once put in motion for the purpose of arresting this extraordinary chieftain. But while they were engaged in looking for him, he and a company of Seminoles, attended by a number of Exiles and black persons, previously held in bondage by the Creeks, were rapidly wending their way towards their new settlement.[2]

1852.]

This visit of Wild Cat to the Western Country occasioned much excitement in that region, as well as astonishment at Washington, and constituted the occasion of a protracted correspondence between the War Department and our Military Officers and Indian Agents of that country. Wild Cat was denounced as a " pirate"— " robber"— " OUTLAW;" and nearly all the opprobrious epithets known to our language were heaped upon him, for thus aiding his fellow men to regain those rights to life and liberty with which the God of Nature had originally endowed them.

During the year 1852, while our commissioners, appointed to establish the boundary between the United States and Mexico, were engaged in the discharge of their official duties, a small party of

(1) This number has been increased by fresh arrivals from the Indian Country, since 1850.

(2) Vide Manuscript Letters now on file in the Indian Bureau at Washington.

armed men was in attendance for their protection. Some eight of these were said to have been engaged in patroling the country, when they fell in with Wild Cat and a portion of this band of Exiles, who were at all times prepared for friends or foes. The whites were made prisoners without bloodshed, and taken to their village. A council was called. Abraham was yet living, and the white men declared that he was regarded as a ruling prince by his people. They were evidently suspicious of the intentions of our men; but upon inquiry and consideration, they became satisfied that no hostile intentions had brought our friends to that country; they were accordingly treated with becoming hospitality, and dismissed. These brief statements appeared in some of the newspapers of that day, which constitutes our only authority for stating them.

Complaints were subsequently made through the Texan newspapers, that slaves escaped from that region of country 1853.] and found an asylum in Mexico, on the other side of the Rio Grande; and intimations were thrown out that a party of volunteers, without authority from the United States, were about to visit the settlement, which thus encouraged slaves to seek their freedom. The suggestion was so much in character with the slaveholders of Texas, that it excited attention among those who were aware of the settlement of Exiles in the region indicated. It was believed that those men who were about to visit Wild Cat and Abraham and Louis and their companions, for the purpose of seizing and enslaving men, would find an entertainment for which they were not prepared.

Some few months subsequently, a brief reference was made in the newspapers of Texas to this expedition, giving their readers to understand that it had failed of accomplishing the object intended, and had returned with its numbers *somewhat diminished* by their conflict with the blacks.

As was naturally expected, after the lapse of some six months, great complaint was heard through the public press of Indian depre-

22

dations upon the frontier of Texas.   Plantations were said to be destroyed; buildings burned; people murdered, and slaves carried away.   This foray was said to have been made by Camanche Indians, led on by Wild Cat.   He appears yet ready to make war upon all who fight for slavery; and many of the scenes which were enacted in Florida, will most likely be again presented on our south-western frontier, where the same causes exist which formerly existed in Florida, and the same effects will be likely to follow.